NO FREE LUNCH

One Man's Journey from Welfare to the American Dream

NO FREE LUNCH

One Man's Journey from Welfare to the American Dream

RODNEY J. CARROLL

President and CEO of the Welfare to Work Partnership

WITH GARY KARTON

ONE WORLD
BALLANTINE BOOKS | NEW YORK

A One World Book
Published by The Ballantine Publishing Group

Copyright © 2002 by Rodney Carroll

www.ballantinebooks.com/one/

Library of Congress Cataloging-in-Publication Data is available
upon request from the publisher.

ISBN 0-345-45229-1

Designed by Ann Gold

Manufactured in the United States of America

First Edition: May 2002

10   9   8   7   6   5   4   3   2   1

This book is dedicated to my grandmother

LULA LUCAS
September 7, 1904–December 15, 1999

Acknowledgments

I would like to thank my friend and writer Gary Karton who believed in this project when no else did. He is a brilliant writer who "gets it." During the many times when I was trying to convey my painful memories; it was his "way with words" that made it possible. Like my grandmother used to say, "it's not the beef and vegetables in beef stew that makes it taste good, it's the spices and seasonings." Gary provided the spices and seasonings. Karl Weber was the first person outside our immediate families that thought someone would want to read this book. He provided invaluable guidance. I remember our first meeting with our editor, Anita Diggs. She understood what we were trying to do before we even opened our mouths.

I'd like to thank my friend and mentor Eli Segal. Also Jonathan Tisch, Gerry Greenwald, and Tommy Thompson, whose innovative W-2 program was a constant reminder for me and the rest of the country that Welfare to Work can help both businesses and communities thrive.

To Courtney and Cheryl, growing up together was quite an experience. I'm thankful that we've survived. I'm also glad that we've grown even closer together. May God bless you.

To Christian, Charity, Chanel, and Chase. I love you more than anything in my life. I always think of you and I pray for your happiness, your safety, and general well-being. You guys make me smile. I am so very proud of each one of you.

To Tondalaya, I never knew that there could be someone who could understand me so thoroughly. I praise God for you.

Finally, to my Lord and savior Jesus Christ, for any success, any good fortune, any anything, I give You all the praise and honor. You, who loved me before I was born, who continue to intercede for me, I love You and I attempt to be like You.

—Rodney Carroll

❧   ❧   ❧

I'd like to thank Rodney Carroll for giving me the opportunity to help tell his incredible story. I spent many late nights in my basement transcribing the notes from our talks about the book and what stands out most is the amount of time we spent laughing. Even through the toughest times, Rodney always found a reason to laugh.

This book is about the power of believing—in yourself and in others. I'd like to thank all the people who believed in me during the process of writing my first book.

That list starts with my mom, who worked with me on several treatments for a book about welfare to work. She is also the best editor I know. From there, Eli Segal, after consulting with his good friend Peter Osnos, gave the project the go-ahead and Rodney and I began a process neither of us knew anything about.

Mr. Osnos introduced us to literary agent Karl Weber, who was the first independent person outside of the Partnership to believe in this project. Karl endured constant questions and phone messages from me and still always returned my calls—eventually. He introduced us to agent Christie Fletcher, who found the perfect publisher in Anita Diggs, from Ballantine Books. Anita's passion for the topic was an ideal fit.

I want to thank my friends at *The Washington Post*, especially Ken Denlinger for his time and counseling. Of course I would have never had a job at *The Post* without Bob Levey and Neil Greenberger.

Thanks to Susan Hannen for her encouragement and everyone at the Partnership for making it fun to come to work.

Lastly, thanks to Dixie for all the different ways she helped—from waking up early with Jake and Brody to late-night editing. And all she asked in return was a supersize fries and an oreo McFlurry.

—Gary Karton

Foreword

By Former President Bill Clinton

I've been extremely fortunate in my life to have a career that has allowed me to meet remarkable people whose stories are so inspiring that they cause others to change their lives. People who have faced adversity that most of us couldn't imagine and persevered. People who are blind to stereotypes and see the potential within every American. People who dedicate their lives to helping others see the potential within themselves.

Rarely do I meet a person, like Rodney Carroll, whose story combines all of these elements. His is much more than a tale of rags to riches. Rodney's story shows us that anyone, given an opportunity and the will to succeed, can reach their dreams, and teaches us that we all have the power to help others reach their dreams as well.

Rodney's story also concerns a topic about which I am very passionate. When I was governor of Arkansas, I had the chance to go to welfare offices, talk to caseworkers, and talk to recipients. I spent hours talking to welfare recipients, asking them what would it take to make the system work for them and listening to them tell me all the manifold ways in which welfare discouraged work and independence.

At the time our country was engaged in a great debate concerning our welfare system. For some, the welfare system was our last line of defense against abject poverty. To others, it was Exhibit A of America's decline. Clearly, it had become a system that undermined our cherished values of work and family.

So in 1996, I asked the American people to join me on a crusade to transform our system of welfare into a system of work. I asked the American people to change course, to restore with all of our people the fundamental bargain that we ought to have opportunity for all in return for responsibility from all our citizens, and to include everyone in America's community.

Together, I wanted to transform a system of dependence into a system of independence, to prove that people on welfare could succeed at work if given a chance and the tools to succeed and to give a whole generation of Americans the opportunity to earn the dignity that comes from earning a paycheck.

When we passed the landmark welfare law, it was clear that moving Americans from welfare to work would take the commitment of every element of our society, not just government, but businesses, faith-based organizations, community groups, and private citizens.

So I asked my longtime friend Eli Segal to start the Welfare to Work Partnership to help rally the business community so that people coming off welfare could have the same job opportunities as you and me.

After five years, we are seeing the signs of the transformation everywhere. Inner-city buses that used to be empty at rush hour are packed. Tax-preparation services are moving into abandoned storefronts helping former welfare recipients fill out the first tax forms of their lives.

There are more subtle changes as well. Mothers collecting their mail with a little more pride because they know they will see a bank statement, not a welfare check, and children going to school with their heads held a little higher.

From now on, our nation's answer to this great social challenge will no longer be a never-ending cycle of welfare, it will be the power and the ethic of work. Together we took a historic chance to make welfare what it was meant to be: a second chance, not a way of life.

Through it all, we knew there would be millions of personal stories that would touch us all. Stories that prove the indomitable power of the human spirit. Stories of people like Rodney Carroll.

Welfare to work is working thanks to individuals like Rodney who dedicate their lives to helping others succeed. His story is one of perseverance and courage that transcends political and social boundaries. He is an example to all Americans—not just those on welfare—that even when things are at their worst, we must continue to fight. That we all have the potential to make a positive impact on the world.

Rodney's commitment and vision continue to help the Welfare to Work Partnership move people from lives of dependence to lives of independence. Under his leadership, we will continue to work together to ensure that everyone who works hard and plays by the rules has a chance to live the American dream.

NO FREE LUNCH

One Man's Journey from Welfare to the American Dream

1. One, Two, Three—You're My Man

In exactly twenty-four hours the president of the United States is scheduled to step up to a podium and say, "I'd now like to introduce a man who knows about welfare reform from every conceivable perspective. He's a truly remarkable man and we are grateful for his services. I'm happy to introduce Rodney Carroll." That's when I will walk on stage, shake President Bill Clinton's hand, and speak about a topic that has consumed my life.

The event is a town hall meeting and the White House staff is leading our first and only rehearsal. Since the signing of the new welfare reform law on August 22, 1996, thousands of people have moved from welfare to work. For the first time in history, our country is working together to change a dysfunctional welfare system that has slowly destroyed generations of American families, and at the core of this quiet revolution are inspiring stories of courage and perseverance. Tomorrow, former welfare recipients, politicians, Fortune 100 CEOs, small business owners, and community leaders who represent these stories will be joining President Clinton in Chicago in a demonstration of what can happen when you have the courage and opportunity to change your life.

My boss, Eli Segal, who started the Welfare to Work Partnership at the President's request, told the White House that I would be the ideal person to moderate the town hall meeting with President Clinton and in twenty-four hours I will have my opportunity.

The final touches are taking place and the empty warehouse at Navy Pier on Lake Michigan in Chicago is starting to resemble a venue befitting the president of the United States. The stage reminds me of one of those old Roman gladiator movies where two guys are fighting down in a pit with the fans cheering from above. It is a

1

circular arena, surrounded by ten rows of bleachers, where cabinet secretaries, governors, mayors, and those who have moved from welfare to work will be waiting their turn to tell their success stories. Two sixty-foot banners reading WELFARE MOTHERS MAKE RESPONSIBLE WORKERS and WELFARE TO WORK IS A PROGRAM THAT CREATES INDEPENDENCE hang from the rafters behind the stage. A huge camera riser faces the stage prepared for the television cameras and national media. Thousands of chairs line the warehouse floor while pigeons watch from the rafters above.

Looking up, I notice three rows of floodlights. It is a hot August day and I am already perspiring through my sports shirt. I am sure that with the lights shining down tomorrow, it will be even hotter. There are four sixteen-foot television screens placed strategically throughout the audience so the people way in back will have no problem seeing me sweat.

When I first came to Washington, I was hoping to get close enough to the president so I could get a picture with him. My ninety-three-year-old grandmother in Philadelphia would have gotten a kick out of that. I had never dreamed I'd be sharing a stage with the president of the United States. But as the rehearsal progressed, I began to wonder if I might not have been better off with just a picture.

"No," shouted Sharon, the White House staffer in charge of the event, when I asked if I could use the podium after the president. "No one can stand behind a podium with a presidential seal after the president. That's the way it is."

Sharon reminded me of an army sergeant. It was obvious she was good at her job. Her voice was thunderous and her manner forbidding. She was a no-nonsense woman and had her own idea of how the event should run.

Her job was to make sure that the president looked good. Welfare reform was the president's idea. He had worked with Congress to push the legislation through and this was his time. Who the heck was I?

"A prop," a colleague suggested, trying to build my confidence. "A simple prop."

My role, as Sharon described it, was to walk on stage after the president introduced me, shake his hand, and introduce the first welfare-to-work success story—Wendy Waxler, a former welfare recipient with a disabled child. After Wendy told her story, President Clinton would make a few appropriate comments and then I would introduce the next participant. There were to be seventeen participants in all.

There would be two seats on the stage—one for the president and one for me. My instructions were clear. If the president chose to sit, I should sit as well. If he decided to walk around the stage, I should just stand. If he wanted to use a handheld microphone then that's what I, too, would have to use. If he walked across the stage I was to make sure I didn't wind up in front of him. And I should never have my back to the president. And, I should also never turn my back to the audience. It was like playing the political version of Simon Says.

Sharon covered every possible scenario. As with all presidential events, nothing would be left to chance. The event was beautifully choreographed, the stories would be inspiring, and the president would be at his usual best. But as Sharon kept defining my own role, I became more and more uncomfortable.

Sharon told me that in addition to introducing the success stories, my job would be to keep the program moving on schedule. That meant that I might even have to cut the president off.

The program was to run ninety minutes, not one minute more. At ninety minutes, the Secret Service would give me the cue and the program would end. Anyone who hadn't spoken would be excluded. Former welfare recipients, who had flown all the way to Chicago to tell the president their stories might not get a chance to speak. And in order to avoid this, I had better be prepared to say:

"Uh, excuse me, Mr. President, but you seem to be rambling on too long. I'm afraid I'm going to have to ask you to stop right there. No hard feelings? Okay?" I could not imagine ever doing that. What I had was an impossible task. I couldn't get all the stories in, keep the president at bay, and yet not cut him off, not get in front of him and also not walk behind him, maintain eye contact with the president without turning my back on the guests. I couldn't do it. Even as I look back now, I'm convinced that it can't be done. It was your classic Washington scenario, where you are told, "we have a ninety-minute speech and we want you to get it done in forty. Don't leave out any words and make sure you speak slowly."

I took a deep breath.

"Sure, it will be difficult," I told myself. "But I've been through tougher times. This is a great opportunity and I must make it work."

I abandoned that resolve when Sharon handed me the final script. As I went through it, two things struck me. One, it was well written—every story was clear and concise. Two, I couldn't read that script because it wasn't me.

"I thought I was up here because I was a person who had lived this and worked this," I protested. "Where is all that in this script?"

"The president will take care of all that in his introduction," Sharon assured me. "Whatever you do, don't ad lib; every word is in there for a purpose. You have to trust us."

"But surely I can't say something that is not me," I persisted.

"You just stick to the script," Sharon said bluntly. "Bring a sheet of paper, or three-by-five note cards, and just read it as written. Listen, all you have to do is read the questions as we have written them, let the president make his comments, and then you go to the next person."

Sharon explained that there were times when someone like me might experience stage fright, go off on a tangent, or call the president Bill, or cause some other kind of embarrassment. "It's our job to make sure that doesn't happen," she said.

After she got done with me, Sharon turned to the other participants.

The speakers at the town hall were a mixture of welfare-to-work success stories, corporate executives, service providers, and elected officials. The rehearsal was mainly for the participants who used to be on welfare—the others had representatives to take last-minute notes.

The first person was Wendy Waxler, an account associate for Xerox. According to the script, Wendy's key message was that she was on welfare because she had to take care of her disabled child.

I read the first question as it was written in the script: "So, Wendy, it must be exciting to be at a fax processing center. How has your family's life changed since you got the job?"

"Well, it is exciting," Wendy answered proudly. "My daughter is three years . . ."

"What about your daughter?" Sharon interrupted. "Isn't there something about your daughter that you want to tell us?"

"Oh, yeah," said Wendy. "She has a disability."

"No," corrected Sharon. "Not a disability. A handicap. She has a handicap."

"Okay, she has a handicap," repeated Wendy, the pride gone from her face.

The next person was Rena Burns, who had grown up on welfare with a single mother. Without a college education, Rena had started her own business and now hired people off welfare. Earlier in the day, Rena had told me a great story about a former welfare recipient who had worked for her as a receptionist. The woman, who didn't have a high school education, asked Rena why her company didn't bid on a particular project.

"We are a small company and don't have the resources to respond to every request for a proposal," Rena explained.

The former welfare recipient had asked if she could try in her spare time. A month later, they got the account. Today the woman works exclusively on finding new business. I was anxious for Rena to tell that story at the town hall.

But Sharon's script was explicit. "I'm a small company without a human resources department, yet I can still successfully hire people off welfare," Rena said on cue.

"Don't forget to mention that you won the Small Business Association Award," prompted Sharon.

"Rena, why don't you tell us about some of your workers," I said, ignoring the script.

Sharon cut me off. "No Rena. That was perfect. Right on schedule."

And so it went. Tiffany Smith, a UPS package sorter went on too long. Antoinette Patrick, a pharmacy technician at CVS, focused on the wrong aspect of her job.

"Please," Sharon cut in, "just stick to the script."

Bill Simmons was next. He was the CEO of Masterlube in Billings, Montana. He hired welfare recipients with substance-abuse problems. Once hired, he prepared them for more lucrative jobs in other fields. It was an inspiring story because most businesses try to reduce employee turnover to lower training costs. Bill understood that it wasn't everyone's dream to change oil. For substance abusers, however, it was a good place to gain work experience. His former employees had gone on to become accountants and office managers. One young lady was a Ph.D., another worked in a bank, and yet another worked for a consulting firm in Washington, D.C. He celebrated their success on a "wall of fame" outside his office.

One of his employees was Tyler Left Hand, a Native American who had made the decision to leave the reservation to provide for his daughter. As the script had it, Tyler represented a father who was taking responsibility for his child—something fathers of welfare children didn't always do. But Tyler wanted to speak about his experience leaving the reservation.

"My family disowned me," he said. "They would have preferred that I stayed on welfare and on the reservation."

"We don't want any of that in here," said Sharon.

By the time we got to Maria Mercado, she was so nervous tears were running down her face. Maria was a Hispanic woman who had worked as a merchandising sales associate at Marshall's, an affiliate of TJX. She represented someone who had received industry-based training at Goodwill, a national service provider. Basically, Goodwill had taught her how to be a salesperson before she got to TJX. So her first day on the job, she was ready to work. It was a great example of how businesses can team up with community-based organizations.

But Sharon was only concerned about the length of the program, and when Maria started crying, the White House staff wondered whether it might not be better if she was only seen on stage, but not heard.

"Well, let's hear her story," I said, disgusted that that option had even been broached. The atmosphere got so tense that Maria couldn't open her mouth, and the tears continued to stream down her face.

At this point, it was obvious that things were not going well and so we took a break. The problem was that Sharon and I had different perspectives. Sharon was putting on a show. She saw the town hall participants as mere actors, representing the people who had moved from welfare to work. I was more engaged because I saw them as real people who had made the great leap from total dependence to absolute independence, from living on handouts to honest work.

For my part, I was getting less and less excited about this "opportunity." I knew that I couldn't do well reading, unless I was reading my own work. I knew I couldn't speak passionately unless I was speaking from the heart. I knew that if I read the script as it stood, I would be doing an injustice to myself, to Eli, and to every other participant in the event, including the president.

To Sharon, I'm sure I seemed argumentative and probably unreasonable, but the truth is that I believed there were people out there that were just waiting for me to fail. The president was going to introduce me as a former welfare recipient. So if I stood up and mixed up my words, stuttered, or seemed nervous, in my mind I would be telling the thousands of people in the audience and the millions more who watched on television that welfare recipients were not smart enough to be with the president. I could already hear people talking: "See, people on welfare are not capable of something like this."

As I looked around the empty bleachers, I visualized where everyone would be sitting the next day. To my right would be Secretary of Transportation Rodney Slater. Jim Kelly, the CEO of UPS and the person who was ultimately responsible for the welfare-to-work success at UPS, had never heard me speak. I wondered what he would think. Not to mention all the people who had heard me speak in different venues and thought I was good. "How's he going to do now?" I imagined them saying. "Of course he can do well at a little luncheon or a college. But this is the big time."

I kept thinking this is not going to work. I must have said that a thousand times. It's never going to work, it's never going to work. How could I ignore my own instincts and pretend to be someone I was not?

I had made that mistake before when I faced an even more daunting task than speaking before the president of the United States. When I was nine, I had to speak in front of all the parents on my grandmother's street.

She lived on Gratz Street in North Philadelphia. My sister, Cheryl, brother, Courtney, and I visited her for weeks at a time and spent summers with her. It was a tough neighborhood. Rival gangs ruled the streets. Shootings and street fights were commonplace. The next street over, Cleveland, was especially dangerous. Even today I get nervous walking down Cleveland.

There were no large houses on my grandmother's street. Families and extended families were packed into three-bedroom town houses, most with a small kitchen, single bath, and living room. The summers were exceptionally hot, so, to clear some space, the parents sent us out to play by nine in the morning and we didn't come back in until it got dark.

Once you were out, you couldn't leave the safety of the street. That was too bad, because there was a park just four blocks away that had plenty of room for kids to run and play, but it was too dangerous for us to go by ourselves. We were safe on Gratz: the parents watched out for us and the gangs stayed away, for the most part.

Gratz was not a big street—a couple of football fields long at most. The street was cramped with parked cars lining one side so a passing car could barely squeeze through. The sidewalks were filled with old lawn furniture, flower beds, and these tiny trees that the people planted to make the street look more presentable. It was difficult to find a clear space to play where a window, flowerpot, or random resident was not in the way. But we tried.

Every month or so, the parents held a neighborhood meeting at which they discussed ways to improve the block. It might be painting the curb, planting a tree, or removing graffiti off a wall. The whole area knew that Mr. Walker, who lived two houses down from my grandmother, was a drunk. Mr. Walker stumbled through the neighborhood, tripping down stairs and slurring his words. He was famous for saying, "I'm not drunk." The kids actually called him "Mr. 'I'm not drunk' Walker." So every couple of months, when Mr. 'I'm not drunk' Walker lost his latest job, the other parents used to take up a collection to help his family. On the surface, the meetings seemed like a great way to work together and improve the neighborhood. But we kids knew different. It seemed each meeting ended in a ban on one of the games my friends and I loved to play.

I played with the same guys almost every day. Karl was my best friend. He was one of the smarter kids on the block, but he was also a Goody Two-shoes. He was the kind of guy who walked the extra ten feet to cross the street at the crosswalk. Melvin, who wore thick Coke-bottle glasses that were held together with a pound of tape, was tough as nails. He was shorter than the rest of us and had to be extra tough to hold his own. It seemed like he could fall from a skyscraper, get up, and keep playing. Melvin was a loyal friend. Ronnie was Melvin's younger brother. Ronnie was as shy as Melvin was tough.

Herb was your classic momma's boy. Many guys called him big-boned to his face, but he was just plain fat. He always had to be in an hour before curfew. His mother had an incredible voice that carried through the entire street. When she wanted him in, she stuck her head out the window and called, "HER-BERT." We always made fun of him for that, but everybody loved him. Elsworth was the slowest of the bunch, which hurt him in most of our games. He was the catcher in baseball, the center in football, and the goalie in street hockey. He tried hard. There was David, who we called "The Spider" because he was the one that always got the ball off a roof; Roger Spotward, who for some reason wanted to be called Tony, and finally, Roger Watters. Roger was the stereotypical nerd. He wore glasses, he liked to read and play chess, and he was not very athletic. Roger just wanted to be accepted, and for most games he was the umpire or the referee.

Most of us grew up on welfare, or without much money. Of course, we didn't know enough to understand how poor we were. We created our own fun with whatever was lying around the neighborhood. It still amazes me how creativity grows in direct proportion to poverty—at least for kids.

Instead of racing bicycles—which no one could afford—we'd designed our own scooters, which basically consisted of a pair of adjustable roller skates and a thick stick about three feet long. We pulled the roller skates apart and nailed two wheels to each side of the board. A wooden milk crate completed the scooter and we were ready to race. We designed obstacle courses around cars and between trees and held time trials. These scooters could really fly, but the steering wasn't always the most responsive. The parents were forever complaining about the noise. They didn't want us on the sidewalk because young children could get hurt, and they didn't want us in the street because it blocked traffic. The monthly meeting at Melvin's house ended in a ban on scooter races.

During baseball season, we played a game called half ball, using an old rubber ball and a broom handle. We'd cut the ball in half, split into teams of three, and play a modified version of whiffle ball. With the oblong shape of the ball, you could create several different pitches. If the flat side was facing left, the ball curved to the right. If the flat side was down, the ball rose. Pitching was a real art form. I had a side-armed sinkerball that was unhittable. Of course, we didn't have a big field to play on, so the idea was to hit the ball off the houses and try to catch it on the carom. The half balls banged against the windows and left marks on the walls. For some reason, the parents didn't go for that. The meeting at Herbert's house ended with a ban on half ball.

Basketball was fun but extremely short-lived. We used to cut the bottom out of a milk crate and nail it to a telephone pole. Looking back, I can see why inner-city kids are so good at basketball, because if you could shoot a basketball through a milk crate, with no backboard and only a half-an-inch leeway on any side with eight friends trying to tackle you, then you could certainly drill a twenty-five-footer with a glass backboard and regulation rim in an indoor gymnasium. Melvin was remarkably quick and adept at swiping your shot. The problem was that most times, the ball ended up in a flower bed or went through a window. Parents' meeting at Tony's: no more basketball.

But our all-time favorite game was called One, Two, Three—You're My Man. The game was created because tag was too boring and led to arguments about whether or not you were actually touched. There was no room for doubt with One, Two, Three—You're My Man, and it never got boring.

The game started with everybody in a circle. One person—usually Herbert—chanted: My-mother-and-your-mother-were-hanging-up-clothes. With each word, Herbert pointed to a different person. Whomever he was pointing to when he said the word, "clothes," was eliminated. Herb continued: My-mother-punched-your-mother-right-dead-in-the-nose. Another person was eliminated on "nose." What-color-was-the-blood? Red, R-E-D. Eliminate one person and continue.

Finally, we ended with one person, whose job was to chase down the rest of us. We had five minutes to hide anywhere on the block. Just touching the person wouldn't do, you had to catch 'em and hold 'em long enough to say, "One, Two, Three—You're My Man." If a guy was grabbed only for "One, Two, Three—You're," and then got away, he was free. So you'd have to grab, tackle, sit on, or do something else to hold him down.

Once a person was caught, he joined the "chaser." Now there were two people to chase everyone else down and so on until there was only one person left. That person was the winner. This was our favorite game because it could take an entire day to play one game. By the end of the day, the whole neighborhood would be chasing down one person. And you'd never know when someone was going to jump out from a car, or a street post, or a basement window to tackle you.

The game turned a little dangerous when the old abandoned house on the corner became fair game. The only entrance to the house was through a dark alley that was littered with broken glass. It was a three-level house, and there was a perfect escape route through the window on the third level to the roof of the second level. Then, with a running jump, you could cross the alley to the roof of the adjacent house to safety.

The gap was only about four feet wide, but it was two stories high and if you missed you could fall to your death. We played for weeks without ever considering that option until one day Robert Speaks slipped and was hanging on to the ledge screaming for his life. Luckily, Karl and I grabbed him by the shirt and pulled him to safety.

Robert Speaks was killed in a gang fight a couple of years later—I liked him.

I'd usually do pretty well at One, Two, Three—You're My Man. Most guys spent their energy trying to catch the first person they saw. But there was no way anyone was going to catch Melvin or Karl and certainly not Clyde. He was the fastest guy I ever saw in my life, and he proved it by running away from cops. He used to run drugs and from time to time we saw him flying through the neighborhood. The next thing you knew a couple of cop cars—with lights flashing and sirens blaring—came cruising after him. No one was going to catch Clyde, except the cops. He spent most of the last thirty years in jail.

When I was the chaser, the first thing I did was catch all the slow people and build my numbers. Elsworth and Herbert were slow, but had tremendous grips. So if they ever got their hands on you there was no escape. Tony was fast but he didn't have stamina. So we used him to finish people off once they were tired of running from us. There was quite a science to it.

The problem was the parents didn't like us flying through the neighborhood, and when that close call with Robert got around, we suspected it would be the end of One, Two, Three—You're My Man. And that was something we were not prepared to let happen.

The way we saw it, we were kids—not angels. We were outside for twelve hours, the sidewalks were narrow, the streets were packed, and if a flowerpot got broken, a car got scratched, a window got marked, or a younger child run over, so be it.

We knew the next parents' meeting was at Karl's house and we gathered on our usual corner in front of the abandoned beauty shop to plan our strategy. We agreed to attend the meeting and ask that once a week, the parents take turns walking us to the park so we could run and scream and play One, Two, Three—You're My Man as much as we liked.

"They're not going to let us all speak," said Karl. "We need a spokesman."

Everyone looked at me. "Rodney," they said in unison. "You should be the one."

"You gotta be crazy," I told them. "I'm not speaking in front of all your parents." My grandmother was never at the meetings because she worked every day as a cleaning lady across town.

I should have walked away then. But before I could, Karl put his arm around my shoulder and whispered, "Look, Rodney. If you do this we'll get to go to the playground and the parents won't be blaming us for messing up the neighborhood. Everybody wins and it will be because of you. You'll be a hero." Karl knew me too well.

I was nervous, but Karl was right. I liked the idea of being the hero. My grandmother had told me stories about Martin Luther King, Jr. and John F. Kennedy. She told me how millions of people listened when they spoke and how the two men had been willing to die for what they believed in. When I was old enough to read, I found a book in her house called, *Heroes of the 20th Century*, describing their lives. I also read about people like Paul Revere and George Washington. To this day, my favorite quote is by Patrick Henry, who said, "Give me liberty or give me death."

I learned that heroes have moments in their lives where they find the courage to do something that others are unwilling or afraid to do.

This was my thinking when I agreed to represent the group at the parents' meeting.

"What if they say no?" I asked, trying to prepare for every possibility.

Good old Michael Caldwell was quick to reply. "Tell them that if they don't agree, then we're going to trash the block."

"What?" I said. "I'll get killed if I threaten them."

I offered an alternative. "What if I try this approach: 'We're keeping this neighborhood pretty clean now. But we can make it spotless. All we're asking is that you take us to the park once in a while.' "

But everyone else felt that we needed the strong-handed approach.

"We gotta have something. We're the ones that dirty up the block," said Herbert as he finished his Popsicle and tossed the stick in the bushes. "We have to let them know that we mean business."

I had a bad feeling, but we all agreed that the final plan was for me to say that kids have rights, too, and demand that they take us to the park. If they said no, then I would counter with our threat about trashing the neighborhood.

We marched to Karl's house for the meeting, united on our grand mission.

Karl's house was packed. The parents filled the living room while the kids sat on the stairs. There was never any food at these meetings; they took place during the day when it was hot, and the idea was to take care of business and get out. No one wanted to linger in a stuffy room full of sweaty bodies.

Mr. Jimmy led the meeting. Mr. Jimmy was about five-foot-two inches tall, 120 pounds, and always wore a flannel lumberjack shirt with both suspenders and a belt holding up pants that were two sizes too big. Despite his size, he tried to be a tough guy in the neighborhood. Mr. Jimmy led the discussion about how to improve the things around the neighborhood. They talked about boarding up the abandoned house on the corner. They decided to call the city to replace a broken stop sign and they debated whether or not to take a collection for Christmas lights this year—in the past only a few families could afford them. The whole thing took only twenty minutes, but for me, it seemed like a couple of hours.

The parents were about to discuss the condition of the neighborhood and were getting ready to ban yet another game when Melvin yelled, "Why don't we hear from the kids now."

"Okay," said Mr. Jimmy without an ounce of patience. "So are we going to hear from all of you?"

"No," said Karl. "Rodney is going to talk for us."

I got up from my perch on the stairs, took off my hat in a show of respect, and inched my way down.

Everyone stared as if I was wasting their last five minutes on earth.

"First of all, we're happy that you let us come to this meeting. You are our parents and we love you very much." I decided to finesse them a little.

"And we really want to be good children and do what you want us to do, but we have to play. That's what kids do. We play. Parents work." Then I remembered that most were on welfare and quickly covered with, "or work around the house. You work hard and cook meals and wash clothes. But kids play. We have to play."

I kept my head up, making eye contact with as many parents as possible.

"Every time you have these meetings, the result is you end up banning another game we play. First it was no scooters, so we played half ball. Then half ball caused too much damage so we played basketball. Well, we're running out of things to play. So we have an idea that we'd like to share with you."

I decided to start slow.

"Not all the time, but maybe every Saturday, just for a little while, we were thinking maybe some of you could, perhaps, just walk us to the playground so we can play there."

Immediately I heard Mrs. Poindexter yell, "Oh, no, we're not going to the playground."

Mr. Jimmy interrupted, "Let him talk, let him talk."

I continued.

"It will be great. That way, Mrs. Hall, you won't have us yelling outside your window. Mrs. Poindexter, we won't play ball near your flower beds. Mrs. Livingston, we won't be on your steps." Mrs. Livingston was notorious for yelling at us for sitting on her steps. They were like golden steps. Even if you leaned against them, Mrs. Livingston went crazy.

I tried to build support. "Mr. Caldwell," I continued, "we won't bump into your car." Mr. Caldwell was a classic. He lived in our horrible neighborhood but owned a gorgeous Ford LTD. It was maroon with a white interior. It had big whitewall tires, and the chrome was always clean and shiny. And it had two furry dice that hung from the mirror. He spent all his time protecting his car, and I don't think I ever saw him drive it.

I concluded my plea with, "We would really appreciate it and we will be very happy children if you do this for us."

The room went quiet.

Finally Mr. Jimmy said, "Well, that was a nice proposal, but I know that I don't have the time to take you kids to the park." Then he turned to the rest of the parents and asked, "Does anyone here have the time to take these kids up there?" Dead silence.

"Okay. Well, thanks for coming to the meeting. We're not going to have the time to take you to the park. You kids are going to have to play right here without stomping through Mrs. Poindexter's flowers, without leaning on Mrs. Livingston's steps, and without scraping Mr. Caldwell's car. So run along."

The other children started to filter out in defeat, but I put my hat back on my head—backward—and said, "I have just one more thing to say."

Mr. Jimmy did a double take and I could feel the temperature in the room shoot up ten degrees from the parents' collective stare. I stood strong and spoke slowly and clearly.

"We kids know it's important to keep the neighborhood neat and we've been doing a pretty good job except for a couple of times. But if nobody wants to help us play, all of us kids feel like we're going to go out of our way to make sure that the neighborhood is a mess."

I had said it. I took a deep breath and waited for the parents to see the error of their ways. Unfortunately, it didn't quite work out that way. "Rodney Carroll," said Mrs. Trower, Karl's mother. "You are showing a great ignorance today. When your grandmother gets home, she will be surprised and disappointed at your behavior."

Mr. Waters, who chimed in from the back of the room, was a little more aggressive.

"You know what he needs is a good whuppin'. Who do you think you are, talking to adults like that?"

This was not good. I was getting slammed from all directions. I was looking for support from my friends, but found none.

"Roger," I said. "Why don't you say something?"

"Well I just want to play," said Roger, sheepishly. "But if they say no, then . . ."

Traitor, I thought as I glared in his direction. And the barrage continued.

"You have too much mouth on you," said Herbert's mom.

"You're too smart for your britches," yelled Robert's dad.

"You shouldn't worry about playing," threatened Mr. Davis. "You should worry if you're ever going to sit down again."

"You should be on punishment for a week." I could swear that came from Karl.

Mrs. Livingston clawed her way to the front of the room, got right up in my face, and said, "I remember the day when you asked where you could play. Well I can think of where you can play now, but I'm too much of a Christian woman to tell you." She was just warming up. "But I'll tell you one thing, the next time you go near my steps, I'm going to throw hot water out the window."

Mr. Jimmy mercifully stepped in. "The meeting is adjourned. This is a waste of time anyway. This is not kid stuff. This is grown-up stuff. Why don't you kids just get on out of here? And remember, anybody that throws any trash on the ground will be in serious trouble."

As we left the house I was about ready to cry. My friends and I went back to the curb to figure out what went wrong.

"Why did you say we would trash the neighborhood?" asked Karl.

"Why did I say that?" I was shocked at the question. "You told me to say that."

"Yeah, but you should have saw that it wasn't going so well," responded Robert. "When Mr. Waters stood up you should have known there was trouble. Weren't you scared when he stood up?"

"Yeah."

"Well, why did you say it then?"

I scanned my friends. I couldn't believe they were blaming this on me.

"You didn't say, if you're scared don't say it," I said. "The plan was to just say it."

"Yeah," said Karl. "I could tell that once they didn't go for it the first time that they weren't going to go for it after you threatened them. You have to be able to read the situation."

"I knew you weren't going to do well," said Barry. "I knew you would mess up."

"Didn't you see Mr. Davis in the back," said Herbert. "This guy was really mean. I'll tell you right now, I would have never said that to Mr. Davis. I thought he was going to get up and slap you himself."

"Why didn't someone stop me then?" I asked, although I knew this conversation was pointless. The damage was done and it was obvious who was taking the heat.

"You're in major trouble now," reiterated Karl.

In a last attempt to garner a little unity I said, "What about the rest of you guys?" But they just walked away shaking their heads.

Later that night, Karl's mom made good on her promise and told my grandmother what had happened. I sat on the top of the stairs and heard the entire conversation. Mrs. Trower took the liberty of exaggerating things a little. She said I was disrespectful. She added that I had talked loud and said things that made no sense. She said that I was going to single-handedly trash the neighborhood. She didn't know what had gotten into me.

"Oooohh, you're in trouble," said my sister Cheryl.

"Wait until I tell everyone," said my brother Courtney. But he was too late. The entire neighborhood already knew. I was already branded as an outlaw.

When Karl's mom left I came down to speak with my grandmother.

"What happened?" she said. One thing about my grandmother, she always listened to both sides of the story.

I told her what happened. I was going to be a hero like Patrick Henry. The parents were going to praise me for my intellect and my friends were going to admire me for my courage.

"Instead, the parents want to lynch me and my friends want to disown me," I said.

My grandmother shook her head. She always seemed to have a way of putting things into perspective. This was not the first time my conviction had gotten me into trouble with authority and it wouldn't be the last. But after each one, my grandmother was there to talk it through with me.

She started with a question.

"What made you say that if you didn't get your way, you'll trash the neighborhood?" she asked.

"It was the plan," I told her.

"Who's plan?" she replied. She stressed the word "Who's."

"My friends," I answered. "I had a different idea." I told her what it was.

"Why didn't you do it your way?" My grandmother asked.

"Because I wanted to follow the plan. They elected me as the leader and I thought I should follow the plan."

My grandmother leaned down so we were at eye level, put her hands on my shoulders, and said in a stern voice: "Next time someone wants you to be their leader you tell them, 'I'll be your leader, but I can't lead your way, I have to do it my way. Or you get someone else to lead.' "

I remembered those words as the rehearsal for the town hall event with President Clinton concluded. In twenty-four hours, I would be in the position I had dreamed about since the days when my grandmother told me stories about how John F. Kennedy and Martin Luther King, Jr., had captivated audiences with their inspiring speeches. This was my once-in-a-lifetime opportunity, and I was only sure of one thing: I needed to find a way out of it.

===

Not far from Navy Pier is a high-rise public housing project called Cabrini-Green. If you are a poor family living on welfare in Chicago, you are likely to live here. Following the rehearsal, I took a ride to clear my head and I found myself heading toward Cabrini-Green. It wasn't hard to tell when I got there. It is located just a few blocks from one of the richest residential neighborhoods in Chicago, yet Cabrini-Green is home to drug traffickers and deadly gangs.

The walls in Cabrini-Green apartments are warped and crumbling. The linoleum floors are cracked and pockmarked.

These are places where little boys and girls cannot walk on their way to and from school because the surrounding areas are controlled by gangs. Every child in Cabrini-Green has a choice: join a gang to get protection or spend your childhood in fear.

When kids leave Cabrini-Green and go to school, they attend what one of our former education secretaries called "the worst public school system in America." A system riddled with crime and drugs, with buildings so dilapidated they ooze asbestos. If they get sick, poor families in Chicago must try to find a clinic that accepts Medicaid patients, but the system is so swollen and clogged that you cannot hope for an appointment. So you wait until the illness is so far advanced you have to go to the emergency room. At least there you can get treated.

Kids in Cabrini-Green aren't running and playing the way we did thirty years earlier although it is eighty degrees and sunny. They aren't doing anything. They have no vision of a future outside welfare. And when you can't visualize something, you can't reach it. On one corner four older kids, with their collars pulled up and their heads held low, see me and try to hide drugs. On another corner an eleven-year-old girl is smoking a cigarette while her friend drinks a beer. I know she's eleven because I asked her.

"What are you? A cop?" she asks sarcastically as I walk past.

The adults are out as well, but the sight is even more striking. They are out in their house slippers and bathrobes with curlers in their hair. Like they're going to be around all day—no sense in getting ready to go anywhere.

The area is filled with fear. Drive-by shootings aren't front-page news but they happen here every day. "Children in our inner cities are getting killed," said President Clinton. "They don't get killed in bunches so that they make the news, just one here and one there."

It is these kinds of neighborhoods where it happens. Just a stray bullet or a fight that gets out of hand. Two months ago I got a call from a friend whose son was killed in a drive-by shooting. They were sitting on the steps of their apartment on a day like today in a place like this. There was a fourteen-year-old girl who lived next door. Her nineteen-year-old boyfriend was angry for some reason or another. He and some friends drove by and started shooting. My friend's son happened to be in the way and he got shot. He was nineteen. He was a decent kid. Who knows what he could have made of himself?

I was in Chicago, but I might just as well have been in a similar place in New York or Los Angeles or any other big city in the United States. Or even where I grew up in Philadelphia. I sat down on a park bench.

This could not have been FDR's vision when he started welfare, I thought to myself.

During the Great Depression, welfare was used to help alleviate some of the hardship experienced by many in our nation. It seemed reasonable at the time. America, the richest and most technologically advanced nation on earth, needed to do more to help its poorest citizens.

The problems started when welfare moved from being temporary assistance to being a way of life. When families became completely dependent on government to survive. When poor people were herded into large public housing projects.

What's even worse is the effect welfare had on our nation's children. Even the children from welfare families that stayed out of gunfire and away from gangs had to walk a near-perfect line to escape the path of welfare or worse.

I looked back at the kids hanging out on the corner. I thought of all the things that had happened in my life, and had taken me from where they were to where I am now. Then I walked back to Navy Pier.

2. Old Blues Songs

For the first six years of my life, I lived with my mother, Roselyn, sister, Cheryl, and brother, Courtney, in a one-bedroom apartment of the Richard Allen Homes in the projects of North Philadelphia. My dad, James, worked as a cook at Hahneman Hospital at Broad and Vine. Well, I always called him a cook, but he insisted he was a chef. I visited him at work a couple of times a year. He made me the same thing each time—a bacon, egg, and cheese sandwich on white toast. He politely asked how I was doing in school, but during our periodic meetings it became clear that James had no interest in being a dad.

My mom made a determined effort to keep James out of my life for as long as she could. Every few years, he sent a Christmas present and maybe by February, my mom allowed me to open it. No matter what questions I asked about him, my mom always gave the same answer, "He's no good." To this day, I'm not sure that my parents ever got married. I have never seen a wedding picture and the few times I asked my mom, she snapped back, "Don't you worry about it." James died of liver disease when I was twenty-nine.

My mom worked nights at the U.S. Post Office as a mail sorter and made pretty good money. But she had a severe drinking problem and most of her paycheck went for booze, so we stayed in the projects.

The Richard Allen Homes were one of the toughest parts of Philly and still are. There was glass and broken bottles strewn all over the sidewalks. There were drug dealers and violence twenty-four hours a day. We didn't know our neighbors. We had no friends and we lived by my mother's only rule: never go outside. We didn't have toys, and since we weren't allowed outside, we spent our time staring out the window and watching the older kids throw the ball or play kick-the-can.

When I was eight, my mom married Stan Carter, a fellow employee from the night shift, and for a short while, we lived, what I called, "the good life." We moved out of the projects to a middle-class neighborhood in West Oak Lane. It was only five miles away from my old neighborhood and my grandmother's house in North Philadelphia, but it might as well have been on a different planet.

We lived in a three-bedroom house that had central air-conditioning and heat. The streets were wide and clean and I had a black English-racer bicycle that I rode all over the neighborhood. This bike wouldn't have lasted five minutes in my old neighborhood. I think my best friend Karl described it best to his wife years later when they were considering moving back to help renovate the old neighborhood. When his wife, Denise, asked where their nine-year-old son, Joshua, was going to ride his bike, Karl replied, "Don't worry, he won't have it very long."

There was no threat of violence or crime around our new house. Our front yard was covered with grass and we had a driveway and a garage. The neighborhood had large trees and gardens and we lived across the street from a school with a playground, basketball court, and a four-square court. My friends all had brand-new bikes. Henry, who lived next door, even had a minibike. Each house on our block had a large, covered porch, so even in the rain, we could jump from porch to porch without getting wet.

Whenever I left the house, I made sure to walk past Debbie Coleman's, six houses down. Debbie was eighteen months older than me and I had a crush on her from the time I was nine.

I was excited about my mother's second marriage and hoped Stan would be a real father to me. I dreamed of playing catch or throwing the football, but quickly learned that Stan was not interested. I loved sports but Stan wasn't athletic. Other fathers were scoutmasters in the Cub Scouts, but for Stan it was always "I'm too tired," or "I'm too busy," or "Maybe next time."

After the first eight months of their marriage, Stan and my mom separated and for the next six years they were on-again, off-again, depending on how long mom stayed sober. When Stan didn't live with us, he stayed with his parents—his father was a doctor and had plenty of money. We continued to live with mom, but "the good life" was over.

My mother could be a wonderful person when she was not drinking. She could be compassionate and caring. She made us cookies. She read us stories and acted out all the characters in the books. She did a killer version of *The Cat in the Hat*. I considered my mom an intelligent woman—she enjoyed reading and was a good writer. She was a great cook—spaghetti and meatballs was her specialty. She played the piano and loved to sing. When we were young, my mom sang jazzed-up versions of all the children's songs. "The Itsy Bitsy Spider" was my favorite. Of course, I was right there to tell her that the melodies she sang were different from those we learned in school.

"Don't be afraid to try to make something better," she answered. "Sometimes, you have to add a little soul."

But Cheryl, Courtney, and I rarely saw my mom's soulful side. As long as I can remember, my mother had a severe alcohol problem. And when she drank, her personality and mood changed. She became cold and heartless and mean.

"Who told you to wear that blue shirt?" she asked as I left for school, her eyes barely open and still wearing clothes from the previous night. Most of the time she was hungover in the morning and she didn't have the energy to help us prepare for the day. When I tried to answer, she snapped, "Don't talk back to me when I'm asking you a question."

Even when she was pleasant in the morning, I was nervous about coming home after school because she drank all day.

"Guess what? Guess what?" I yelled as I walked in the door. "I got an 'A' on a test."

"Why you making so much noise?" she yelled back. "I'm trying to get some sleep here. You guys just shut up and sit down."

We were looking for love and support and when my mom was drinking we were slammed to the ground—both verbally and physically.

Courtney, Cheryl, and I earned good grades—it was rare to bring home even a "B." One of my few "B's" in school came on a spelling test because I misspelled "received." I put the "i" before the "e." When my mom saw the paper, she pounded her fist and yelled, "How can you spell received wrong? Anyone can spell that."

She crumpled up the paper and threw it to the floor. Perhaps she forgot that I needed it signed and returned to the teacher. I picked up the paper and smoothed it out.

"Will you sign it?" I asked.

"I'm not signing no paper!" she answered, staring in disgust. "I only sign A's."

My mom always found some reason to abuse us. If we didn't eat the food on our plate quickly enough, my mom got so frustrated that she threw the plate against the wall.

At six, Cheryl was learning cursive handwriting. After reviewing one of her homework assignments, my mom forced Cheryl to stay up all night to rewrite her work. Cheryl sat hunched over the dinner table trying as hard as she could to make it perfect.

"No," my mom yelled as Cheryl fought back tears. "Do it again."

It broke my heart.

When my mom wasn't drinking, she handled things differently. If I brought home a "B" in spelling, she said, "Okay, now remember, 'i' before 'e' except after 'c.' Or if we didn't eat our carrots, she said, "You have to eat your carrots because they are good for your eyes. Why don't we put a little sugar on your carrots?" Or she suggested that for every carrot we ate, we could have one bite of a cookie. Or if Cheryl was struggling with her handwriting, my mom placed her hand on Cheryl's and said, "See how I'm doing this? I'm taking the 'c' and I'm touching this line and I'm coming down and touching this line." My brother, sister, and I clung to those times.

But as we got older, the drunken stupors became more and more frequent and she acted less and less like a mother. She refused to wash or iron our clothes. I had no money for books because my mom spent it all on alcohol. I missed field trips because my mom refused to sign the release forms. The school accepted fewer excuses. In fourth grade they said, "Well, we'll let you slide this time." But in eighth grade, suddenly you're sitting in the principal's office while the rest of your class is at the planetarium.

Kinsey Elementary School was located directly across the street so it took only a minute to get home. I dreaded that minute walk and I did anything I could to prolong it. In junior high, I played sports, but before that, I went from teacher to teacher asking for extra work. I begged my teachers to let me clean the blackboards or clear the desks. If we were doing numbers the next day, I'd ask to write the lesson on the board. My teachers thought I was an eager student, but early on, my motives had little to do with school. But the more I stayed, the more I realized that I liked learning. I liked knowing things. Most kids learn a great deal from their parents and I wasn't learning anything of value at home.

The first teacher that had an impact on me was my fourth-grade teacher, Mrs. Parker. She told me, "You're as smart as you want to be."

My mom wasn't interested in my passion for learning and she was suspicious when I came home late.

"The teachers asked me to help with tomorrow's lesson plan," I told her proudly.

"Those teachers get paid good money," she insisted. "You don't have to help them."

No matter how long I managed to stay at school, at some point I had to go home. The worst part was that I had no idea what to expect. Would my mom be sober or drunk? I prepared myself by looking for the signs outside of our house. Are the blinds open or closed? Is the mail picked up? Is the door locked?

The best indication was to put my ear to the door and listen to the music. If it was playing, mom was drinking. You could be sure of it. She listened to all kinds of music, but it was mostly old blues songs and soul by B.B. King, Aretha Franklin, and Otis Redding.

Coming into the house was similar to those old monster movies—where the music tells you something bad is going to happen. In the movies, it's the music that scares you as much as the monster, and that's the way it was for us. If I heard music, I walked slowly through the house with an eerie feeling, not knowing where my mom might be.

The goal was to sneak quietly from the front door through the living room, up the stairs to my room to start homework before my mom found something to pick on. Occasionally, she drank so much that she passed out, which was a godsend. There wasn't a hot cooked meal, but jelly bread—peanut butter and jelly sandwiches without the peanut butter—was good enough for us. If she was asleep and if we were quiet enough, we could avoid her abuse for the entire night.

One night, Cheryl, Courtney, and I noticed my mom falling asleep on the couch. Cheryl, who was wise to my mom's routine, noticed that the music was still playing. My mom needed complete quiet to fall into a deep sleep.

"We have to cut the music off," she said.

We all agreed and Courtney and I convinced Cheryl to make the move. Cheryl sneaked down the steps with Courtney and me coaching from above. She crawled on her hands and knees across the living room, around the couch, and up to the stereo. Today, the record player, tuner, and speakers could fit in a shoebox, but our unit was four feet high, in a large wooden cabinet that weighed about one hundred pounds. Cheryl had to lift the lid and hook the latch to keep it open before turning off the stereo. If the hook wasn't latched properly, the top slammed down, making a loud bang.

"Don't forget the latch," I whispered. I should have also advised her to gradually turn the music down, because when Cheryl cut the music, it startled my mom. She quickly sat up and grabbed Cheryl's wrist. Cheryl let out a shriek of pain and fear that I'll never forget.

"What are you doing turning that music off!" my mom yelled as she squeezed Cheryl's wrist.

"We wanted you to sleep in peace," said Cheryl.

My mom didn't buy it and squeezed harder. Cheryl tried again.

"Rodney made me do it," she pleaded.

"Where is he?" my mom screamed, and Cheryl pointed our way. Courtney and I bolted for our room. My mom stormed up the stairs and into our room, dragging Cheryl with her. She picked up a shoe and chucked it at Courtney. "Don't you ever disrespect me in my house," she said as she threw Cheryl to the bed. I tried to explain, but she hit me with the back of her hand and said, "Don't talk back to me." She took another swing, but I ducked out of the way. She was out of control.

Usually we could expect one hit each before my mom cut off the lights and sent us to bed without supper. But tonight was different. My mom swung at me as I jumped for cover on the top bunk. Courtney and Cheryl darted behind a dresser. My mom chased us around the room for a few seconds before she had enough.

"Don't try hiding from me," she yelled. "I'm going to get my belt."

When she left, the three of us bolted out of the room, down the stairs, and into the basement. But running only made it worse. The physical pain of being whipped didn't hurt nearly as much as the anticipation. Suddenly my mom appeared at the top of the steps.

"I'm not going to keep chasing you," she yelled, breathing heavy. "You have five seconds to get into bed." My mom started counting and we knew enough not to test her any further. As we ran past her to go upstairs, she took a swing at each of us. She hit me in the back. Courtney got nailed in the head and Cheryl was whipped in the back of the leg. That one was the loudest.

We went to bed with our clothes on. Courtney was crying so hard that the bunk beds shook.

"Stop crying or I'll give you something to cry about," Mom yelled.

"Courtney," I said as I leaned my head over and saw the tears pouring down his face, "put your face in the pillow." The bunk beds still shook, but the pillow muffled the cry enough to appease my mom.

The next morning I awoke to the smell of pancakes and sausage. I rubbed my eyes to make sure I wasn't dreaming.

"Courtney," I yelled, peeking my head over the edge. "Courtney, wake up. Mom's making breakfast."

In a second Courtney was alert. We both knew that if mom was cooking, it meant she wasn't drinking.

Courtney sniffed the aroma from the food. These were his favorite moments. "Oh, I hope she has the cinnamon applesauce for the grits," Courtney said.

We hopped out of bed and met Cheryl in the hall. We sneaked down the stairs. The lamp next to the couch was still tipped over. We crept down like little puppies who had just been hit with a newspaper. We were desperate to race into the kitchen with our tails wagging but cautiously waited for reassurance.

When my mom said, "Come on in, breakfast will be ready in five minutes," we cruised into the kitchen. We took turns hugging her.

"I'll get the plates," said Cheryl.

"I'll get the juice," I said. Courtney clung to my mom.

My mom cooked a fantastic spread of pancakes, eggs, sausages, and grits—with cinnamon applesauce. We ate and laughed and sang.

But before Courtney could finish his second helping of grits, my mother wiped her chin and stood up.

"I have to run to the store," she said. By now, we knew what that meant. Too many times she went to "the store" and came back drunk.

"No, please don't go," cried Courtney. "Stay here with us."

"Nope, I have to run a couple of errands," my mom answered, bending down on her knees to give Courtney one more hug.

"Then take us with you," said Cheryl. "We can help you."

"No, I can go faster on my own," she said.

With that, my mom grabbed her keys and left.

Before the door slammed, Cheryl threw down her plate and yelled, "I hate liquor."

"Yeah, me, too," said Courtney. He didn't know what he was talking about. He said "me, too," to everything.

"Why do you hate liquor?" I asked Cheryl.

"Because it's the liquor that does something to her. Mom is nice. See how Mom is? This is Mom. It's the liquor that makes her mean. I'm never going to drink any as long as I live."

"Me, too," said Courtney. "We're never going to drink because if we drink, then we could be mean."

The three of us put our hands together and made a pact. "We will never drink as long as we live."

But nothing seemed to deter my mom from drinking. Throughout her entire life, she never believed she had a problem. Several times, she went to rehab, but only as a means to keep her job. Rehab usually lasted six weeks. During that time, we stayed with Grandma. When my mom returned, it didn't take long before she started drinking again and a few months later, she'd go away again.

"She's on vacation," my grandmother told us, trying to protect us from the truth.

"Can we go? Can we go?" we asked.

When my mom called from her "vacations," she said all the things you want to hear as a kid. "I miss you. I love you." And we cried when we hung up the phone because it made us believe everything would be all right. But it never was.

My grandmother's full name was Lula Lucas but we called her Mom Mom. Mom Mom would give you the blood out of her veins if she could. Even when my mom was out of rehab, every six weeks or so, we spent a weekend at my grandmother's house.

We loved to go to her house and we cried when it was time to go back home. The more we cried, the less my mom let us go over. In retrospect, it probably would have been smarter to say, "Oh, Mom, we missed you. It's so good to be back home."

My grandmother made us feel like the most special kids in the world. Although she lived in poverty, she had a positive attitude. She was patient, creative, and had a great sense of humor. She worked full-time as a house cleaner and made eighteen dollars a day, plus bus fare. She always reminded us that it was, "plus bus fare."

We had the same routine every visit. On Friday night, my mom dropped us off around 8:00 P.M. She walked us to the door, but rarely stayed more than a second. We carried our clothes in a shopping bag and when we walked in the door, our grandmother directed us straight upstairs to put our clothes in our room before dinner. Courtney and I shared a room, and Cheryl slept on the couch. It seemed like we were forever hungry at home, but my grandmother loved to cook for us. She cooked fried chicken or pork chops.

We went to bed around 9:30 and always fell fast asleep. Our stomachs were full, the house was warm, the bed linen smelled fresh, and we still had the entire weekend ahead of us.

Saturdays with Mom Mom were the best. We woke up early, grabbed a quick breakfast, then took a bus to the subway, and the subway downtown to Center City, Philadelphia. The subway dropped us off in front of Gimbels, a huge department store with a discount level in the basement. We had a blast trying on different outfits and laughing. One day I tried on a blue shirt that my grandmother said made me look like a movie star.

"How much is it?" she asked.

"Fifteen . . ." I answered.

"You know," she replied, "now that I think about it, you'd look much better in this." My grandmother held the ugliest Hawaiian shirt you ever saw. "All for only two dollars." We all started laughing.

It was a silly time. Every joke was funny because we were happy.

"How do you think this looks?" I asked my brother as I walked out of the dressing room in a three-piece suit, including shirt, shoes, and clip-on tie.

"You're looking good," he conceded. "Let's get me one."

"Ooh, don't I look pretty?" added Cheryl, emerging from the dressing room in a yellow dress with big ruffles on the sleeves. As she pranced around the dress bounced up and down, exposing her three-year-old sneakers.

Although we were there for hours, for some reason, nobody gave us a hard time. Wearing new clothes made us feel important. When we were in the basement of Gimbels, I forgot about a life of patched-up jeans and secondhand shoes and envisioned a future of pin-striped suits and leather briefcases. When I dressed up, I imagined myself wearing a suit and tie to work every day. I liked that look. My grandmother told me how handsome I was. She said I looked like a businessman or a minister. One time I put on a black suit and she said I looked like Martin Luther King Jr.

To be compared to Martin Luther King Jr. was the highest compliment you could get from my grandmother. My grandmother loved him and everything he stood for.

"Martin Luther King Jr. was arrested yesterday," she told us. She made sure we always knew the latest news. "They're treating him real bad."

"Why does he do this?" I asked. In my mind, going to jail was not good.

"He's fighting for a cause," my grandmother replied. "If you really believe in something, sometimes you have to be willing to die for it."

I didn't have any concept of the greatness of Martin Luther King Jr. other than the reverence with which my grandmother spoke. But I knew I wanted to be a person that someone like my grandmother admired.

The hours passed quickly, but it seemed like we lived a lifetime in the basement at Gimbels. We were home for dinner by 5:00 and by 6:30 we were in the living room talking and playing games, like Candy Land and Old Maid. My grandmother was the best at Old Maid. Her secret was to stick the Old Maid a little higher than the rest of the cards to entice us to pick it. For months, we fell for it until one time she put it up and we all started laughing. We laughed so hard that we couldn't finish the game.

At 7:30, we turned on *The Jackie Gleason Show*, but it was mostly background noise as my grandmother talked to us about life.

"Do you want to be a good person?" she asked. We all said yes. "Then do unto others the way you want done unto you." She said it over and over again. "If you want to be treated well, then treat other people well."

We talked more about Martin Luther King Jr. and John F. Kennedy. She updated us on the Civil Rights movement and we discussed other current events. Cheryl listened the best she could, but had difficulty following everything. Courtney was still very young and usually fell asleep on my grandmother's lap after the second game of Candy Land. But I was riveted by every word. I was at a better age to understand what my grandmother was preaching. I pride myself on my memory and today I remember her words clearly and distinctly.

"Dr. King is a minister and God told him to help the poor people," she said. "Now you always want to help people when you grow up." She explained why JFK was popular. "He's a president who cares about *all* the people." She said both Dr. King and President Kennedy were doing what God wanted them to do.

"A lot of people don't do what God wants them to do," she said.

"What does God want me to do?" I asked her.

"You have to find that out for yourself," she said. "But he has a plan for you. I know that for sure."

My grandmother did not like Malcolm X, however, because, in her mind, Malcolm X was violent.

"There are good leaders and not good leaders," she told us. "The good leaders are people that lead others to do the right thing." She believed that Malcolm X was leading people to sometimes behave violently. "It's bad to act violently yourself," she continued. "But it's worse to lead someone else to do it with you."

I daydreamed about my future when my grandmother talked. I wondered what God wanted me to do. I remember listening to JFK give his famous speech.

"Ask not what your country can do for you, ask what you can do for your country."

I was mesmerized by the country's reaction as much as by his words. People were clapping because of what he had said. Later I became fascinated with the Gettysburg Address and other inspiring speeches.

Long before Martin Luther King Jr. was assassinated, my grandmother told us he was going to be killed, but that didn't make his death any easier for her. We didn't go downtown shopping that Saturday. It was a terrible weekend. For my grandmother, it was a tragedy. She couldn't hold back the tears as she tried to explain it to me.

"Why are you so sad?" I said. "Don't you think he'll go to heaven?"

"Yeah," she answered.

"Then why aren't you happy for that?"

"He is going to go to heaven," she told me. "But I'm sad because he still had more work to do here." It was one of the few times I saw my grandmother sad. "He was a great man who was doing a lot of good. I don't know if there will be anyone else to come along that can make the impact that he did."

"What did he do?" I asked. Although I had an idea, I knew it made my grandmother proud to talk about him.

"He was a man who came from humble beginnings and established a benchmark of greatness," she said. "He gave the country a conscience. He said that all people were created equal. And that's why he was killed."

3. The Final Hearing

I never wanted our Saturday night conversations to end. It was those nights that inspired me to make something out of my life. To be strong in the face of temptations. And most of all to make my grandmother proud of me.

By the time *The Ed Sullivan Show* was over, two hours after *The Jackie Gleason Show*, it was time to take our baths and go to bed. Sunday morning meant a pancake breakfast and church. I wasn't especially religious but I liked the Bible classes because I remembered the verses easily. I got a reputation for being smart. And I liked that feeling. The people at the church were supportive of my grandmother and brought us toys and sweaters.

After church, we had the afternoon to play with our friends. I usually cruised across the street and four houses down to Karl's house. When I was five, my dad sent me a train set for Christmas. Karl also had one, so most of the time, we played trains until dinner. Karl had a traditional household. There was a mother, father, and three children living on almost no income—seventeen thousand dollars a year—in a tiny three-bedroom house. They mixed real milk with powdered milk. The rule was one slice of bologna per sandwich. They didn't own a car and never went on vacation. Karl's mom sewed most of his clothes. But, no matter what else happened, the entire family sat around the table for dinner. They passed the food, talked about their day, and laughed together.

Sunday dinner at my grandmother's was served at 5:30 P.M.— usually roast beef or ham or turkey wings. There was always plenty of food and we could eat as much as we liked. We tried to sneak leftovers home and we usually got away with it, but one time, my mom caught us and threw the food away.

The weekends with my grandmother were a haven, but sure enough, Sunday night came along and it was time to go back to life with mother. If my mom was scheduled to come at 7:00, Courtney started crying around 6:30.

"It'll be alright," I told him. "It'll be alright."

Then we begged my grandmother to let us stay one more night. It was no secret that my grandmother was disappointed with the way my mother lived her life, but she didn't speak ill of her.

"This was a special weekend," she told us. "And we'll do it again soon."

Our only hope depended on my mom's sobriety. My grandmother didn't let us go with my mom if she had been drinking. Mrs. Poindexter ran a makeshift bar across the street, and my mom usually stopped there on her way to get us. We knew mom had been drinking if my grandmother sent us upstairs instead of kissing us good-bye. The three of us sat on the top step listening to every word.

"You're in no shape to take them back," my grandmother would tell mom.

"I'm taking these kids. These are my kids," my mom screamed.

The argument usually escalated until my grandmother was forced to call the police. Just one police car never comes to North Philadelphia. It's always four or five, and that caused a big scene in the street. Mrs. Poindexter was furious because she feared her private bar would get busted. By the time the cops arrived, mom was hysterical and out of control. My grandmother was always calm.

"She's been drinking and I'm afraid she's going to harm the kids," my grandmother told the cops.

I guess back then, drinking and driving wasn't a big deal because about half the time the cops made us go back with mom.

"Nope," they said. "She's the legal mother."

Before they could walk away, I cruised down the steps and got right in their faces.

"We're going to have an accident," I screamed. "Is that what you want? We're going to get killed."

"Get in the car, kid," the cop replied.

Cheryl, Courtney, and I grew extremely close during those times. We learned how to take care of one another. We did our own laundry. We walked to the store together to get milk or spaghetti or laundry detergent. I learned how to cook. At nine, I could cook pancakes and bacon. Not much later, I graduated to dinners—and not just jelly bread. I cooked chicken, spaghetti and meatballs, baked beans and hot dogs, and Beefaroni. I once tried to cook a roast beef but I failed miserably. It looked great on the outside but when we cut it up, blood leaked out everywhere. The problem was compounded when I panicked and tried to hide the roast in the cabinet next to the oven. When my mom found that I got a major spanking.

At dinnertime, Courtney, Cheryl, and I sat quietly at the table so we didn't wake up my mom. Then we cleaned the kitchen spotless. Ninety percent of the time, the next morning my mom wasn't feeling well enough to hassle us on our way to school.

"I'm sick," she said. "Get yourself ready." And we did. We started to need my mom less and less. I learned to sign her name. One time Cheryl came home with a "C." "You can't go to Mom with that," I said. "Give it to me."

As I grew older I felt sorry for my mom. But I could never understand why she was so mean to us. As much as my grandmother built us up, my mom tore us down.

I started to tolerate her "sickness" less as well. I wasn't a meek little kid listening for music at the front door after school. I grew bigger and stronger and at twelve, I was at least her size. If she took a swing at me, I blocked the punch and said, "There's no need to hit me. I'll do whatever you need me to do."

Finally on April 10, 1970, when I was twelve, I reached my breaking point. I earned a Junior Achievement Award and was preparing to attend the banquet. My mom had signed the permission slip but for some reason she said that I couldn't go.

"You're not going anywhere," she shouted from the couch, too tired to open her eyes.

"I'm going," I said and continued to get ready, figuring she would fall asleep.

"I said, you're not going," she yelled as she pulled herself up.

I quickly snapped back, "Yes, I am."

My mom didn't answer. She stumbled to her feet and walked past me to the front hall closet. Her head was down. Her fists were clenched. She opened the door and grabbed the aluminum baseball bat that I had found in the garbage the previous summer.

"You think you're too big for me to hit you?" she said as she cocked the bat.

"Let's not get into this," I said, dismissing her threat.

As I turned to leave, my mom swung the bat and cracked me in the back of the head.

"You're not going anywhere."

I stumbled forward and braced myself against the front door. I was in shock. I felt a lump forming rapidly on my head. I started crying but didn't look back. I ran out the door, down the steps, and down the street. At the end of the block I saw Debbie. She saw I was crying.

"Rodney, what's the matter?" she asked.

I couldn't speak. I just kept running and crying.

I ran as fast as I could. At first I didn't know where I was going but I ended up at the police station. My biggest fear was that one day I was going to defend myself and strike my mother back. I never wanted that to happen.

"I can't stand this anymore," I mumbled as I approached the desk.

"Can I help you?" said the policeman.

"Yeah," I answered. "My mother hit me with a bat."

The policeman didn't seem shocked. "What did you do to make your mother hit you with a bat? I think you should just go back home," he said. "Where do you live?"

I told him.

"You ran all the way over here?" he asked. It was twenty blocks through bad neighborhoods.

I explained the situation again, emphasizing the aluminum bat part. I even let him feel my lump, but he didn't seem impressed. I tried to persuade him to call my grandmother.

"Don't I get one phone call?" I demanded. "I want to call my grandmother."

"No," he said, "you're not a criminal so you don't get that one phone call."

"This is my mother's mother and I'm sure she'll want to know what's going on," I pleaded.

I finally convinced the cops to call my grandmother and she came to get me. I told my grandmother, "I can't go back home. I can't go back home. I can't go back home." My grandmother took me back to her place. She then went to my mom's to pick up Cheryl and Courtney.

When my mom realized what had happened, she was livid and came for us.

"You're not their mother," she yelled at my grandmother. She attacked my grandmother for not being a good mother to her. She said the nastiest things she could think of, but she left without us.

That night, my grandmother and I sat down and talked.

"We'll figure it out," she said as she put ice on my head. The bump had grown to the size of an orange. My head ached for weeks.

The police made a report of the incident. The report went to the child welfare agency and then the courts got involved. The courts agreed that my mother was an unfit parent and decided to put us in a foster home.

"No," my grandmother said. "I'll take 'em."

We proceeded through a series of court hearings until a judge awarded my grandmother custody. She explained to us that our mother had a disability and she was unable to care for us, but she was still our mother.

At the final hearing, my mother was sober. She was crying and the police kept us apart. The judge recognized that, financially, my grandmother could not afford to take care of three children and needed the state's assistance.

We saw my mom sporadically after that day in court. She kept drinking and rarely kept our dates to spend time together. It didn't bother me much until she missed my high school graduation. I was angry because it was a big deal for me. I had a cap and gown and as I came off of the stage, she was the only one not there. She had told me she would be there. She had promised. I knew that she was drinking. After the ceremony, she stopped by my grandmother's house to apologize. I saw her leave Mrs. Poindexter's house and met her on the front step.

"You need to get help," I told her solemnly, before she had a chance to speak. "You should get help for your sickness."

My mom started crying.

My mom died in 1987 when I was thirty. She had a brain aneurysm caused by the alcoholism. She had wasted away. She looked like she didn't even have the strength to pick up a bat, let alone swing it. She went into a coma, then on life support, and finally died eighty-two days later. When I heard the news, I was sad. I realized that my mom had drunk herself to death.

4. Black English Racer

I loved my black English racer. It represented my freedom. It was perfect for the wide streets and relatively safe neighborhood of my mom's home of West Oak Lane. But it had no place at my grandmother's on Gratz Street. The sidewalks were too narrow, the streets barely had room for the cars, and it would be only a matter of days before it was stolen.

But leaving my favorite bike behind was a small price to pay in exchange for a home where I was loved. To some extent, Courtney, Cheryl, and I sacrificed a part of our childhood when we lived with my mom. Emotionally, we were constantly on edge, never knowing what to expect.

That was never a concern at my grandmother's, where we received constant love and encouragement. Every school day, my grandmother woke us up at 6:00 A.M. by gently knocking on our door.

"Time to wake up," she would say. "It's another glorious day."

I was thirteen years old and in the middle of seventh grade when we moved in with my grandmother. Rather than switch schools, I continued to attend Wagner Junior High in my old neighborhood. Like most schools, Wagner had its share of trouble with gangs and drugs, but it wasn't nearly as dangerous as Gillespie Junior High School, which most of the kids in my grandmother's neighborhood attended. The families of the children that attended Wagner certainly weren't rich, but they weren't on welfare either.

Courtney, who was seven, and Cheryl, who was eleven, both went to the local elementary school. Mrs. Smith, who lived across from Herb, served as the local day-care provider. She walked the young kids in the neighborhood to school in the mornings and home in the afternoons.

We started every morning with a prayer—usually something traditional: "We thank God for waking us up safely this morning. We ask that You go with us this day and keep us safe from harm." But every now and then, my grandmother interjected a personal touch: "Thank You God for waking me up with my right mind."

We ate a hot breakfast together every morning—usually raisin and cinnamon oatmeal—and my grandmother created a theme for each day.

"Today is 'give someone your smile day,' " she said. For the rest of the morning we practiced our smile. After school, we reported, "I gave someone my smile today."

"Today is 'how do you know God loves you day.' " Or "Today is 'idea day.' Come home with an idea on how the world could be a better place."

Cheryl loved animals. Her idea usually involved finding safe, warm homes for all the stray dogs and cats on the street. Courtney loved fried chicken. One night, with crumbs on his face and grease on his mouth and fingers, he enthusiastically waved his drumstick and decreed, "I think every day should be fried chicken day. We'd all be happy. No wars, no fights. We don't need police officers, because everyone would eat fried chicken. This world would be a better place."

"That's great," my grandmother said. "Here, have another wing."

"What's your idea, Rodney?" Cheryl asked.

My commute to school consisted of the bus to the subway to a trolley that dropped me off two blocks from school. On the way to and from school, I saw vagrants beg for food and money and the homeless sleep in refrigerator boxes. On my own block, I saw people steal to feed their family or to support a drug habit.

I had no concept of the middle class when I was thirteen. I believed that people were either rich or poor. It didn't seem right.

"The world would be a better place if nobody was allowed to be poor."

"That's a good suggestion, but being poor isn't only about money," my grandmother said, adding a little perspective. "Some people have money and are still poor. And some people don't have money but are rich in other ways. We don't have a lot of money, but we have each other."

I didn't accept that so easily.

"How can you have money and be poor?" I asked.

"Having a nice house and plenty of food doesn't always make you happy," she tried to explain.

"Well, maybe we should try it and see how happy we'd be," Cheryl suggested.

After school I hung out with my friends. Now that we were teenagers, Karl, Tony, Elsworth, David, Melvin, Herbert, and I didn't need adult supervision to play at the park. Between games of basketball, football, and of course, One, Two, Three—You're My Man, we sat on the bleachers and dreamed about our future.

"You see that car?" Elsworth said, pointing to a Chevy Impala. "I'm going to get one like that."

"That's nothing," said David. "I'm getting a Ferrari."

"I'm getting a Porsche," said Herbert.

"Your mom won't let you drive no Porsche," joked Tony. "You'll be lucky if she lets you take the training wheels off your bike."

"What are you getting, Rodney?" asked Karl.

"I'm not spending my money on a car," I said. "I'm saving my money to buy a nice place to live."

"You're not going anywhere," said Melvin. "You're going to be right here with us."

Melvin never saw a life outside of Gratz Street. He wanted to work at the local factory like his older brother, Nelson.

"I'm not getting a job at a factory," I said.

"What are you going to do, Mr. Big Shot?" he asked.

"I'm going to go to college."

"Yeah, right," said Melvin. "You're going to go to college? What college you going to go to?"

"I don't know, yet," I said. "But I'm going to college and learn."

"Learn what? How to work at a factory?" said Tony.

"I'm going to be a scientist," I said proudly.

"You know, Rodney," Melvin added, "you're no better than us. You're no smarter than us."

Before I could respond, two uniformed police officers approached us.

"Any of you seen a tall, thin guy? Wears gold glasses and answers to Lucky?"

"Nope," we said in unison. "Never heard of him."

But everyone knew Lucky. He was a drug dealer who lived on Cleveland Street. He was called Lucky because whenever there was a problem—whether it be a shooting or a raid—Lucky was nowhere to be found. "You're lucky you weren't here," we told him. "The cops were looking for you."

If Lucky wasn't such a successful drug dealer, he could have easily made the transition to politician. Everybody liked him, even the adults. He was a tall, good-looking guy who had big sideburns, wore fancy clothes, a gold watch, and always wore sunglasses—day or night. He had an easygoing, inclusive personality. He made everyone feel like they were his best friend.

What Lucky did was wrong, but he made it seem cool. To some degree, a part of me admired him. Morally, he had no problem dealing drugs. He believed it was his only chance to succeed in life. He said that because he was born black and poor, he didn't have access to the same opportunities as other kids. He dropped out of school when he was fourteen because, "the public school system is like a jail. After four years, you leave in no better shape than when you started."

To Lucky, dealing drugs was a business, and he ran an efficient operation that any shareholder would be proud of. He called himself a sophisticated drug dealer—if there is such a thing. "I never actually touch any drugs," he bragged. "I don't deal drugs, touch drugs, smell drugs. There are no drugs on me, in my house, in my car."

Other drug dealers I knew—as well as number runners, loan sharks, and pimps—were usually violent people. But Lucky didn't come across as dangerous. He never carried a gun, although I knew he had one. Everything about him was cool and calm.

Before Lucky sold drugs, he pawned stolen goods. Every few weeks when the cops weren't around, he approached us at the park with an "opportunity" as he put it.

"Anyone want a television?" he asked. "Just fifteen bucks. Or how about a new bike for twenty bones? Hey, I got the new army jackets for just six bucks."

Lucky was smarter than most criminals. He never touched the stolen merchandise. He only facilitated the deal. The cops knew Lucky broke the law, but they couldn't catch him.

"Yeah, I'll take the bike," said Elsworth. "You got it with you?"

"Hey, I don't have the bike," Lucky explained. "I just know where you can go get it. I'm just trying to help you guys out."

"Where can you get it?" said Elsworth.

"Well, if you're interested, be at the park behind the church at 8:00 P.M. Somebody will drive up with a new bike. You give 'em the twenty and it's yours."

"How do you know about this bike?" Herbert asked.

"Hey, it pays to know things," said Lucky.

Elsworth bought the bike. Michael Caldwell got a jacket. David bought a television, but his mother knew it was stolen and made him return it when he tried to sneak it into his room.

"What television?" said Lucky. "I never sold you a TV."

Even when they weren't buying stolen goods, the guys looked forward to Lucky's visits. I called him the human time-out because every time he came to the park, my friends stopped playing basketball to check on Lucky's latest opportunity. I usually kept shooting.

Lucky and I didn't have much contact except for a few conversations on the court. Melvin told him about my plans for the future and he liked to give me a hard time.

"So I understand you're going to be a scientist? What are you going to do, wear a white coat?"

"That's right," I said without making eye contact.

"Keep dreaming," he said.

As the years went by, Lucky made a habit of talking to me before he left the park.

"Hey, it's the dreamer. What are you dreaming about today?" he said. "You gonna save the world? You going to be president? Whenever you're ready to come out of dreamland and get into reality, we can talk."

"Yeah, yeah, yeah," I said.

But Lucky was harmless and I was completely occupied with my plans for an honest future. With my home life stable, I was primed to make an impact on the world. My plan was to get good grades, go to college, and become a scientist. I focused my full attention on school. I was obsessed with learning. I paid close attention in class and studied diligently at home.

Homework was as much about learning as it was about spending time with my grandmother. My grandmother was an extremely wise woman, but she didn't have a formal education. Of all my classes, math was her weakest, but she tried nonetheless to participate.

"Question: $2x + 3 = 17$. What's 'x'?"

"The problem is that you have an 'x' in there," my grandmother said. "Letters are for writing, numbers are for math. You're confusing the two."

"No, Mom Mom. The letter is part of the problem," I tried to explain.

"You got that right," she said. "It is the problem."

But no matter how hard I tried to convince her, she refused to accept that there were letters in mathematics.

"Tell her that it's new math," said Mr. Borum, my math teacher, when I told him the situation.

It didn't work. Even on the easiest problem, my grandmother and I were like Abbott and Costello debating the integration of numbers and letters.

"Question: $5+y=9$. What's 'y'?"

"You have to take the 'y' out of there," my grandmother said.

"That's the object," I said. "What's 'y'?"

" 'Y' 's a letter," she said. "You need a four in there."

"Right," I said. "That's 'y.' "

"What's 'y'?"

"The answer."

It got sillier and sillier and after a couple of minutes, we were both cracking up. My grandmother loved to keep the joke going. At our morning prayer, my grandmother prayed, "God help Rodney understand that letters are for writing and numbers are for math."

Over the weekend, Karl and I went to Earl's Market for a Tastykake and soda. I asked my grandmother for twenty-five cents. She gave me a piece of paper with an "x" on it.

"What's this?" I asked.

"Just tell Earl the 'x' equals twenty-five cents," she said. "It's new math."

My grandmother had a great sense of humor and kidded Cheryl and Courtney as well. Courtney, especially, loved to be included in the joke. If he had a tail, it would have been wagging all the time. He loved to be hugged and my grandmother gave him lots of warm hugs.

He had big, bright eyes and was a silly kid. He liked to entertain. He made grand entrances to our living room by pretending to trip over the rug and then waited for a reaction.

In seventh grade, I played a police officer in the school play. When I practiced my lines at night, Courtney wanted to be included.

"There's no part for you," I told him.

"I'll just be the other person that rides with the police officer," he begged.

"Alright."

"So what are you boys doing here on the corner?" I said in my most official voice while my grandmother and Cheryl watched from the couch.

Before I could finish my line, Courtney stepped in front of me and pointed. "Yeah, what are you doing on the corner?" He hammed it up. I bet he could have been a great actor.

———

Wagner Junior High was divided into two groups: those who chose to take a language—German, French, or Spanish—and those who didn't. The students who took a language were typically more motivated and therefore shared a homeroom.

I was unaware that English didn't count as a language and I started seventh grade in classes with the "more difficult" students.

Mark E. Young was the meanest kid I've ever known. His nickname was Devil. He was sixteen and still in the seventh grade. He had sideburns. He was notorious for pounding kids in the bathroom and throwing their clothes out the window. He was just plain mean.

But Devil had beautiful handwriting. On the last page of every test was a form that we were required to sign to signify that we didn't cheat. During social studies, I finished my test early and was about to sign my name when Devil grabbed my arm.

"Rodney, give me your test," Devil said. "I'm going to put my name on it and turn it in."

"What?" I whispered. We all knew that Mrs. Sacksman's only concern was keeping the class under control and I didn't want her to think I was cheating.

"Give me your test," he ordered.

"I can't do that," I whispered.

"Look," he said, pounding his fist on the desk. "You either give me your test or I'll meet you outside."

Devil was part of the Summerville gang—one of two gangs that ruled the area surrounding the school. The other gang was called Clang. I didn't want to cheat, but I knew I couldn't take on Devil in a fight.

"Mark," I said. He gave me a dirty look.

"Sorry. I mean Devil. Your handwriting is too fancy. I have average handwriting. The teacher will know right away because yours is so much nicer than mine."

He thought about it for a second.

"Good point," he said. "Let me see your . . ." Before he finished explaining Plan B, Mrs. Sacksman lifted her head. "No talking back there. Only five more minutes and I'm watching you two." It was a close call but I escaped without any trouble.

A week later we received our report cards. In each class, there were three grades. One for test scores, one for work habits, and one for behavior. I picked up my card from homeroom and headed home to show my grandmother. I didn't bother to look at it. My test scores were impeccable. My work habits were top-notch and I was practically the teacher's pet. The worst thing I ever did in class was read a comic book in Mr. Borum's class after I had finished my work—something I would never admit to because reading a comic book in school was practically considered a federal offense.

I handed my grandmother the report card before dinner. She read the comments out loud.

" 'Rodney continues to excel in class. He's a good student and classmate. He's a pleasure to have in homeroom.' " I basked in the accolades.

She looked over the four pages of grades. She smiled and kissed me on the cheek.

"Great report card," she said. And she signed it.

That night I flipped through my report card before going to sleep. Just as I expected: AAA in math. AAA in science. AAA in English. Then I turned to social studies. Work habits—D. Test scores— C. Behavior—E (my school used "E's" instead of "F's"). I rubbed my eyes and looked again: D-C-E.

"This is impossible."

I double-checked the name on the page, but it was mine. I ran downstairs to tell my grandmother.

"Did you see these grades?" I asked her.

"Yes," she said. "I'm very proud of you."

"But it says I got a D-C-E in social studies."

"You can't always get good grades," she said. "You still have a great report card here."

"No," I said shaking my head. "This is wrong. This is a mistake. She's got me confused with someone else."

My grandmother sensed the frustration in my voice. Like always, she was calm and positive. "Okay," she said. "Tomorrow morning, ask her. I'm sure you'll work it out."

I went to bed, but couldn't sleep. This was an outrage. A tremendous injustice. I felt like I'd been robbed. I earned "A's," not D-C-E. I could not live until I remedied the situation.

I got to school early the next morning and headed straight for Mrs. Sacksman's room. Surely she would admit to making a mistake and adjust the grade immediately.

"Nope. Those are correct," she said matter-of-factly.

"How can that be?" I was in disbelief.

"When I tell the class to be quiet, I need the whole class to be quiet," she explained.

"I am quiet," I said.

"No," she repeated. "The whole class. You're part of the class."

"I can't control the class," I said. "What about the other grades?" I reminded her that my test average was ninety-four.

"Those are your grades," she said. "Just like everyone else. You're dismissed."

It was obvious that Mrs. Sacksman viewed everyone in the class as the same. To her, I was no different than Devil, an unmotivated, disinterested troublemaker. I stormed out the door, took an immediate left, and barged into the principal's office three doors down. It would be the first of many incidents in that office.

"Rodney, what's the matter?" said Principal Shoemaker. Principal Shoemaker was around fifty years old, he wore a three-piece suit every day, and he hated his job. He believed everyone who entered his office was wrong and deserved to be expelled. Unfortunately, he was usually right.

I showed him my report card. He read it.

"Not too bad," he said. "Except for social studies. You got some work to do there."

"Work to do?" I said and explained the situation.

"What do you want me to do?" he said.

"I don't know, but somebody better do something," I threatened. "Because this is an injustice."

"Well, I think you should just work harder," he said. "Mrs. Sacksman is a good teacher and if you work harder, you'll be fine. It's still a good report card." Again, I was dismissed without the problem being resolved. I grew angrier and angrier. I viewed my grades as my ticket to college. How was I going to make an impact on the world with D-C-E on my report card? I was being cheated out of what I rightfully deserved.

I spent the rest of the day telling anyone who would listen about my trials. I told every teacher, but always got the same response.

"Well, you got a good grade in my class. Just try harder next time."

Even my friends missed the point.

"You have to get out of that class," said John Daniel and Michael Rice, my two best friends in school. "Why don't you just take a language? Then you won't be in these classes."

"I do take a language," I insisted. "I take English."

"You have to take another language," said John.

"The point is that she's out of her mind."

"What are you going to do?" said Michael. "You've already seen Mr. Shoemaker."

"I don't know," I said. "But I'll tell you right now, somebody's going to fix this."

On the way home, I plotted my course of action. A crime had been committed, and when there's a crime, you call the police.

I walked in the door and headed for the phone.

"I'd like to report a problem," I said, when the sergeant answered the phone.

"How old are you?" she asked.

"Thirteen."

"What's the problem?"

"A teacher gave me a bad grade."

Click.

I called back and got a different person. Perhaps they didn't understand the gravity of the situation.

"There's been an injustice," I charged.

"What are you talking about? What is the injustice?"

"Someone graded me unfairly."

"Who?"

"A teacher."

Click.

The third time, I tried a new approach.

"I want to report a crime." That got their attention.

"I'm a student and a teacher committed a crime against me."

The sergeant took my information.

"We'll be at your school first thing in the morning," she said.

That night at dinner, my grandmother asked about my day. If the police had responded to my first call—the one in which I had merely said that I received a bad grade—I would have gladly told her everything. But I had a feeling she wouldn't approve of my exaggeration to the police.

"Everything is fine," I told my grandmother. "It's all been taken care of."

I slept like a rock that night, anticipating the sweet justice that would soon be mine. I was already awake when my grandmother knocked on the door the next morning. I knew my method was suspect, but I believed that in the end, I would be a hero—or at the very least have my grades changed.

"Mess with me?" I thought to myself. "We'll see what happens."

When the bell rang at 8:10, a teacher's aide entered my homeroom and called my name.

"Rodney Carroll. You're needed in the principal's office."

"That's what I call service." I proudly walked through the rows of desks, out the door, and down the hall.

Just outside Mr. Shoemaker's office was a small waiting area, where two police officers stood—one woman and one man. They were in full uniform with badges and guns and billy clubs. Their faces wore blank expressions. They escorted me into the main office, where Mr. Shoemaker and Mrs. Mayfair, the guidance counselor, waited. There was a single chair in the middle of the room, where Mrs. Mayfair instructed me to sit. It was like a classic interrogation scene from those old movies—minus the bright light overhead—and I loved every minute of it.

"We want to talk to you," said Mrs. Mayfair, motioning me to sit down. Mrs. Mayfair was an elderly woman with glasses and she wore her grayish, white hair in a bun. I waited for the police officers to ask the questions, but they sat quietly in two wooden chairs by the door while Mrs. Mayfair conducted the interview.

"So just tell us what happened," said Mrs. Mayfair in a sympathetic voice.

"Where do you want me to begin?" I said.

"At the beginning." She sat down and slid her chair closer to mine.

I knew this had to appear more important than merely my grades so I started with a larger issue.

"The classroom is out of control," I said. "There are people screaming. The teacher is hollering. I was threatened during a test."

"Threatened by Mrs. Sacksman?" Mrs. Mayfair asked.

"No," I said. "By another student"—I wasn't about to name him. "But the point is that the class is out of control."

"Did Mrs. Sacksman ever scream at you?" Mrs. Mayfair asked, trying to get back to the complaint at hand.

"Not directly," I said.

Finally Mrs. Mayfair got to the point. "What exactly did she do to you? Did she ever hit you? Were you ever alone with her? Did she ever keep you after class?"

"Well, I was alone with her just a couple of days ago," I said. One of the police officers sighed as if to say, Okay, now we're getting somewhere.

"And what happened?" Mrs. Mayfair asked.

"I had a problem and she was unbelievable." Again, I tried to make it as dramatic as possible.

"Unbelievable how? Did she touch you?"

"No. She grabbed a paper out of my hand." I hoped that counted for something. I suspected this wasn't going well.

"What exactly was the paper?" Principal Shoemaker interjected.

"Well, it was my report card," I said meekly. "She gave me grades that I didn't deserve." Then I said the word that ended the charade. "It is a total injustice."

At that point, I heard the two wooden chairs grate against the floor. Mrs. Mayfair stood up, and Principal Shoemaker threw his hands in the air and turned his back.

"Are you telling us that this whole issue is about the report card?" snapped Principal Shoemaker.

"Most of it," I said.

"So she never touched you?" asked one police officer.

"Nope."

"She never threatened to touch you?" asked the other.

"Nope."

"We're outta here," they said and walked out of the office. Mrs. Mayfair and Principal Shoemaker quickly followed, leaving me alone.

I probably should have made a break for it, but instead I slid my chair close to the door to hear what they were saying. Principal Shoemaker and Mrs. Mayfair were apologetic.

"Sorry for wasting your time."

"Thanks for coming down."

The officers were not amused. "Try to clean it up," one of them said.

Mrs. Sacksman waited outside the office. The police probably figured that when I formally accused her of molesting me, they would arrest her. Principal Shoemaker sent her back to her room before returning to his office alone.

"What the heck do you think you're doing? I'm going to call your grandmother. You're wasting the police officers' time. You're embarrassing the school, you're embarrassing me, you're embarrassing the teachers."

I didn't back down. "I'm embarrassed," I said. "I'm embarrassed by these grades. My grades are very important to me."

Mr. Shoemaker was not interested in my opinion and told me so. He finally concluded his tirade. "I'm going to expel you." He stormed out of the office and came back two minutes later. "You're lucky. Mrs. Mayfair says I can't expel you because you haven't broken any official school rule. Get out of my office."

I left in time to make my social studies class with Mrs. Sacksman. Apparently, she never knew the real reason for the meeting. I slinked to the back of the class and sat quietly next to Devil. On my way out, Mrs. Sacksman stopped me.

"I'm standing by those grades," she told me. "You're not going to get them changed."

"Fine." I took a step toward the door.

"But I will do something for you," she said. "I'm recommending that you be transferred to a different homeroom so that you'll be with better students—where you belong." A slight smile came over her face. "It means you'll have to take a language, but I've spoken with your other teachers and they don't feel you'll have a problem catching up."

"Fine." I walked out. The next week, I transferred to John Daniel's homeroom and learned German. To this day, those grades are on my report card and to this day, I want them changed.

When I got home from school, my grandmother was waiting for me. She had heard from Principal Shoemaker.

"Tell me about it," she said. I told her the whole story.

"Why didn't you tell me this before?" As usual she was calm. She made it easy to tell the truth.

"Because I had a feeling you would have talked me out of it and I felt like I had to stand up for my rights."

"I'm proud of you for standing up for your rights," she said. "But it's wrong to mislead people." She told me the story of Rosa Parks— one I already knew.

"Rosa Parks stood up for her right, which was to sit on the bus." We both chuckled at the pun. "But she didn't mislead anyone. She didn't ignore an open seat and then argue that she wasn't allowed to sit like everyone else. You have to tell the truth or your stand doesn't mean a thing."

Perhaps my grandmother's greatest gift was that she could enlighten without criticizing. She emphasized that sometimes my actions were flawed, but never my heart. It was a tough lesson—but my spirit was intact. And as my grandmother said, "That's the most important thing."

5. The Draft

I was one of the few people at Wagner Junior High School on welfare. No one else knew the embarrassment of using vouchers for the bus, the shame of buying canned goods and bread with food stamps, or the indignity of rushing out to the street to receive blocks of government cheese from the Health and Human Services truck.

Our income consisted of our monthly $303.00 welfare check and my grandmother's cleaning job, which paid eighteen dollars a day—plus bus fare. Somehow my grandmother supplied the basic necessities, but extra money was scarce. At one point, I tried to help out with a part-time job, earning $1.25 an hour for sweeping up at H&P Meats on Susquehanna Avenue. But the job was short-lived because of a daily commute through dangerous neighborhoods.

At first, my grandmother found creative ways to mask the differences between me and my classmates. She covered holes in my pants with football-shaped patches. Instead of birthday gifts, I showed up at parties with my grandmother's homemade cookies. Her golden moment came during the shoe fiasco at the start of eighth grade. The cool shoes in school were Converse Chuck Taylor All-Stars. All the kids had them. They cost seven dollars and for once, I wanted to wear the latest style.

"We can either feed the family or buy those shoes," my grandmother told me when I asked for the money. "Which do you think is more important?" That was an unfair question for a thirteen-year-old who was worried about his image.

Gimbels sold a Converse imitation called John Smith, which cost $3.50. The only difference was that the Converse logo was not on the high-top version of the shoe—a flaw that any eighth grader would easily notice. But that's why my grandmother was so clever. She observed that the low-top Chuck Taylor didn't have the logo—there was no place to put it. The only difference between the low-top John Smith and the low-top Chuck Taylor was a tiny mark on the back of the heel. I admitted it was an extremely small difference. But she went a step further. She pulled out a pair of black laces from her sewing drawer and laced my new shoes using one black lace and one white lace. It was revolutionary.

"There's no way anyone will notice the mark now," she said. "They'll be too busy looking at your laces."

The next day at school, I sported new, black-and-white-laced, John Smith low-tops. They were a huge hit. In no time, everyone was wearing black-and-white-laced, low-top shoes.

But as I got older, the differences between my classmates and me were more difficult to hide. My appearance became more important. I started liking girls and I wanted a haircut more than three times a year. The other students started the year with new books and folders and backpacks. I had used books—albeit with new book covers that my grandmother created—last year's folders and a raggedy book bag that my grandmother found at Goodwill.

While my classmates went on field trips to the museums in New York or the monuments in Washington, D.C., I stayed behind because we couldn't afford the cost—usually around thirty dollars. When we saved up ten dollars so I could make the trip to the World Trade Center in New York, the teacher didn't give me a permission slip.

"I'm going on this one," I told her. "We saved so I could go."

"That's okay, Rodney," she said sympathetically. "You don't have to go."

"I want to go," I said. "I can get ten dollars."

"Yeah, we're sure you can," she replied. "But don't use it for this. You need that money for more important things."

Even when I finally made a field trip, it was awkward. Our trip to Gettysburg cost five dollars. Most of the class ate lunch in the battlefield cafeteria, but my grandmother packed me a lunch. At the end of the tour, the class reenacted the battle with authentic Gettysburg muskets that sold for fifty cents in the gift shop. I was the only one who ran around shooting people with my finger.

Debbie Chase was the prettiest girl in the class. She was an only child. Her father was a doctor and her mother stayed at home. Every boy in my grade had a crush on Debbie, including me. At Christmastime, our class held a pollyanna. Each student picked one name out of a hat and spent up to three dollars on a gift. I casually kept picking until I drew Debbie Chase.

To ensure that I didn't waste my golden opportunity with Debbie, I consulted her best friend, Cheryl, about the perfect gift.

"A silver choker with a peace sign," she said.

My grandmother gave me $1.50 toward the gift. I had fifty cents left from my working days.

"Everyone is spending three dollars on the gift," I told my grandmother. "Please, I really need more money."

"God wouldn't want us to use this money foolishly. There's a lot of ways to do nice things without spending money." She suggested that I make Debbie a present or bake more cookies. I didn't have the heart to tell my grandmother that the homemade cookies were beginning to wear thin.

"I really like this girl," I said. "I want to get her something nice so she can like me back." My grandmother gave me the dollar without any more questions.

I spent the next week scouring the city for a silver choker with a peace sign. Finally a day before the exchange, I found the perfect one at a local drugstore.

"That's the one," I said, pointing through the glass. "I would like to purchase this one right here."

"An excellent choice," the man behind the counter said. His name tag read Stan. "Six dollars and ninety-nine cents please."

"What? Six dollars and ninety-nine cents? I don't have that kind of money."

"Sorry," Stan said, laying the choker on the counter.

"Wait. I have three dollars. Suppose I give you the three dollars now and pay you a quarter every two weeks until the choker is paid off? Please, I really need that choker."

He looked at my face and took a deep breath.

"Alright," he said. "Give me the three dollars and I'll write up an agreement."

I reached into my pocket and pulled out one crinkly dollar bill, three quarters, six dimes, nine nickels, and twenty pennies.

"Here you go," I said. "It's all there. You can count it."

I started to reach for the choker. Stan pulled it away.

"Alright," he said. "You're all set. I'll put that aside for you."

"What are you talking about? I need to take it with me."

"You can't get it until you pay the entire six dollars and ninety-nine cents."

"I told you, I'll pay you."

"Yeah, I'll hold it for you. The price won't go up and I won't sell it to someone else. But you can't take it out until you pay the money."

This wasn't going to work. I needed a gift in twenty-four hours. I needed the choker. I offered to sweep the floor or stock the shelves to earn the money, but to no avail. Then Stan pointed out that the peace sign alone sold for $3.39. "I'll even let you slide on the extra thirty-nine cents."

"Done," I said. I thanked Stan profusely. Now I needed to get creative. My grandmother gave me three pieces of colored wire—like a pipe cleaner—out of her sewing drawer and I meticulously weaved the different colors to create my first and only original piece of jewelry.

I was so busy admiring my handiwork that I didn't notice two small flaws in the design. First, the choker wasn't completely smooth. There were a couple of sharp edges where the wire pierced through the wrapper. And second, I miscalculated the length of the choker. I didn't consider the choker needed to go over the head, so I made it the size of my neck.

The night before the gift exchange, I placed the choker on a green piece of tissue paper inside a little jewelry box my grand-mother had lying around the house. I wrapped the box in purple pa-per and put a red bow on the top.

The next morning, when Debbie's name was called, I stood up proudly with her gift in hand. I didn't realize that Cheryl had blabbed to the entire class—including Debbie—that I was Debbie's polly-anna. She further blabbed that I was getting Debbie the silver chain with the peace sign that she wanted so badly.

I walked to the front of the class through a chorus of ooohs and ahhhs from my classmates. I handed Debbie the box. She looked it over from top to bottom. She shook it. She twisted it. She even smelled it for effect.

"Let me guess what it is," she said with a wink. "Maybe a necklace? What do you think?" The class cheered.

The smile on Debbie's face quickly faded and her face sank when she opened the box. "Pipe cleaners?" she said in disbelief. "What's this?"

I tried to explain. "You see the peace sign?"

"Yeah, I see the peace sign," she said. She turned to Cheryl. "What did you tell him to get me?" She handed Cheryl the gift.

"I told him to get the silver necklace. That's what I told him. I don't know where he got this. What is this wire?"

The room was silent. Michael Rice tried to defend me. "You know Rodney can't afford no necklace. You're lucky you even got that," he said. I felt three inches tall. "It took a lot of time and effort for Rodney to make that chain. So why don't you put it on and see how it looks."

Cheryl handed the necklace back to Debbie. She begrudgingly tried to slip it over her head, but as she did, the pipe cleaners scratched her face. I sank into my chair. I don't know how I made it through the rest of the day.

At dinner, my grandmother asked how the gift exchange went. I told her.

"If she can't see that you really care about her and tried to do the best you can then she doesn't deserve you," she said. It was a small consolation. The next day was Friday. I was sick. I couldn't go to school. I couldn't face my classmates. I couldn't face Debbie.

By the following week, I gathered enough courage to return to school. I didn't like the idea of missing classes. In fact, I was even more motivated to study, get to college, and become a scientist. I became introverted and kept mostly to myself. I excelled in German and even got my grandmother speaking a little. Despite my social disasters, my education in school was flourishing, but my education in reality was just beginning.

At West Oak Lane, I was free to travel almost anywhere at anytime without risk. At my grandmother's, the terrain was not as safe.

The biggest adjustment to living in North Philadelphia was not the lack of money or insecurity in school. It was learning "the rules."

Karl, Herbert, Melvin, and the others kids who lived in the neighborhood had mastered the rules long ago. They grew up like most inner-city children: always on guard. Always suspicious. Never trusting anyone. Through the weekends and summers at my grandmother's, I knew the basics:

"Don't stay out after dark."

"If you see a group of people, head the other way."

"Don't wear nice sneakers to the park or they will get stolen."

"Never walk down Cleveland Street. No matter what."

My friends taught me the more complicated rules.

"The answer is always, 'No,' if someone asks if you have change for a quarter."

"Don't leave the street after 5:30 on a weekday or anytime on Saturday. That's when the gangs are out."

"Don't let change jingle in your pocket. If people know you have money, they will take it."

I learned the most serious rules from Leon, who was in several gangs.

"Always walk on the side of the street that doesn't have parked cars. There's less room to get ambushed."

"Don't go down to the subway until you hear the train coming. It's the perfect place to get jumped."

Even my grandmother reinforced the rules.

"If you're ever in trouble with a gang, run into the street or run into the closest business, church, store—the first public place you can get to."

It was like growing up in a minefield. You could survive, but you needed a detailed map of all the dangerous areas. And you had to follow it.

Johnny's Steaks on the corner of Susquehanna and Gratz had the best steak sandwiches and French fries in the area. The fries were cut fresh from real potatoes. We couldn't afford steak sandwiches, but for fifteen cents, we could get a large cup of fries. Everyone knew that one of the rules was, "Don't go down Susquehanna on Saturday. Several people had been attacked, robbed, harassed, and stabbed by a local gang. It was moderately safe on any weekday and on Sundays. The only problem was that we had school during the week and Johnny's was closed on Sundays.

One Saturday afternoon, Karl came running through the neighborhood screaming until he got to my house.

"Rodney, Rodney. Get out here," he said, pounding on the door.

"What's the matter?" I said. Karl told me that he was jumped. Two guys had stolen his fries.

"What were you thinking? It's noon on Saturday," I lectured.

"I wanted some fries," he said. "I thought I could quietly slip in and slip out."

"Well, who was it?" I asked.

"Blue Monk and Jason," he said. We knew these guys from the neighborhood. Neither was bigger than Karl. Blue Monk talked a tough game, but he rarely backed it up.

"You let Blue Monk take your fries," I said, mocking Karl.

Ninety-nine percent of the time, Karl was the smartest, nicest guy in the world. But if anyone crossed him, he turned into Dirty Harry. "There were two of them," Karl said. "And that's not the point. We have to go back and get revenge."

"I'm not going back there for some french fries," I said. "By the time we get there, they'll have eight or ten guys waiting."

"Then we'll get Marvin and Herbert to go with us," Karl said. "Come on. How many guys do we need? We can take them."

I told Karl to wait a minute. I walked inside, told my grandmother the story and came back with fifteen cents.

"Listen, Karl," I said. "Who knows who'll be waiting for us if we try to find those guys. I have fifteen cents right here. Let's just get some more fries."

Gerald, an eighteen-year-old who lived down the block, escorted us safely—his fee was half the fries.

If I had been jumped, I would have been just as angry as Karl—probably more so. I wouldn't have stayed reasonable and calm. I would have wanted revenge. I know this because it happened to me for the first time the next week. In Karl's case, ignoring the rules only meant losing a fifteen-cent order of the best fries in the city. For me, it was much more costly.

Growing up in North Philadelphia, there was unbelievable pressure to join a gang. There was a different gang in every section of town, and they were always trying to recruit new members. Many joined for the protection. Many joined for a sense of belonging. No matter what the reason, one thing was for sure: once you were in, the gang ruled your life—no matter how long or short that might be.

My grandmother continually warned us about the danger of gangs. Almost nightly, there were stories about gang stabbings or shootings on the news.

"Only cowards join gangs," my grandmother told us. "Remember, you want to be a leader, not a follower. And if you get in a gang, you're going to be a follower."

But not joining a gang wasn't a matter of simply saying, "No, thank you, but thanks for asking."

Gangs actively pursued new membership. They targeted the toughest kids, who they thought could make their gang stronger.

Our street played regular football games against other streets in the neighborhood. The games usually included gang members so I knew many of them and they knew me. I was fast, I could hit hard, and most people knew that I took some karate lessons so I was a good candidate for a gang.

"It's cool to be in a gang. We'll protect you. Girls will like you if you're in a gang," were the standard pitches.

When those didn't work, gang leaders tried scare tactics.

"Well, if you get jumped by Twenty-first and Norris, don't come to us for our help," said Cool Breeze, leader of the Diamond Street gang. Cool Breeze was a tall, stocky kid who always wore a vest, but no shirt. The name Cool Breeze was tattooed on his right forearm. His head was shaved and he wore an earring in his left ear, which was daring for the early 1970s.

When that didn't work, you were bombarded every day by gang members advising you to join. At the park, at the subway, at school, even at my own house—there was no escape.

"Diamond Street wants you to be part of them," said Leon Caldwell, blocking my way as I walked out of my house one morning. He wasn't even in the gang, but he liked to build favors to cash in on later. "Cool Breeze wanted me to tell you that they got your back."

"Tell them I don't need anyone to have my back," I answered, pushing past him.

"I don't think that's smart," Leon warned, his voice rising as I kept walking. "You might as well let him have your back because you may need him sometime."

Gang leaders like Cool Breeze don't give up, and when all else fails, the gangs rely on the draft.

The draft is when a gang spray-paints your name on their logo. Usually it's on the turf of a rival gang.

"Diamond Street was here," they would paint. "We're taking over." Then each gang member sprayed his name around a Diamond.

"Spiderman."

"Cool Breeze."

"Iron Knuckles."

"Switch Blade."

When they wanted to draft you, they painted your name as well. I didn't even have a cool name like the others.

"Rodney." It kind of stuck out.

Now, when the rival game saw my name, they assumed I was with Diamond Street. And it was difficult to explain that it was just a misunderstanding.

From that point on, every time Diamond Street spray-painted their logo, they included my name.

Most people succumbed to the draft—on the surface it was easier than running for your life every day. But once you join, you lose the ability to think for yourself. You have to steal when they tell you to steal. You have to fight who they tell you to fight. You ditch school when they tell you to. As you get older, you drink and do drugs together. It is a dead-end street.

———

Stromman's bakery, on the corner of Twenty-second and Glenwood, was located directly across the street from the Diamond Street projects—one of the toughest areas in the city. To this day, UPS drivers use a police escort when delivering packages in the Diamond Street projects.

The rule for Stromman's was simple: Never go by yourself.

Stromman's cooked fresh bread Monday through Saturday. On Sunday, they sold Saturday's leftover bread for half price. But in addition to bread, Stromman's made homemade donuts, irresistible cupcakes, and my personal favorite, melt-in-your-mouth sticky buns with raisins.

Most of the time my grandmother and I picked up the bread after church. Throughout dozens of trips to Stromman's, my grandmother and I never had a problem.

One Sunday, my grandmother asked me to go by myself—she wanted to get a head start on dinner. Maybe I was a little too confident, or even cocky. Maybe I was focusing too much on those sticky buns, but I agreed. I figured I'd slip in, get the bread and buns, and slip out.

I walked down my street—on the side without the cars—through the park to Twenty-second Street. I passed an antiquated building and was shocked to read, "Rodney was here—part of the Diamond Street Gang." It was spray-painted in blue and black paint.

I had been drafted.

I knew what came next. Anytime a member of the Diamond Street approached me, they would ask, "Where you from?" The proper answer was, "I'm from the Diamond Street."

I put my head down in disbelief. The sticky buns didn't seem that important anymore. When I looked up, ten guys were walking my way. Half were wearing dark jackets that read Diamond Street across the front. They walked with the same strut, using the same posture, wearing the same tough-guy expressions on their faces. They looked like actors from Michael Jackson's *Beat It* video.

Cool Breeze walked right up to me and took off his sunglasses. He put his face in mine as if to emphasize that he had finally won.

"Where you from?" he asked. I had learned to fear those three words. I tried to ignore the question and keep walking, but the rest of the gang blocked my path.

"Where you from?" Cool Breeze repeated.

I knew it was only a matter of time before the confrontation escalated.

"I'm from 2366 Gratz Street," I answered, clearly not following the draft protocol.

"You're part of Diamond Street," he decreed.

"No, no," I answered, trying not to show fear. "I'm not into that."

"Is that right?" he said. "Well, we'll see about that. Give my boy a box."

A "box" is basically fighting with one of the gang members—usually a new member who is still trying to prove himself. The rules are simple. A nine-by-nine-foot box is drawn around both fighters. In this case, the gang simply surrounded us. If you leave the box, the rest of the gang jumped you.

I was a relatively big fourteen-year-old—five-foot-eight, 150 pounds and solid. And I was in good shape from playing sports. My opponent was bigger than I was—probably five-foot-ten—and outweighed me by twenty pounds.

I knew that no matter how well I fought, there was no escape. There would be no dancing around the ring like Sugar Ray Leonard. This is a box. You fight until someone can't fight anymore. If I get the best of the box, then I have to give another gang member a box. My main goal is to try to not get killed, but also to not kill the other person.

"Remember, no hitting in the face," Cool Breeze reminded us. My opponent had an awkward stance and I could tell he wasn't used to fighting. I tried not to be too aggressive. When he punched, I counterpunched.

I remembered my grandmother's advice to run into the middle of traffic. My plan was to look for openings in the box and run. I might be able to escape.

We exchanged a few punches in the arm as the gang cheered.

"Kill him, Jimbo."

"He's a punk."

"He's a sissy."

"Get 'im, Jimbo."

Then Jimbo hit me in the jaw. My lip started bleeding.

"Hey, just the body," said Cool Breeze, clearly an honorable gang leader.

A hit in the face during a box leads to something called a slide for a slide. When Jimbo hit me in the face, that's a slide. So technically, I was entitled to a slide back.

"No," I said. "Let's keep going." I knew that if Jimbo looked bad at the end of the box, then I got beat up even worse by the rest of the guys.

The fight continued. I watched Jimbo with one eye and looked for an opening to run through with the other. I landed a couple of jabs in his ribs, he got me good with a rabbit punch.

Then he hit my face again, grazing my left eye.

"That's it," I said. I put my hands down.

"Where you going?" yelled Jimbo, grabbing my shoulder.

"That's it," I repeated. "You hit me in the face. I'm done."

"You're not going nowhere," he answered. The gang closed in. Two guys bent down to grab knives out of the inside cuffs of their pants. That was my chance. I bowled through them and darted in front of traffic on Twenty-second Street. One car swerved to miss me. Another skidded to a halt less than a foot in front of me. I pushed off the hood and ran a block and a half the other way into Earl's Market, a corner store at the end of the block.

Everyone in our neighborhood considered Earl an extortionist. His was the only store in the area that was open holidays and Sundays, so when you were desperate for milk or bread or butter, Earl's was the only choice—and you were forced to pay the incredible markup.

The Diamond Street gang was right behind me when I slid through Earl's front door and pretended to look for milk. Cool Breeze walked in and put his face up to mine.

"You'll have to come out eventually," he said. "We'll be waiting."

Cool Breeze walked out and leaned against the window. A few others were hiding knives behind their backs. Jimbo punched himself in the arm like he was psyching himself up for another fight. The rest paced the sidewalk. I ran to Earl.

"Those guys are going to jump me," I said in a panic, pointing out the window. "Can you call the police?"

"I don't want no trouble," Earl said. "Get out of my store."

"You're not going to get any trouble, just call the police," I pleaded. But Earl refused.

I looked for a back exit, but there was none.

"Get out of my store."

I was nervous leaving Earl's store, but I figured that when Cool Breeze and the gang jumped me, Earl would notice and break it up. We were in a busy part of the neighborhood and worst-case scenario, another adult would call the police. If I could hold my own for a few minutes, I'd be fine.

As soon as my foot hit the pavement, I got jumped. I threw one guy off as the others grabbed me and pushed me into Earl's window. The window broke.

At that point, I should have stayed on the ground, but my adrenaline was flowing. I got up swinging. It was to no avail. I was punched from almost every angle in every conceivable place—my neck, the back of my head, my shoulders, and my arms. I was stabbed in the forearm and blood ran down my arm. I was hit in the back of the head with a bottle and there was broken glass down my shirt. Through all the abuse, there were no attacks from in front of me. Nobody had the courage to take a direct shot, it was always from behind or the side. My grandmother was right. They were cowards.

Finally I dropped to the ground and covered up to protect myself. My arms were around my head. I knew my body would heal, but I'd seen too many people suffer permanent damage from being repeatedly kicked in the head during a fight. They took turns kicking me and throwing boxes and bottles at me.

I didn't hear anything. I just lay there waiting for it to stop and wondering why it didn't. The fight took place on the steps of Earl's store. There were adults walking by watching ten guys beat on one. Nobody called the police. Nobody tried to help.

Eventually, a woman from a nearby house yelled out her window, "Hey, you hoodlums, get out of here or I'm going to call the police." That's all it took. As soon as Diamond Street heard "police," they ran.

I had been beaten from head to toe. I had two black eyes and my face was swollen. I could only take half breaths because of cracked ribs. Both hands were swollen and I couldn't bend my fingers. My knee was throbbing and my clothes were covered with blood.

As I lay flat on my back, Earl finally came out.

"Get out of here before I call the police and have you arrested for breaking my window," he yelled. I got up and walked away.

Tears poured down my face as I limped home. The Rodney Carroll that was so calm and reasonable through Karl's ordeal had been beaten out of me. I wasn't thinking clearly. All I could think of was revenge.

When my friends saw me, they rushed over.

"I got jumped by Diamond Street," I said without breaking stride.

"Why?" asked Karl.

"I wouldn't join their gang," I answered.

Just saying the words made me even angrier. What kind of place am I living in when I get beaten for not joining a gang?

Courtney and Cheryl were the first to see me when I got home. Cheryl started crying. "Oh my God, oh my God." Courtney was speechless, standing with his mouth wide open. They were both scared to death. I headed directly to the bathroom, bracing myself on the railing to climb the stairs. My grandmother rushed in to find the bathtub filled with blood.

"What happened?" she yelled. I told her.

"Why didn't you run?" she asked.

"I did. I ran into Earl's store. He wouldn't call the police. He kicked me out."

My grandmother left the bathroom. Even with the water running, I heard her yelling at Earl on the phone. "What were you thinking, kicking my grandson out of your store?" A few minutes later she came back in the bathroom with fresh towels and bandages.

"He said he didn't want any trouble in his store," my grandmother informed me. "He said if he called the police, then the gang would have broken his windows."

"They broke the window anyway," I said sarcastically, "with my head."

My grandmother barely stopped the bleeding in my forehead when she decided I needed to go to the hospital. My knee was the size of a softball and she was concerned about the stab wound in my arm.

The hospital was eight miles away. We didn't have a car, we couldn't afford a taxi, and I was in no shape to take the bus. My grandmother called 911. She described the injuries to the operator and gave our address for the ambulance.

"Those injuries are not serious enough for an ambulance," the operator said, and hung up.

Next my grandmother called the police. She told the sergeant the story, and how 911 reacted.

"We'll send a car," the sergeant said.

An hour and a half later a police car showed up in front of my house and drove us to the emergency room. I left the hospital with a big white bandage to cover the stitches. When I looked in the mirror, I was embarrassed because I knew that everyone would know that I got "jacked up." We took the bus home.

It wasn't long before Diamond Street spread the word about the fight. Their message was simple: "Anybody that messes with us will suffer the same fate."

I was raging mad. At Diamond Street for beating me. At Earl for not calling the police. At the other grown-ups for not stopping to help. At 911 for not sending an ambulance. At the police for taking ninety minutes to get to my house. I was even angry at my grand-mother for sending me to get the bread in the first place.

On top of everything else, I knew my gang problems were not over. I knew that Diamond Street would be back, convinced that their beating had forced me to change my mind about joining their gang. Instead I was more determined than ever not to join.

The next morning I gathered all my friends—Karl, David, Tony, Elsworth, Robert, and Michael—on the corner in front of the aban-doned beauty parlor. We wanted Herbert to join us, but as soon as his mom saw him huddling with five other guys on the corner she yelled, "HERBERT, get in here," and he went running.

"I'm never joining a gang," I told them. "I don't care what they do, I'm never going to join. But I'm never going to get beat up again either." Gangs usually picked on one or two guys. So I figured if we had six guys together they would leave us alone.

"I think we should all stick together for protection."

"Great," said Tony. "What's our name going to be? Gratz Street gang?"

"No," I said in disgust. "We don't have a name. We are not a gang. We'll just be ourselves."

Lucky listened from nearby. The drug-dealing business was booming and Lucky had moved away from Cleveland Street to a safer neighborhood in Germantown, near West Oak Lane. But he still came back to North Philadelphia for business. He drove a shiny, new red convertible and bragged about his house with its garage to keep his car clean and safe.

"What are you guys talking about?" he asked. We told him.

"I wouldn't do that," he advised. "You want to stand on your own." He was a nonviolent, nonconfrontational drug dealer.

"Yeah, then we'll get jacked up like Rodney," said David.

"Just don't go where the gangs go," Lucky advised.

"Don't go to school?" said Karl.

"Works for me," Lucky said. "Would you rather get killed?"

Despite Lucky's advice, we agreed to look out for each other. And the strategy worked well for the first couple of days. We traveled in groups of at least three. We let the others know when we were leaving the neighborhood. We even practiced boxing techniques. Through it all, I convinced myself and the others that we were not a gang.

But the illusion became more difficult when Leon joined. Leon was already in two gangs. One morning before school, Leon informed us that he got in a scuffle with one of his gangs. He told them that he was part of the Gratz Street gang and that we would back him up if there was any trouble.

"We don't have your back," I said. "This is not a gang."

"Come on, Rodney," said Elsworth. "We just can't let Leon get beat up. He's on our street."

"We got your back," Michael told Leon.

I agreed that if the other gang came on our block, we'd help.

"We're not looking for trouble," I said.

But Leon was trouble. He was the self-proclaimed toughest kid in the neighborhood. He had the gang look down pat—he wore a black scarf over his head that made him look like a pirate. He cut the sleeves off his shirts to expose the tattoo of "L.C." on his arm.

When Leon joined us, he and I got into an immediate power struggle for leadership. He showed the guys what it was like to be in a real gang. He taught them how to fight with knives and pipes. We all walked with the same cool strut and spoke in the same slang. Everything was choreographed. I felt like one of the Sharks from *West Side Story*.

But I had other things on my mind besides Leon. My focus remained on revenge. I knew Jimbo attended my school. I knew that one on one, I could beat him in a fight. And I knew that I needed to make sure that the rest of the school knew it also.

I planned to catch Jimbo after school when he was alone. But

Jimbo rarely came to school and when he did, he traveled with the others from his gang. Every day, I became more and more anxious to find him alone and more and more frustrated when I couldn't.

Finally, I saw him alone walking to class after first period. I dropped my books. He must have seen the crazed look in my eye because he immediately turned the other way.

"Don't even think about running," I yelled.

He took off, but I ran him down and tackled him. I turned him over and started swinging. He was trying to defend himself, but it was no use. I continued to punch him in the face and in the body. Each punch was full of fury. A week ago, I wouldn't have been capable of delivering such a merciless beating, but today, I couldn't stop.

"What you got now, Jimbo?" I yelled.

Finally, a nonteaching assistant pulled me off of him. He helped Jimbo off the ground and escorted us both to the principal's office.

"What happened?" asked Principal Shoemaker calmly.

The NTA explained as much as he knew and I filled in the remaining details, convinced I was justified in my attack. Principal Shoemaker disagreed.

"We've had enough of this," he said, pounding his fist on the desk. "You know, Carroll, everyone says you're a good kid, but you're just like the rest of them. You're just a thug. Fighting is against the rules. This time, you're going to be expelled."

That's when it occurred to me that everything I had worked so hard for was going to be ruined. "You're going to Boone," said Principal Shoemaker. "You're going to Boone."

Going to Boone was like going to jail. It was seventy years old and constructed of huge cement blocks. It had a twenty-foot iron gate surrounding the grounds, graffiti on the walls, and no rims on the hoops in the basketball court. There was no hope of college after Boone.

"That's right," said Jimbo. "I'll tell you right now, we're going to get you. I'm gonna kick your ass."

"See," I said to Shoemaker. "That's what I'm talking about."

Before Shoemaker could respond, his assistant interrupted.

"Rodney's grandmother is here," she said.

The first thing they do is call your parents. Principal Shoemaker left the office. He came back a minute later with my grandmother.

She had missed work to come get me. Principal Shoemaker asked her to have a seat, but my grandmother refused.

"The problem is this other guy," she said. "He's picking on my grandson."

"That's not what we heard," said Principal Shoemaker. "We heard that Rodney ran this guy down in the hallway, tackled him, and started punching."

"No," my grandmother answered. "That's not true."

Principal Shoemaker looked at me and I told my grandmother the truth. She was in shock. She couldn't believe that I would do such a thing.

Principal Shoemaker explained to my grandmother that fighting was unacceptable and that I was going to be expelled.

The room was silent. Principal Shoemaker's accusation that, "I was just like the rest of them," kept echoing in my head. It was a devastating comment. The perception was that if you're a welfare recipient, if you're poor, if you're from a certain neighborhood, then you're going to be nothing. To Earl, everyone was a hoodlum. To Principal Shoemaker, everyone was a juvenile delinquent. You're going to be in a gang, you're going to do drugs, you're going to jail, and you're going to die.

═══

Walter Borum was fresh out of college when he took the job as math teacher at my junior high school. He was smart and energetic and drove a brand-new green Super Beetle. He could have taught anywhere, but his parents still lived in the heart of Philadelphia and he was determined to work in the inner-city school system.

Math came extremely easy for me. One time I completed a test before Mr. Borum finished handing them out. Mr. Borum falsely accused me of cheating. When I proved my innocence by acing an impromptu test in Principal Shoemaker's office, Mr. Borum felt terrible.

From that point on, Mr. Borum became my unofficial big brother. During class, he gave me extra-credit work, which kept me busy. He taught me trigonometry, which kept me challenged. A few times a year, he took me to 76er's games.

It wasn't long before Mr. Borum heard about my fight with Jimbo and he heard what Principal Shoemaker wanted to do. Mr. Borum stood up for me that day. Thanks to him, I was not expelled. I was suspended for three days. My grandmother and I left the school together. We walked to the bus stop. I knew a million thoughts must have been going through her mind, but she was silent for almost a mile. I wanted to say something, but I didn't know what. Finally, she sighed and then spoke quietly while still looking straight ahead.

"What would make you do this?" my grandmother asked. "You know better than that."

"I had to go to school," I answered, looking down. "They were threatening me every day."

"If you don't listen to me, you're going to end up in much more trouble than this," she said. "This is only the beginning. People die."

"I was only protecting myself," I explained without regret.

"Violence for violence never gets anything," she preached. She quoted the passage from the Bible in which Jesus says if someone hits you on the left cheek, show him your right cheek.

Then I'd have two swollen cheeks, I thought to myself.

"You have to be strong-minded," she said.

While my grandmother spoke, I had mixed emotions. I respected her message, but I was proud of myself. I knew that most of the school saw the fight and those that didn't had heard about it. I felt like I was going to be a big shot because I hadn't let the gang take advantage of me.

"I'm telling you right now," I said to my grandmother, trying to educate her about the ways of the street, "it doesn't look good now, but that guy will never bother me again. He knows I can hold my own. He knows I'm not a punk."

My grandmother stopped dead in her tracks and stared at me. I'll never forget that stare. It was filled with so much disappointment.

"Is that what you really think?" she said. "Let me tell you what's going to happen. They're either going to get bigger and stronger guys to come back for you or they will try to get you to join their gang. Either way, it's not over."

"No way," I said. "I'm not going to be part of their gang. That's it. I'll get respect and that will be it."

My grandmother grounded me for a month.

My suspension started Wednesday and by the following Monday I was back at school. I felt vindicated. My grandmother didn't understand. The problem was solved.

"Jimbo is after you," yelled John Daniel as I entered my first class.

"What are you talking about?" I said. "Just calm down."

"He's embarrassed. Diamond Street gang told him that he better take you out or he's out of the gang." I went from feeling invincible to scared to death in about thirty seconds.

I went back to Principal Shoemaker.

"Remember the guy I fought with?" I said. "He's going to take me out." As outrageous as it sounds, it wasn't uncommon for people in my school to be stabbed or thrown down a flight of stairs.

"You started it," he said. "If you didn't attack him in the first place, he wouldn't want to get even. That's what you get."

I wasn't satisfied with Principal Shoemaker's answer, so I tried Mr. Borum. None of the Diamond Street gang was in my classes so, if Jimbo and his cronies were going to jump me, it was either going to be in the lunchroom or after school. Mr. Borum let me eat lunch in his classroom. For the rest of the semester I stayed after school with different teachers. I joined the chess team. I did extra-credit work. I always left school accompanied by a teacher.

I spent the majority of my time with Mr. Thomas, my science teacher. Mr. Thomas was a tall, gangly man with a beard that covered most of his face. When I stayed after school with him, we mostly talked about what it was like in college, fraternity parties, and all-nighters. He told me he wanted to be a scientist, but he got married instead of getting his masters degree.

It was the afternoons with Mr. Thomas that fueled my desire to be a scientist. I read all the books in his classroom. Like most kids in my class, I found the experiments the most interesting.

"What would happen if you put these two things together?" I asked. No matter how many scenarios I asked about, the answer was always the same.

"Let's find out."

Sure enough, when the Diamond Street gang couldn't get me, they went after other guys on my street. That caused our gang—or group—to continue to grow for protection. Leon brought other guys into the gang and after a while it was hard to keep track of all the members.

"We need to get jackets," said Leon and instructed everyone to buy the same dark Wrangler jean jacket. I was wary of the way the gang was growing, but I was more concerned about Diamond Street. So I told my grandmother that my other jacket was ripped in the fight and asked for a new one.

Over the weekend, she took me to Gimbels. On the way home, my grandmother noticed that other people on the street had the same jacket, including Leon—he had already ripped the sleeves off.

"How did he get that jacket?" she asked me suspiciously.

"I don't know," I said.

"You're in a gang, aren't you?" she said.

"No. We're not in a gang."

"Then why do you all have the same jacket?"

"Because we're all in the same neighborhood and we want to make sure that we stand for the same thing."

"No," she snapped; it wasn't often that my grandmother raised her voice. But she was growing impatient with me. This was the final straw.

"You're not wearing this jacket," she ordered. I knew that was the end of the conversation. My grandmother went to work. I met my friends out on the street without my new jacket.

"Where's your jacket?" asked Leon.

"I'm with you guys," I explained. "You guys know me, I don't need to wear a jacket."

This was the opening Leon needed. "You ain't nothing but a big punk grandmomma's boy," Leon yelled. "You were probably just lucky when you beat up Jimbo. He probably tripped or something."

I wasn't in the mood to be challenged. "If you want to try me," I said. "Come on."

"Oooh, oooh," yelled the gang, sensing a fight. I always believed that Leon wasn't as tough as he tried to make out, but I soon learned different.

We moved to the middle of the street. Leon danced around and taunted me about being a grandmomma's boy. I punched him in the face with my left hand. He staggered back but quickly regained his balance and tackled me to the ground. We wrestled, then stood up and continued punching. It was a time when there were no grown-ups around and no one else dared break up the fight. We moved throughout the street—over cars, in the bushes. There were no weapons. Half the time we were boxing, the other half wrestling. Neither was getting the best of the other and neither was giving up.

In an instant, Karl yelled, "Police," as a cop car cruised passed our street. We both sat on the curb breathing heavily.

"So what, your grandmother call you in?" Leon said.

"No, she ain't even home from work yet," I responded. "Let's go."

I tackled him to the street and the fight continued. The longer we fought, the less punches were thrown.

Eventually, Mr. Caldwell heard the ruckus and broke us up. I was glad he did. I think Leon was, too.

"Leon, get in the house," Mr. Caldwell yelled. "As for you Rodney, when your grandmother gets home, she's going to kill you. You are turning into a huge disappointment."

When I got home I went back to the bathroom to tend to my wounds—this was becoming an unwelcome routine. The injuries from the fight with Leon were relatively minor—swollen cheek, skinned knee, bloody knuckles. Courtney and Cheryl came to see what was wrong but I yelled at them to leave me alone. I filled my hands with water and washed my face. I stared into the mirror. What was happening to me? I'd had four fights in my whole life and three had been in the last five weeks. I had become a regular in the principal's office. My grandmother was right. Our gang was getting bigger because Diamond Street was getting bigger. Diamond Street was getting bigger because we were getting bigger. Eventually, someone was going to get killed.

But even more alarming was the person I had turned into. I wasn't thinking clearly. I wasn't fighting for dignity or honor or any of the things that Martin Luther King Jr. or John F. Kennedy fought for. I wasn't a person my grandmother was proud of. I washed a few tears from my face and walked back to the corner.

"I'll never hang out with you guys again," I declared to the rest of the gang. "I don't need your protection."

It wasn't long before the Gratz Street gang faded away. Leon and the remaining members joined the Diamond Street gang and made sure they left us alone. Two months later, Robert Speaks was killed in a gang fight. He was stabbed in the back with a screwdriver and bled to death. When we heard about the fight, a bunch of people from my street ran to find him. I didn't leave the porch.

6. Un-Lucky

After two years at my grandmother's, I grew tired of the rules. I started to resent the environment. I wasn't a kid anymore. I was fifteen years old. Why couldn't I walk across the street? Why do I have to sprint for the subway every day? Why can't I go out after dark?

But I knew why. As I got older, drugs and crime became more prevalent among my friends. Some were killed. Others were in and out of jail. I learned we were all just a day away from disaster.

"We have to be absolutely crazy to live like this," I told my grandmother. "We have to move."

That Monday, I passed by Willie's Barbershop on the corner of Nineteenth and York on my way home from school. The Sunday paper was left from the day before. I grabbed the real estate section.

I spent the night searching for a better place. After navigating through the apartments and rental homes and condos, I found the place: a five-bedroom, three-and-a-half-bath house, only three blocks from my old house on West Oak Lane.

I showed my grandmother the paper.

"You really want to move, don't you?" she said.

"It's not safe here," I said, pointing to my wounds. "What about Courtney and Cheryl? We have to move, we have to."

I'm sure my grandmother knew that it was unrealistic to move on our budget, but she agreed to call the real estate agent from work the next day. She learned that the house cost five hundred dollars a month. Even she could do the math. Currently we barely squeaked by paying no rent—my grandmother bought her house for seven thousand dollars with a fifteen-year mortgage in 1950. Our entire welfare check was only $303 a month.

"There's no way this can happen?" I stated in question form hoping my grandmother could use her usual magic to make things better with a simple answer. But this time there were no simple answers. We both knew the reality—we weren't going anywhere—and my grandmother said nothing. She just gave me a hug.

My mind-set quickly changed from getting my whole family out of the area to getting myself out of the area. That meant college. Wagner was a school for seventh, eighth, and ninth grades. During the summer before ninth grade, I applied to Central High School, an elite public high school in Philadelphia with a rigorous curriculum. It was a sure path to college. Mr. Borum assured me that I exceeded all the standards for admittance.

"You should have no problem getting in," he said. He even phoned in my recommendation, but in the end, it wasn't enough. I was rejected.

"I'm very sorry," said Mr. Borum, when he gave me the news. "There simply aren't enough spots for everyone. But we can keep trying. Spots open every semester and we can keep trying." I was shocked to learn that my good friend, Buddy Gabis, whom I tutored through most of seventh and eighth grade, was accepted to Central. His father was an attorney and had made a call to the school board.

In the middle of the semester, Mr. Borum helped me transfer from Wagner to West Philadelphia University City High. It was quite a change from Wagner and I felt good about the transfer. I was re-energized. I studied hard and got good grades.

In the spring of tenth grade, I saw a flyer in my counselor's office for a summer program at Temple University called Upward Bound.

The program was designed to prepare children for careers after college. One week was spent shadowing a doctor, the next a dentist, then an architect. In between we took classes on campus to learn why the humanities courses were important to our future.

Ever since those days dressing up in Gimbels department store, I dreamed of a job where I could wear a suit to work. I had drifted from my mission recently, but I believed this could be a fresh start. I wanted to have an impact on society and I believed entering this program was the first step.

There was only one hitch: the cost. I feared a program this comprehensive would be expensive.

"It's free," said the counselor who handed me the application.

The Philadelphia board of education sponsored the program for all children—primarily those from public schools.

I devoted that Saturday to completing the application. After breakfast, I carefully read the instructions. The application was due the first week in May. Applications were reviewed throughout May and everyone would be contacted through the mail by June eighth. There was an orientation for parents in late June and the program started the week after the Fourth of July.

The next page briefly described the purpose of the program: looking for kids with a hunger for learning. Highly motivated kids who were willing to work hard to accomplish their dreams. The third page described the program: Stay in dorms. Get a chance to taste college life. Meet friends, study, learn.

This program is perfect for me, I thought to myself.

"Come on, Rodney," barked Melvin as my friends stood outside my window. "We're heading to the park."

"You guys go without me," I said.

"Are you still working on that application?" he screamed. "You know you don't have a chance. That's for the rich kids with rich parents. They're never going to accept someone from North Philadelphia."

But Melvin was wrong. There was no doubt in my mind that I was going to get in. The last page of the application required my name, address, phone number, and social security number. There were several lines to list my classes and grade-point average. I wanted to put an asterisk next to my 3.85 average to describe Mrs. Sacksman's quirky D-C-E grading policy, but I resisted. There was a space designated for language and I was proud to write German.

The final part of the application was for teacher recommendations. I wrote down Mr. Borum's and Mr. Thomas's names. They were both enthusiastic to help.

I was anxious to describe my vision of being a scientist, but there was no spot for "future dream or goals." I filled out the application neatly. I read every question twice. I made sure there were no misspelled words or grammatical mistakes. My grandmother double-checked everything, then signed in the area marked parent or guardian's signature.

My grandmother offered to drop the application in the mail on her way to work Monday morning.

"No way," I said. "I'll deliver it myself. You can't trust the mail."

On my way home from school on Monday, I got off the subway at Broad Street and walked two blocks to Temple University. I asked an older student for directions to the Upward Bound office. He pointed me to the office of admissions.

Although the Temple campus is imposing, I navigated it easily. The guard at the admissions building sent me to the second floor. At the top of the stairway was a sign on the door that read, UPWARD BOUND.

I asked the lady behind the desk three times to make sure I was leaving the application in the right place. Finally she showed me a stack of applications to prove it. I handed over the brown envelope containing my application as if I were passing a live grenade.

"Be very careful with this," I said.

She thanked me and dropped it on the pile with the rest.

"We'll be in touch," she said.

It wasn't until I arrived home that I realized how lucky I was to be safe. Without regard for any of the rules, I strolled home through Diamond Street, down Susquehanna, and past Cleveland. I was like Mr. Magoo, oblivious to the dangers around me because I was sky high after handing in my application.

For the next month, I waited patiently for my acceptance letter with an air of arrogance. I lectured my friends about the importance of working hard and staying out of trouble, "like me." I told them I was going to live in a nice house, with a nice car.

"I'm going to make an impact," I predicted. "Just wait and see."

I warned Courtney and Cheryl that I probably wasn't going to be around much this summer.

"I'm going to be at college but if I get a chance, I'll call."

On the evening of June fifth, Courtney yelled my name from halfway up the stairs. I was in my room doing homework after dinner. Like every day, when the mail came Courtney, Cheryl, or I picked it up and placed it on the bowl behind the dining room table. There it sat until my grandmother sifted through it after dinner.

"Hey, Rodney," Courtney yelled. "Mom Mom wants to see you. There's a letter for you."

I wasn't expecting anything for three more days. I barely touched three of the fourteen stairs and narrowly avoided running over

Courtney on my way down. My grandmother waved the letter with a big smile on her face.

I grabbed the letter and showed my grandmother, Courtney, and Cheryl the official Temple University Seal with my name typed underneath. I opened it.

I wasn't the least bit nervous.

"When do you start?" asked Courtney.

"Can we come visit you?" said Cheryl.

I read the first line out loud. "We regret to inform you that this year you haven't been selected for the Upward Bound program at Temple University." It didn't hit me until I saw the look on my family's face. I reread it to myself. "We regret to inform you that this year you haven't been selected for the Upward Bound program at Temple University. However, you are more than welcome to apply next year."

I stared straight ahead as tears poured from my eyes. I tried to fight them back, but couldn't.

"We can try for this next year," my grandmother immediately said.

"Yeah, now you can be with us this summer," Courtney added. The tears kept coming.

"I can't believe this," I whispered. I put the paper down and ran up to my room.

"How can this be?" I said out loud to myself over and over. I replayed the entire process in my head. Everything was in order. Did Mr. Borum and or Mr. Thomas give me a bad recommendation? It was the only intangible.

The next day at school I learned that Mr. Thomas and Mr. Borum were never contacted about the program.

Then how could I have been rejected, I thought. It couldn't be my grades—I had practically straight "A's." It couldn't be my extra curriculars—I played sports, was in the school play, on the chess team. It couldn't be my language—German was one of my best subjects. It couldn't be my references—they hadn't checked them.

"What else is there?" I kept thinking. "The only other thing on the application was my address."

19132 and 19133. Those are the zip codes for North Philadelphia. In the state of Pennsylvania, they are every bit as telling as

90210. Most of the people that live in 19132 and 19133 struggle to survive. Many go to jail. Many do drugs and turn to violence. Many join gangs. There normally aren't many doctors or lawyers or scientists that come out of those zip codes.

It turned out that Melvin was right. The program was filled with kids from the suburbs.

I imagined the admissions committee looking at my zip code and thinking, "It's not likely that a guy growing up in North Philadelphia is going to be a lawyer or a doctor or an engineer, so it's a waste of time to include him."

I imagined they believed that if a person had two parents and lived in a nice neighborhood with good schools, he or she was more likely to become a doctor or a lawyer. And they're probably right.

But the reality is that every child deserves to be in Upward Bound. It is kids like me and Melvin who needed the program the most because we didn't have parents to say, "Be a doctor like me," or "Be a dentist like me."

I brooded over my rejection for months.

"See. You're not going to get anywhere. We're all in the same boat," said Melvin. He hounded me relentlessly.

"All that work isn't doing anything for you," said Elsworth. "You stay after school for what? I'm having fun. I'm trying to get girls. If I studied, I'd get the same grades. But what's the use?"

"You're not going to make an impact," said Leon. "You're going to be right here with us."

And the worst part is that a piece of me believed him.

━━

Despite the setback, I tried to keep my spirit alive, like my grandmother always told me to. I was excited for the school year. West Philadelphia University City High School got its name because it was located in a part of the city called University City—where the University of Pennsylvania and Drexel were within a block of each other. It was brand-new. There were clean lockers, new books, central air-conditioning, and independent-study programs. It was also a magnet school for accelerated students and had all the modern facilities. I was one of the few people on welfare at the school.

One day, I saw some friends walking through the halls with a form letter asking for seven dollars to take the PSATs. I never got a letter. I figured it was a simple oversight, and I went to the school office to ask why I hadn't received a request for seven dollars to take the PSATs. The woman there was helpful, checked my file and told me that I didn't have to take the test. Naturally, I thought that meant I was so smart that I didn't have to take the PSATs. I was going right into the SATs.

I was feeling pretty good about myself until my friend, Chan, approached me and asked if I was going to take the PSATs.

"I don't have to take the PSATs," I said. "They told me I don't have to take it."

Chan seemed confused when I explained that I was so smart that I didn't have to take the PSATs. He said everyone had to take the PSATs. Now, coming from anyone else I would have laughed and walked away, basking in my own brilliance. But I considered Chan to be one of the few people who was even smarter than I was.

I walked quietly back to the office and this time asked to speak to my high school counselor, Mrs. Adams. Everyone considered Mrs. Adams the most compassionate person in the school. She was the kind of person that gave you her lunch money if you lost yours. Or if she didn't have any money, she'd share her sandwich.

Girls would talk to her about sex. "I'm thinking about having sex," they said. "What do you think?" How many school counselors do you know who make students feel comfortable enough to ask about sex?

I had a great relationship with Mrs. Adams. One time I was supposed to take a math test. But I was working out in the gym for football and I lost track of time. My teacher wasn't going to let me make up the test, which would have ruined my average. When I spoke to Mrs. Adams about it, she went to the instructor and made sure that I got a makeup test. So there was no doubt in my mind that Mrs. Adams would clear up the misunderstanding.

It was a free period, and Mrs. Adams was in her office with the door open. I walked right in as I normally did and sat in the chair in front of her desk.

"Can I help you, Rodney?" she asked.

I explained to her that I had been talking to Chan and he had insisted that everyone had to take the PSATs, regardless of how smart you are. Mrs. Adams closed the folder she was reviewing, then got up and closed the door.

"You only have to take that test if you're going to college," Mrs. Adams said as she sat back down at her desk.

What was she talking about?

"I am going to college," I answered passionately. I knew that college was the only way out of North Philadelphia; I swore I was going to college. There was never a doubt in my mind. "And Chan said that every college wants you to take this test."

Mrs. Adams paused for a moment like something was wrong. I got anxious.

"I can get the seven dollars," I said, wondering if it was a mere money issue. I knew that seven dollars was a lot for us, but there was no doubt in my mind that my grandmother would find a way to get me the money. "I am going to college," I repeated, looking her right in the eye.

"Well, let's talk about that," she answered in the kind of voice you would use to talk a suicide victim out of jumping off a fifteen-story ledge. "You could take the test. You might do okay—you're a pretty bright kid. But I'm not sure that's a good use of your time."

I was in utter shock. Where was this coming from?

"What do you mean? I'm going to be a scientist. Didn't you know that?"

I didn't wait for an answer, I just told her about my dream: "I can see it now. I'm gonna be a scientist. I have a white lab coat. I'll be introduced at a news conference. The announcer will say, 'We're here with renowned scientist Rodney Carroll, who's just won the Nobel Prize for discovering a cure that is going to save the lives of millions of people in the world.' "

I described my vision the way I had seen it since I was seven. And Mrs. Adams let me go on. She sat there quietly and listened.

"Can't you see it?" I asked with my hands outstretched and a smile on my face, waiting for Mrs. Adams to validate my future.

I waited. And waited. And waited through a long pause. Finally, Mrs. Adams said: "A lot of people won't tell you the truth. I'm going to tell you the truth."

My grin faded as she said, "No, you're not going to be a scientist.

The truth is you're not going to any college. I know this is disappointing to you, but a person who comes from a background like yours is lucky to even be in high school. If you try to do something that is probably not going to happen, you're only going to set yourself up for disappointment later. You'll thank me one day for being straight with you and for telling you the truth."

She spoke for no more than five minutes, but it seemed like an hour.

When she finished I said, "Thank you," and I walked away. It slowly dawned on me that I must have been crazy to think that I was going to be a scientist.

I went home from school and sat at the beat-up piano in the living room. I often sat there and daydreamed. Sometimes I would go into a daydream for hours.

My grandmother often asked me what I was thinking about. There were all kinds of things. I used to think about what I would say if people asked for my opinion on different situations.

I sometimes imagined that I was on television with Walter Cronkite. In those days, reporters stuck a fat microphone in your face after they had asked a question. I imagined Walter Cronkite had asked me about whatever the hot topic was in the news.

"So, Rodney Carroll, what do you think about the space program?"

I'd grab the microphone from his hand—the way I had seen Dr. King do it—and respond with some type of humanitarian answer like, "Well, I understand that it's important to compete in outer space. But what about giving the people down here some attention as well."

When my grandmother came home on the day I learned I couldn't be a scientist, she asked, "What are you thinking about?"

"What kind of job I'll get," I said solemnly. "I'm not going to be a scientist, you know."

"What do you mean?" she asked. My grandmother had heard me talk about being a scientist for years. "Why would you say you can't be a scientist?"

"Some people don't feel I can do it," I answered meekly.

"Did the kids at school say that?" she said.

"No," I answered. "It was the school counselor." My grandmother was shocked.

I explained that people who grew up like me don't go on to college and don't become award-winning scientists.

"How many times do I have to tell you that you can be whoever you want to be," my grandmother said. "If you really want to go to college, and put your mind to it, you'll figure a way to get there."

She said all the right things, and that was the problem. She always said the right things. For years she had told us everyone had the potential for greatness, it was just about getting the opportunity. She said all of us had a talent, but many of us didn't know what it was or how to use it. "Eventually," she said, "you'll get an opportunity and then you need to make the best of that opportunity. But you mustn't give up."

I figured this was typical grandmother stuff—straight from the chapter on how to encourage your grandchild on page 237 of the grandmother's handbook. My grandmother had never been to college or high school. How would she know about this?

But a certified school counselor like Mrs. Adams, on the other hand, knows about who gets to go to college and who doesn't. And that's why she had such an impact on me.

━━

My entire eleventh grade was a waste. The science classes that used to stimulate me didn't interest me anymore. When am I ever going to use this if I can't be a scientist? I thought. No wonder people just drop out of school. What's the point?

I spent the next several months thinking of jobs that didn't need a college degree. An artist, a photographer, an actor, even a factory worker.

At one point I planned to enlist in the military. My cousin Butchy was in the air force. He wore a nice blue uniform. Flying planes would be a cool job, I thought. There was a recruiting office on Broad Street. I stopped by after school one day to pick up a pamphlet and speak with the recruiter.

"What do you want here, kid?" said a man in the same blue uniform as Butchy—he sported several medals on the breast.

"I want to get some information on the service," I said.

"How old are you?"

"Seventeen."

"Come back in a couple of years and we'll be happy to make a man out of you," he said.

He turned his attention back to his paperwork.

"I was trying to get information to see if I wanted to come back," I said.

"Oh, yeah, you want to come back. This is the way to go. You'll see the world. You'll make some money. Uncle Sam will make a man out of you. Look over the brochure."

I looked through the brochure on my way home. It listed several occupations that sounded interesting—radar technician topped my list—but nowhere did it mention pilot.

I called the number on the back of the brochure and inquired about the process for becoming a pilot.

"What kind of degree you have?" asked the man who answered the phone. His tone seemed much nicer than the first gentleman.

"What do you mean, a degree?" I said.

"What college did you graduate from?" he asked.

"I'm not going to college," I said. "That's why I want to go into the air force. Do you have to graduate from college to be a pilot?" I asked, fearing the answer.

"Absolutely," he said. "Call us back when you graduate."

Well, I thought as I hung up the phone. I guess I'm not going to do anything with my life. I'm not going to be anything great.

I walked to Dobbins High School. I hoped that nobody would be around and nobody was. I started shooting free throws when Lucky came by.

"Hey, it's the dreamer," he said. "What are you dreaming about today?"

This time I was out of dreamland. "You're always talking about this reality," I said. "Tell me about reality."

He was surprised that I had finally taken him seriously. He waved me to the bleachers and we started to talk about his business.

"Look," he said. "Before we start, I want you to know one thing. I don't deal drugs, touch drugs, smell drugs. I never keep drugs on me or near me. You can frisk me right now. There's no drugs on me. 'Cause the problem is that people buy their own product, which means they can't think straight. You always have to be thinking in this business."

"So how are you involved?" I asked.

He described his entire operation.

"There are people who sell the product," he said. "Let's call them salesmen. They have something to sell."

"Then you buy," I said.

"No, I don't buy. I give money to other people who buy."

"And then they use the drugs."

"No," he said. "Then they sell the stuff. Since I gave them the money to buy it, they're generous enough to give me a portion of the proceeds when they sell it."

"What do you mean?" I asked. Lucky was very patient with me.

"What happens is that these people who have the drugs need to sell it, and I get buyers."

"People who want to use the drugs," I said.

"No," said Lucky, slowing down. "Listen to what I'm saying. These are not people who want to use drugs, they just want to make money."

"Okay."

"But they don't have money to buy the drugs. You follow me?"

"Kind of," I said.

"So I give them money."

"Why would you do that?" I asked. Lucky shook his head. Apparently this was harder to explain then he imagined. He pulled out a small notebook and pen from his jacket pocket and started writing down figures.

"Okay, look," he said. "Let's try it this way. There are people with the drugs—a lot of drugs. They may have one thousand dollars' worth of drugs. I find people to buy the drugs. Because we buy a lot of drugs at once, we can get the one thousand dollars' worth of drugs for eight hundred dollars. The buyer doesn't have eight hundred dollars. I have eight hundred dollars."

"Where did you get the eight hundred dollars?" I asked.

"Look, if you want to keep interrupting me, we're never going to get anywhere," he said. "Listen to what I'm saying. I give them eight hundred dollars to go buy the drugs. So now, the buyer has one

thousand dollars worth of drugs. I don't have it. I don't touch the
drugs, smell drugs, taste the drugs, see the drugs, hear the drugs, feel
the drugs." He made that point about a dozen times.

"So now the buyer gets the drugs. He breaks the drug down into
even smaller parts called nickel bags. Each nickel bag costs five dollars. He creates two thousand dollars worth of nickel bags from the
drugs we paid eight hundred dollars for."

"Four hundred bags," I said immediately. Lucky took a second to
do the math in his head.

"Yeah, four hundred bags," he affirmed. "See, I knew you were
sharp. Anyway, so now we collect two thousand dollars. The first
thing I do is get my eight hundred dollars back—my initial investment. Then I immediately get back another eight hundred dollars. So
now I get sixteen hundred dollars. And the rest goes to the buyer—
four hundred dollars."

"Why would the buyer want to do that?" I asked. "It seems like a
lot of work for only four hundred dollars."

Lucky shook his head.

"You really don't know this business," he said. "Do you know how
easy it is to sell four hundred dollars' worth of nickel bags? We can't
keep this stuff on the shelf. Look around. These people have nothing
else in their lives. It's like selling water in the desert. We have a waiting list. The buyer makes four hundred in three days—a week at
most. Where you gonna make four hundred dollars a week?"

I have absolutely no idea, I thought to myself while I shrugged
my shoulders.

"Yeah, but you're making eight hundred dollars and you haven't
done a thing."

"Hold it right there," said Lucky, putting his hand on my shoulder. "That's where you're wrong." He flipped the page on the notebook and started listing his risks. "I make the initial investment.
Without my investment there is no cycle. Suppose people don't buy, I
lose money. Suppose something happens, I lose the money. Suppose
the cops intervene, I lose the money. I take all the risk, so the very
least I deserve is double my money back."

We talked for almost an hour before Lucky delivered his
summation.

"I just put people together with what they need. I just take peo-

ple over here who don't want to be over there. That's all I do." He
was smooth. He said he was making enough money so that he could
retire at thirty. He simply wanted to take care of his son.

"Are you interested?" he said.

"In what?" I asked. "What are you talking about? I'm not sure exactly what you're talking about."

"I'm going to give you a business proposition," he said.

"What is it?" I asked.

"You got to tell me if you're interested."

We went back and forth. Finally, he grabbed my arm and asked,
"Are you interested in making five hundred dollars a week?"

"I don't want to sell drugs," I told him. I was disillusioned, but I
wasn't delusional. I knew that the seller or the buyer or whatever
Lucky called them was the one that was going to go to jail. "I'm not
going to sell nickel bags of marijuana," I said.

"That's not what I'm talking about for you," he said in his relaxing
tone that made everything seem okay. "Obviously, you're smarter
than that. I got an altogether different proposition for you. All I want
you to do is ride in the car with me. You interested?"

It was difficult to resist Lucky. Since that day, I have been in hundreds of interviews and heard dozens of sales pitches. But Lucky
gave the most compelling, attractive pitch of them all. This was not
some drug dealer on the corner saying, "Here's a joint, go sell it." He
outlined the operation as a legitimate business proposition. He talked
about supply, demand, and marketing. He played on my emotions.
He made me believe in him. He was honest about the risk and the re-
ward. The only thing missing was a PowerPoint presentation. The
fact was drug dealing was a serious business—it was illegal and im-
moral, but it was serious.

"Yeah, I'm interested in making five hundred dollars a week,"
I said.

"Well then." A victory smirk appeared on Lucky's face. "I'll pay
you five hundred dollars a week for four weeks. All I want you to do is
ride in the car with me. We'll talk. We'll see how things are. We'll see
if you like it. After a month you'll have two thousand dollars cash in
your pocket. If the job is not for you, you can walk away."

It seemed too good to be true. "What exactly do I have to do?"

"Nothing," Lucky said. "You come over in the morning. We'll

talk. I'll introduce you to a few people. You'll get to see things. You'll see how things work. The more you see, you'll know if it's good for you or not. Are you in?"

Deep down, I knew what Lucky was offering. I knew this wasn't drug brokering, or facilitating. I knew it was drug dealing. But I also knew that my own dreams were gone. According to Mrs. Adams I wasn't going to college because I couldn't afford it. I couldn't be a scientist because I had no money. Two thousand dollars cash for one month's work was serious money. And Lucky's life didn't seem so bad. He had everything I wanted. He had moved out of the neighborhood. He wasn't concerned about walking from Cleveland to Broad Street. He didn't have to follow the rules. He had his own car. He could come and go as he pleased. He was his own man. Playing it straight hadn't gotten me anywhere. So why not give this a try? What did I have to lose?

What I know now is that this is exactly how good kids go bad. Kids from bad neighborhoods are looking for opportunities. They see people who are into crime or drugs with lives that appear to be better because of it. They have cars. They have clothes. They go on vacation. They move out of the neighborhood into nice houses.

They're not eating baked beans and hot dogs every night; they're eating steak and lobster. It's tough to turn down. It's very seductive.

The perception is that people on welfare are not looking for opportunities. The truth is that people on welfare don't get as many opportunities as others. And the ones they do get usually are the wrong ones.

"Sounds great," I said. "When do we start?"

"Meet me right here Monday after school," he said.

As Lucky walked away, I yelled, "Hey, who's going to know about this?"

"Don't worry, dreamer," he said. "This is just between you and me."

Over the weekend I thought about what Lucky had said. I understood the concept. I saw his point. I began to understand the operation and its vast potential. It seemed brilliant to me. I even thought of ways it could be expanded. For the first time in a long while, I was excited about my future.

I was convinced I could be a great drug dealer—good head for numbers; never used the stuff myself; a clear vision of the future.

"What the hell are you doing?" Karl yelled, busting into my room. He was every bit as angry as he had been when he got jumped. "I heard what you're up to and I'm just telling you, if you do that, you're going to be messed up."

I looked him in the eye and lied. "I don't know what you're talking about. Whatever you heard is wrong."

I couldn't believe how quickly Karl had heard about Lucky and me. I hadn't told anyone so Lucky must have. It shocked me back to reality. I couldn't trust Lucky. What was I about to do? Would John F. Kennedy do this? Would Martin Luther King Jr.?

I could have made an argument for selling drugs if I was going to take the money and help someone with it. But this was not about helping others. Everything about it was completely selfish.

Monday came and I went to meet Lucky.

"You ready to go?" he asked. "Get in the car."

"I want to talk to you," I answered, backing away.

"Get in the car."

"I want to talk."

"Get in the car."

I got in the car. I was anxious to tell him the news. I wasn't going to question him about Karl. I wanted to break it off with no hard feelings.

"I don't want to do this," I said.

"What?"

"I changed my mind. I'm not interested anymore."

"You just got cold feet," Lucky responded. "Just relax."

"No, seriously," I said. "I was thinking about it over the weekend. It's not for me."

"Can't you just take one ride with me?" he asked. His voice took a sinister edge I'd never heard from him. "Just take a ride. What? You don't like this fine car?"

"This is a very nice car," I said. "But I'm telling you I can't do this. I don't want to be involved in this." I never thought Lucky had a temper. He was always so cool. Under control. But he lost his patience with me.

"So you mean to tell me that I came all the way out here to get you and you're going to back off. Man, dreamer, I never thought you were the kind of guy that would back down on a promise. I thought you were a man who, when he said he would do something, did it. I think you should take a ride with me. End of conversation."

We turned left on Twentieth Street and then right on Norris. Lucky stopped the car at a red light and without thinking, I jumped out of the car and started running.

"Where you going?" I heard Lucky yell, but I didn't stop. I ran and ran and ran as fast as I could.

It was a couple of weeks before I had the courage to face Lucky.

"You punked out," he sneered. "You could have been making good money. You're never going to be nothing. This was an opportunity for you. Turtle's with me now. He's making your money."

A year later, Turtle was in jail serving a three-year sentence—I'm not sure what for. Lucky's luck ran out, too. He was killed by some other drug dealers.

Although my drug-dealing days were over before they got started, my interest in school continued to decline. Throughout eleventh grade, my grades slipped from "B's" to "C's." My favorite subject shifted from science to lunch.

Keith Grant was one of my best friends in high school. Although we were in different curriculum tracks—mine was concentrated on math and science while his focused on English and history—we shared the same lunch period. Every day for two years, we met for lunch.

Keith lived in Wynnefield, the equivalent of West Oak Lane only on the southwest side of town. His father was an accountant for the Marine Corps and his mother was a nurse.

I looked forward to lunches with Keith. We played cards and talked about girls and sports. Part of my welfare benefits included a coupon for lunch every day. The cafeteria served great food and my coupon entitled me to as much as I wanted. One day was spaghetti and meatballs, a soda, banana, and dessert. The next was hamburgers, French fries, soda, and pie.

I was still trying to hide the fact that I was on welfare and had become deft at cruising through the line without anyone in the school knowing I was using a welfare coupon. Keith loved my lunches. He received a weekly allowance from his parents, but spent most of it on albums and movies, leaving little for lunch. So while I routinely feasted on ham and cheese, soup, juice, chips, and pie, Keith usually got by with a soda and chips.

Eventually, I started sharing my lunch with Keith.

In the middle of our junior year, Keith received his driver's license. His father agreed to let him drive the family car during the day.

"When are you guys getting a car?" he asked.

"We're not getting a car," I said.

"Why not?"

" 'Cause we can't afford it."

I told him that I was on welfare.

"Wow," he said, never suspecting a thing. "How'd that happen?" I told him the whole story. He told his parents, and they started including me on family outings. They took me to Phillies games. When they bought Eagles' shirts for their kids, they bought an extra one for me.

Finally, one day it dawned on Keith.

"If you're so poor, how can you afford those great lunches every day? My God. Look at this lunch. This doesn't make sense."

"It's because I'm on welfare," I said. "I get this voucher." I showed it to him. It was about the size of a credit card.

"Does that pay for it?" he asked.

"When I show it," I explained, "it's free."

"You get all this stuff for free, every day?" he asked in disbelief.

"Yeah," I said. "I go up there with the coupon, they know me by now and they automatically fill up my tray with all the food."

"Man, that's really cool," he said. "I wish I had that. I really wish I could be on welfare."

"What did you say?"

"I wish I could be on welfare," he repeated.

"No, you don't," I said.

"Yeah, I do. I wish I could be on welfare so I could have a free lunch."

"Trust me," I said. "It's no free lunch. This lunch cost more than you'll ever imagine."

"What do you mean? You just told me that you're not paying for it."

"I'm getting the lunch," I said. "But look at the cost. I live in one of the toughest neighborhoods in the city. That costs me. I don't have freedom to leave my block. If I walk down the wrong street, I get beat up. Do you want to trade my house for your house?"

"No," he said quietly.

"Do you know that I'm not going to college? They won't even let me take the PSAT. Are you going to college?"

"My dad has a college fund," he said. "He's been putting money away since I was a kid."

"I don't have any dad doing that," I said. "So I'm not going to get a college degree and I'm not going to have a good job. And I'm not going to make a lot of money and I'm not going to live in a nice neighborhood. I'm probably going to live in the same crummy, crime-ridden, drug-infested, sloppy neighborhood for the rest of my life. That's probably what's going to happen to me."

"I had no idea," he said.

"You haven't heard the half of it yet," I continued. "Until a couple of years ago, I believed I was the smartest person that ever lived. If there was a question, I was the first to raise his hand. I studied. I loved knowledge. Now, I don't see the point in being smart. Somebody can just give me D-C-E. I can get passed over for a summer program. I won't get selected for the best high schools. I won't get the same opportunities as everyone else.

"When you're on welfare you're alone. You're embarrassed. How long have you known me? All of this time I've been getting these free lunches and you never knew until now. That's because every day I came in and tried to hide it because I was worried about you seeing it. Let me tell you something. Being on welfare makes you feel like your life is hopeless. You don't believe in yourself. And God knows nobody else believes in you. People used to say I was a dreamer. I used to dream of being a scientist. Of making an impact. Not anymore. I'm not going to be a scientist. I'm not going to make an impact. I've run out of dreams.

"So I'm telling you right now, you want this lunch, you can have this lunch. But trust me, it's not free."

The loneliest moment in my life came when I finished that tirade. I finally gave up on myself. It wasn't caused by one event, or even two or three. I had lived with my grandmother for four years and in that time it slowly sneaked up on me—the D-C-E on my report card, the rejection to Temple and Central High, the fights, the drugs, the temptations—until I simply stopped believing. I accepted that all my grand dreams were just that—dreams.

To everyone else, however, I was still the same kid. I continued to live my life—I still went to school—and did just enough to earn average grades. I still played sports—and was an all-state linebacker. I still hung out with my friends on the corner in front of the abandoned beauty parlor.

During the summer, it seemed like the entire neighborhood hung out on that corner. As hot as it was outside, it was even more uncomfortable inside. On any given night there were people pitching pennies, shooting craps, listening to music, drinking or smoking, or talking on one of the four corners of Gratz and York.

One particular August night in 1974 seemed to be hotter than the rest. I was about to start my senior year of high school. Herbert, Karl, Melvin, and I played two-on-two basketball on a hoop we hung to the light post. Suddenly, Gerald and James flew down York Street. We knew what was next and right on cue, a cop car came around the corner. Soon another one drove the wrong way down a one-way street to surround Gerald and James at the intersection of York and Gratz.

"Put your hands on your heads," the cops yelled from the megaphone.

This was just the distraction people in the neighborhood needed, and they slowly walked to the corner to see what was going on.

"Get your hands off me, pig," said Gerald. He had never been known for his tact.

"I told you to keep your hands behind your back," the cop yelled, taking exception to Gerald's comment.

"I don't listen to no pigs," Gerald yelled back, pulling his hands away.

With that, the cop cocked his billy club and cracked Gerald in the forehead. Gerald fell to the ground. The police officer picked him up and cuffed his hands. Blood poured down Gerald's face but he continued to struggle.

Word of Gerald's clubbing spread quickly and within minutes an angry crowd formed. "What the hell are you doing?" yelled Leon. "You goddamn pig, you had no right to hit him."

"Yeah," piped in Mr. "I'm not drunk" Walker. "Who the hell do you think you are? This is our neighborhood and you can't come busting in here."

More people starting streaming in from the 2300 block of Gratz Street, from Cleveland, from Nineteenth Street. The crowd of fifteen or twenty had turned into an angry mob of fifty or sixty. Little kids, big kids, mothers, dads, all around. Mr. Jimmy, Mrs. Pondexter, Mrs. Livingston, Mr. Caldwell, Leon, were all there. Courtney and Cheryl watched from our window.

"What are you pigs doing?" screamed Mr. Jimmy. "Why don't you go catch some real criminals?"

"Leave us alone," said Mrs. Poindexter. "You guys cause more trouble than you're worth."

Gerald took advantage of the support to resist even more.

"Hey, you didn't have to hit me," he said. "Everyone saw that. Police brutality. I was coming quietly. You guys all saw that."

The police officers realized they were badly outnumbered and that tension was mounting.

"Get back into your houses," the cops ordered. "Everyone clear the way."

"You don't tell me where to go," yelled Leon. "I live here."

"Stand back, stand back," the police screamed. But it was too late. By now, Gerald's face was covered in blood and the crowd surrounded the officers like sharks.

The cops grabbed their billy clubs and night sticks and shouted at the crowd to disperse.

"Go home, go back into your houses."

The crowd shouted back. "We have a right to be here. You don't tell us where to go. We live here, you don't."

Suddenly a paddy wagon and police van came to back up the police officers. The street was blocked by the crowd so the cops got out and tried to force their way through.

"Get out of the way," the officers ordered. As they went by, the crowd pushed and swore and threw garbage at the cops. The cops pushed back.

"Who you pushing?" yelled Kurt Weaver. "I know you ain't going to push me."

"You want to go downtown?" the cops threatened. "You better get out of my way."

"I'm just standing here," replied Kurt, refusing to move.

The cop grabbed Kurt and threw him to the ground. He pinned Kurt's neck with a billy club.

"Hey, why you have to do that?" yelled Mr. Jimmy. "He didn't do anything. He's been here all the time. He's not a criminal. Somebody call his mom."

As more people came, I was pushed closer to the action. I knew it was a bad situation that was bound to get worse.

"Don't make us pull our weapons," the cops threatened.

"You ain't the only ones who have guns," replied Shorty.

Things just got worse.

The crowd flung bottles at the cops. The cops panicked and started arresting everyone they could get their hands on. Shorty was thrown in the paddy wagon.

"Get back. Get back in your houses," a cop on a megaphone yelled. "More police officers are on the way."

The crowd pushed and shoved, and I was thrown into the back of a cop. He turned and stared at me. "Do you want some of this?" he asked, pointing to his club. I looked him in the eye. I didn't know who was right or wrong in this situation. I knew the cops were using excessive force and I knew the neighborhood felt like it was just protecting its territory. But two things were clear: I wasn't going to jail because I hadn't broken any laws. And I wasn't going to get beat up like Kurt or Shorty. I straightened up to defend myself. But before anything happened, ten cop cars with lights flashing and sirens blaring came rushing down the block. The officer gave me a long look, then walked away.

I took a deep breath.

The motorcade of cop cars took the bravado out of the crowd and the people started dispersing. Ten had been arrested, including Kurt's mom, Leon, and three other adults. The cops pushed them all into the wagon.

My grandmother was relieved when she heard that I was safe.

"You should always listen to the police," my grandmother told me. "If the police say go away, you should go away."

"But who's going to be around to make sure they don't beat people up?" I asked.

After dinner I needed some fresh air. I went outside and sat on the curb across the street. I went through the scene in my head. Tensions had been so high that any loud noise—a car backfiring, a garbage can lid falling to the ground—could have set off an explosion, resulting in mayhem.

I sat on the corner and stared at the bloodstains and broken glass on the street. It occurred to me how fragile my life was. No employer or college admission board would be interested in the details of how a person was arrested. The average person would think, "You only got what you deserve because you must have done something wrong." But the average person doesn't understand that some times, decent people get trapped in dangerous situations. I had been within a second of being arrested. A jail record would have followed me my whole life. In the blink of an eye, I would have become the stereotype of the "welfare kid from the neighborhood." It could have happened just like that, in one devastating second.

I felt hatred welling up in my heart. I was angry—at the police, at the schools, at the counselors, at my mom—all the people who were supposed to help me but hadn't. What did I do to deserve this life? With no one left to hate I turned my anger to God.

"If You're such a merciful, generous, good, kind God, why do You let all this happen?" I didn't care who heard me yelling. "I pray every day. I try not to curse. I go to church. I attend Sunday school, so how come I'm in this situation? I'm a moment away from being killed by a gang or going to jail. And You know the worst thing, God?" I lowered my voice and shook my head. "What's worse is that if I were killed or put in prison it wouldn't come as a surprise to anyone. It wouldn't be front-page news. Because I had done exactly what everyone had expected I would. I was no different from anyone else around here."

7. Loaders and Pullers

In February of 1978, Philadelphia was hit by the worst snowstorm in thirty years. In one night, more than forty-eight inches of fresh, white powder covered the city. Schools closed, roads were blocked, and even mail carriers had trouble making their deliveries.

I still lived with my grandmother and was taking architecture classes at Temple University. Over the previous summer, Herb, who was getting an accounting degree at Temple, had told me about a Basic Educational Opportunity Grant, which awarded fourteen hundred dollars for college. Although I had struggled in my final year of high school, my grades were still respectable and coupled with where I lived, I was a good candidate for the grant.

My latest ambition was to be a city planner. There were no libraries in my neighborhood at the time I grew up. No hospitals or police stations or firehouses. I thought every community should have its own library, police station, and parks—at the very least.

I enjoyed college but the truth was I never believed I would ever become a city planner. My grandmother encouraged me, but deep inside I figured, "What's the point? Once people learn about my background, I'm sure I'll be right back where I started."

On the morning after the blizzard, I was up before anyone else. The streets were empty as the snow continued to fall. There were no footprints, no car tracks, no broken bottles, no drug deals, no gang fights. It felt like something fresh and pure had washed it all away.

I put on an extra layer of clothes and my heaviest boots and trudged down the street to get to Temple. I liked being outside. The last thing I wanted was to be cooped up at home. Even though classes at Temple were canceled, I hoped the student union or the library would be open and I could hang out or read or watch television.

The student union happened to be open, and as I walked through the first set of double doors, I casually glanced at the bulletin board. It carried the typical college advertisements: roommates wanted, tutoring available, used cars for sale. A huge, yellow flyer with black, block letters caught my attention.

WANTED: the flyer read. STUDENTS TO WORK AT UPS. PART-TIME. GOOD PAY STARTING AT $5.00 AN HOUR.

My eyes focused on the five dollars an hour. I couldn't believe any company would be offering that kind of money. Minimum wage at the time was $1.65 an hour and a job at UPS was one of the most coveted in Philadelphia.

UPS started out as American Messenger Service, which delivered messages across town in Seattle. Jim Casey had founded United Parcel Service in 1907 in the belief that the company would be "owned by its managers and managed by its owners." For ninety-two years, UPS was solely owned by its employees. Even today, 99 percent of UPS stock is owned by its employees. Jim Casey believed that if he treated his employees with respect, it would translate to the customers. And it did.

Today, UPS employs more than three hundred thousand people, including forty thousand former welfare recipients. It's the fourth largest private employer in the United States.

At UPS, an employee of any race, creed, or color could start as a part-time loader and conceivably retire a millionaire. Jim Kelly, the current president and CEO, started as a driver. Cal Darden, the senior vice president of operations, started as a part-timer.

Normally, I wouldn't have stood a chance of landing a job at UPS, but thanks to the snowstorm, they were desperate for workers—especially college students. I was hired on the spot.

"Can you start tomorrow?" said Al Brown, the human resources manager in charge of new hires. Mr. Brown was an elderly gentleman with white hair. He always wore a suit and looked like he could have owned the company.

"I can start right now," I answered enthusiastically.

"Tomorrow will be fine," he said with a smile.

The UPS facility was located twelve miles from my house on the south side of town. To get there I took a bus to the train, another bus, and then walked four blocks, but the commute didn't bother me. Eight years on welfare had made me realize that a person growing up on welfare probably wasn't going to make a mark on the world. I accepted that. But even though I was starting out as a part-timer, the opportunity to earn my own living and advance in the company encouraged me.

On my first day of work, I arrived at 12:45 for my one o'clock shift. I wore work boots, blue jeans, and a long-sleeved sweatshirt. The UPS operation was housed in a large warehouse. When I got there, Mr. Brown walked me up the stairs to a catwalk that overlooked the warehouse and gave me a brief description of the entire operation.

"Every package travels through several locations and endures countless confirmations before it gets to its final destination," he told me.

The hub in Philadelphia was divided into eight stations where packages were sorted and distributed to the entire country. The packages traveled from station to station on a horseshoe-shaped carousel. The packages moved from the carousel, down a ramp, and onto a belt. Our station was responsible for the California belt, the New York belt, and the New England belt. Once the packages were on the belt, they were sorted and loaded into the appropriate trucks.

I looked down one hundred feet from the catwalk to the area where I was going to work. I saw twenty men throwing packages and shouting at the top of their lungs. "Hold the belt, hold the belt. I need some help over here." It seemed frantic.

"A new lamb to slaughter," a big burly guy with an Irish accent yelled, and pointed to me.

What have I gotten myself into? I thought to myself. Part of me wanted to quit right then. But then I remembered the five dollars an hour. I'd do anything for that kind of money. I would work hard, save, and eventually, move away from the projects. That was my goal.

Mr. Brown yelled for the supervisor and a guy who reminded me of Sergeant Carter from Gomer Pyle came up the stairs.

"Bill Sauer, meet Rodney Carroll. This is Carroll's first day," Mr. Brown said and left.

Sauer was the supervisor. He was an ex-Army guy with a crew cut. He wore a short-sleeved shirt even though it was freezing.

"See door sixty-five over there?" he said sternly. "Get in that truck and start loading."

I walked down the catwalk, through door sixty-five, and climbed in the truck. It was cold and dark. There was a long roller dividing the inside of the truck. When the packages got to the belt, they moved down the line from truck to truck. There was a guy outside each truck called a puller. He pulled the packages off the belt, read the addresses, and put them on the rollers inside the appropriate truck. I was a packer. My job was to take the packages off the rollers and stack them in the truck.

I wanted to make a good impression on my first day so I took extra time to make sure the packages in my truck were nice and neat—heavy boxes on the bottom, light ones on top.

"What are you doing in there?" the puller yelled.

"I'm loading," I answered. He poked his head into the truck.

"Step on it," he yelled. "We're getting backed up out here."

I tried to go faster, but apparently it still wasn't fast enough and Sauer appeared from nowhere.

"What's your name?" Sauer asked as if we had never met.

"Rodney Carroll, sir," I answered.

"Well listen, Carter, I'll tell you what, you've worked an hour but you ain't going to be around for the second hour unless you start picking up the pace."

"Yes sir."

I grabbed a box and threw it in the back of the truck. I grabbed another box and tossed it on the first. There was no organization, but I was cruising. Even though it was cold, sweat was dripping off my face. As soon as a box came down the roller I grabbed it and threw it in the truck. I worked my way from the back of the truck to the front in about twenty minutes. The truck was packed. Boxes were stacked everywhere, including on the roller, and I was about to close the door when Sauer suddenly appeared again.

"Carter," he yelled.

"That's Carroll," I answered. "Rodney Carroll."

"Well listen, Carter. How you gonna get that roller line out?" Apparently I was supposed to retract the roller line as the truck filled.

"What do you mean?" I said. "Why would I want to get it out? I got it in there good and tight. As a matter of fact, it's bracing these packages over here."

"No, you numbskull," he said. "We're going to need those rollers for the next truck."

"What next truck?" I asked.

"There's a next truck coming," he said. "These rollers come out of this truck and go in the next truck."

He turned away from me. "Cut the belt down!" Cutting the belt caused the packages to gather on the belt while the carousel stopped. It made all the trucks fall behind. Sauer hated that. He ordered seven guys over to my truck and we all worked to heave the rollers out from a mountain of packages. It took ten of us, but we finally got them out. I tried to apologize to the guys, but they didn't want to hear it.

"We're going to get our butts kicked thanks to you," one guy said on his way back to the belt.

We worked at a frantic pace until the shift ended at four o'clock. The full-timers broke for lunch and I was about to get something to eat before heading home when Sauer grabbed my arm and pointed to the New York belt.

"Clean it up," he ordered. Even though the operation was shut down for lunch, we were still backed up. Packages were strewn throughout the belt and all over the floor.

I was happy to do the extra work to make up for my mistake. I filled the trucks, making sure to retract the roller lines as I loaded the packages. I closed the doors. I picked up all the paper strewn on the floor. I put the plastic bags in the garbage. I did everything but clean the bathroom. The place was spotless.

When the guys came back from their break, they were amazed.

"My god," said Sauer. "You're unbelievable. Alright. You can go now. Great piece of work. See you tomorrow."

I clocked out and headed home. The day had started a little shaky, but I had recovered nicely. When I got home, my grandmother had a spaghetti dinner waiting for me. I told her about my day. "It is tough work, but I think I impressed the boss."

I took a hot bath and thought about the money I was going to make. My new plan was in motion. I wasn't going to change the world but at least I would be self-sufficient. "I'll never have to rely on welfare," I said to myself, and sank into the tub.

The next day, the snowstorm had subsided and the buses were back on schedule. I got up early, went to school, and rushed back to work. I tried to punch in, but I couldn't find my time card. Sauer told me it would be with the others, hanging alphabetically in the rack next to the clock. Sauer was reading the sports section.

"Excuse me, Mr. Sauer," I said.

"What is it, Carter?" he was abrupt. I was surprised by his tone. After my performance the previous day, I thought he'd be excited to see me.

"I can't find my time card, sir," I said.

"Didn't someone call you at home?" he replied. He still hadn't looked up from his paper. "Oh, well, you screwed up royally."

"What do you mean?" I asked. "Are you talking about those rollers?"

"No," he said. He folded the paper in half and stood up. "At the end of the day, you just put those packages anywhere. You didn't read them or nothing."

"What was I supposed to read?" I asked defensively. I had no idea what he was talking about.

"You have to read the addresses," he said. "Different packages go in different trucks."

"Nobody ever told me that," I said.

It was obvious that Sauer was not interested in my excuses and I felt I was about to be fired when I saw Al Brown.

Out of desperation, I called his name.

"What's the problem?" he said walking over.

"I don't know," I said. "I guess I messed up real bad."

Sauer cut me off and told Mr. Brown what had happened.

"Nobody ever told me about those things," I said.

"Bill," Mr. Brown said, glaring at Sauer. "Didn't you train him?"

"No, I didn't train him," said Sauer. "Why would I train him? Didn't he already know what he should be doing?"

"No, Bill," Mr. Brown said, like he was talking to a four-year-old. "Weren't you paying attention at the meeting? He just started yesterday, he didn't know what to do."

Sauer turned angrily to me. "Why didn't you tell me you didn't know what to do?"

"You didn't ask," I said. "You just told me to start loading."

I felt my heart beating faster. I knew Sauer was the type of guy who would've said, "Too bad. I'm not going to take the responsibility." But Mr. Brown came to my rescue and, thankfully, I still had a job.

"We'll get you some training and start all over," Mr. Brown said, staring at Sauer. "Take care of it," he told Sauer. I smiled meekly.

Sauer's idea of training was yelling for a six-foot-two-inch dark-haired guy who looked like a heavy from *The Godfather* movies. "Dominic," Sauer ordered, "train this guy."

Dominic Palvino had been at UPS for almost three years. He was Italian and proud of it. He believed that Italians were the best in everything. "We're smarter, we're better athletes, and we're better lovers," he said. Dominic was smart. He was not a particularly hard worker, but he had seniority and knew how to work the system. He was a puller "because you don't want to be in the truck," he said.

Dominic showed me the ropes. He started with the basics—look for a big box for the foundation, build a solid back wall, and "whatever you do," he said, "make sure you bring these roller lines out when you come out. We had some guy yesterday, left the damn rollers in the truck. Can you believe that?"

"Hard to believe," I answered.

The belt was a regular melting pot. There were Irish guys, Italian guys, Muslims, and Jews. And Dominic had an opinion about everyone.

"See that guy," he said. "That's Joe McConnell. He's pretty funny, a real nice guy, but he drinks too much, like all Irish guys." We kept walking and Dominic kept talking. "That's Charlie Moore. He's a good basketball player, but all you blacks are good basketball players. The problem with Charlie is he comes in late sometimes because he's playing ball down the street. He comes in late, now he's backed up and I gotta do his work. You know what I'm saying? The last thing I want to do is his work."

We continued down the belt. "That's Robert," he said. "He's an Indian or he's from India or something like that. The thing with him is he doesn't believe in showers or deodorants. Robbie is a great guy, but whoa, I'm telling you, you can only talk to him for a couple minutes before you got to get some fresh air."

After Robbie was Chauncy Phillips. Chauncy worked the point. The point was the guy who takes the packages from the carousel and directs them to the appropriate belts. They call it splitting the belt. I don't think Dominic mentioned Chauncy's origins, he just called him a drunk and he was right. I never saw Chauncy unless he was high or tipsy. He talked slowly with a soft voice like a burnout: "Hey, man. Everything is everything."

One time, there was a formaldehyde spill and the vapors were unbelievable. Our eyes watered and it was tough to breathe. Everyone ran outside for fresh air. After half an hour, someone asked, "Where's Chauncy?" It turned out Chauncy didn't bother to leave. In fact, he wasn't aware of the spill.

"That's Malcolm," Dominic continued. "He's into some shady business. He sells tickets to strip bars. Stay away from him. Now Bill Sauer is an okay guy, but he's kind of dumb. You gotta make him think he's smart. Because if he thinks that you think he's dumb, then he'll start hollering at you and you don't want him to do that. As long as you come in on time and mind your p's and q's, you'll be alright. You square?"

"That's Larry," said Dominic, pointing to a tall, thin guy with blond straggly hair. "He's always stealing. You don't want to go near him. Whenever he's around, something ends up missing. Stay away from him. Don't bring anything valuable in here. Don't put your stuff in a locker. You square?"

I quickly learned that all his questions were rhetorical. I don't think I said two words all day, but I learned a lot about what it was like at the hub. And it felt good to have a guy like Dominic on my side.

By the end of my fourth day, I had mastered the basics of being a packer. On the fifth day, I arrived fifteen minutes early, as usual, and saw everyone standing around the time clock. I quietly slid over, trying to be one of the guys, when Sauer came down to give a Group Instructional Talk or GIT. We had these talks periodically when something out of the ordinary was going to happen. Sauer explained that it was going to be a heavy day. We had Fingerhut and Spencer Gifts, but if we worked hard, we should be fine. I wasn't worried. Nobody was going to have to cover for me anymore.

I found my time card, which was now where it belonged. I punched in and headed for the belt. Ten minutes later, Sauer came over.

"Carter! Why were you late today?" he yelled. By this time I was answering to Carter.

"What do you mean 'why was I late?' " I said. "I wasn't late. I heard you talk about Spencer Gifts and working hard."

"Nope," he said, holding up my time card. "You couldn't have heard that because this card says you didn't punch in until 1:31. I started talking at 1:25."

"Yeah," I answered. "I didn't punch my card until after that."

"That was dumb," he said. "Why'd you do that?"

"Well you were talking and I didn't want to interrupt," I explained.

"Well, now you're late," he said. "Late is late."

"Is that going to go against me?" I asked.

"Absolutely. Late is late," he repeated. He seemed to be enjoying this. "One more time and you're gone. You got a problem with this?"

"Nope," I said. "I guess I'm late."

"Okay, Carter, get back to work."

I walked back to my truck with my head down. During the thirty-day probation period, you can be late only once. So if I was late one more time, legitimately or otherwise, I was done.

When I got to my truck, Dominic asked what Sauer wanted. I told him.

"Look," he explained. "Punch the time card as soon as you walk in. They're only going to start paying you from the start time anyway. Sometimes I'll punch my card in fifteen minutes early and that way I don't have to worry about it. I go to the bathroom. Then I go in the cafeteria and get a snack so I'm not hungry later. I stroll back for my start time and I'm already punched in. You square?"

I shook my head and took my position as packer on the New York truck. I was loading and listening to the guys talk about women and other people's mothers when Sauer came back to my truck.

"Carter," he yelled.

Now, what? I thought. It was obvious Sauer didn't like me much and from the way he treated me earlier in the day I was paranoid that he was trying to get me fired.

"I want you to come here and pull the Californias because Scott's out," he said. Scott was a puller for the California truck. It was still only my first week, so I didn't note the significance of being promoted to puller so soon. But my coworkers did.

There were several other guys packing that had more seniority than me. When they realized that I was pulling after a week, they walked off the belt in protest. The packages built up to the point that we had to cut the belt again.

John Manning, the shop steward, came over. The stop steward's job was to represent the employees in any disputes. Manning was an older guy, who had watched too many *Dragnet* reruns. He talked in quick, clipped sentences with a deadpan expression. I found myself playing along.

"What's your name?" he asked in a stern voice.

"Carroll."

"Who told you to do this?"

"The supervisor."

"How long you been here?"

"I started Monday."

"It's Thursday," he said. "Do you realize there are people in the trucks that have been here months or a year that want to be pulling?"

"I didn't know that," I said.

"This is a problem," he concluded. Rather than discussing the matter privately with Sauer, Manning pulled everyone off the belt and took me into Sauer's office.

"Why'd you put this guy on as a puller when he should be packing?" Manning asked Sauer.

"Because he can read," said Sauer.

"You trying to say some of these other guys can't read?" Manning said. He seemed to take it personally.

"That's what I'm trying to say," answered Sauer.

Manning called over the two guys in question. The first was Charlie O'Malley, a burly guy in his early forties, who spoke with a thick Irish accent. I recognized him as the guy who had yelled at me on the catwalk that first day.

"Read this," he said to Charlie, pointing at a label marked Brooklyn.

Charlie tried to sound it out. "B-b-b-b-b-br-br-br-brook-brook."

"Brooklyn," interrupted Manning. "Brooklyn, New York. Read this one." It said Rochester. Again, Charlie stuttered as he tried to sound out the city. "R-r-ro-ro-ro-Rockafeller," he guessed.

"Go back to work," said Manning. "You," he said pointing at the other guy. "What does this say?"

The result was worse than with Charlie. Manning gave up.

"When Scott comes back, he goes back," said Manning, and left the office.

I was not comfortable with the situation. Many people on the belt were already mad at me from the roller incident, and now I was upsetting guys that had been there much longer than me. I hoped Sauer would offer some comforting words or a piece of advice, but he just told me to get back to work.

Buzzzzzz, buzzzzzzz, sounded the horn to announce that the belt was starting. All I could think about was how the other guys must hate me.

"You know, it wasn't my fault," I said to Charlie. "The supervisor told me to do it. I had no idea that you were next in line."

"Listen, laddy," he yelled back. "You just pull and you keep your mouth shut. Alright? You think you're hot stuff out there. I'll come out there. You want me to come out there?"

"No," I said. "I'm just telling you."

He cut me off. "You don't tell me nothing. How you going to be here five days and you gonna tell me something. You don't tell me nothin'. I tell you."

Dominic came by and told me that Sauer had set me up. He told me Sauer knew it was going to be a problem.

"Now we got a problem," said Dominic. "Because now they're going to want to get you."

"What do you mean 'get me'?" I said.

"They're going to want to get you back," he explained.

I wasn't ready to get in a fight with a forty-year-old Irishman.

"Maybe I'll talk to him," I said.

"You can't talk to Charlie," Dominic explained. "Charlie don't listen to nobody. The only person Charlie listens to is Charlie. When Charlie talks you just listen and try to stay out of the way."

I decided to heed Dominic's advice and let the matter rest. Besides, it was Friday and I was excited about getting paid. I had worked almost twenty hours and I was anticipating my hundred-dollar payday. A hundred bucks was a lot of money. I had never held a hundred dollars in my hand at one time. I planned to take the check directly to the bank, cash it, and grab a root beer float on the way home. I'm a working man, I thought. I'm going to splurge.

I knew that my grandmother, Cheryl, and Courtney were waiting anxiously for me to get home. I had promised that I was going to buy steaks with my first paycheck. We rarely had steak for dinner and now that I had money of my own, I wanted to celebrate.

When my shift ended, I walked into Sauer's office to get my money.

"No, no," he said. "You don't get paid for this week until next week."

"What?" I said in shock. "You owe me. I worked all week."

"Yes," said Sauer, a little stunned at my naiveté. "We know. We'll pay you. But the way it works is you get paid next Friday for this week."

This made no sense to me. "But then you'll owe me for two weeks," I insisted.

"Listen, Carter," he said. "I'm telling you we'll pay you."

"But you guys owe me," I repeated. "I worked Monday, Tuesday, Wednesday, Thursday, and today and you owe me."

"I know," he repeated. "We're going to pay you next week."

"So you're always going to owe me?" I asked.

"Well, I guess," he said, a little confused himself.

I walked out of his office in disgust. Not only did I have no money, but I had already been clocked late for work, everyone hated me, and there was a forty-year-old Irishman who wanted to 'get me back.'"

I barely had enough money to get home. I caught the bus to the train and was on the last bus home. It occurred to me that my whole family would be waiting for the steaks I promised and I was coming home empty-handed.

When I walked in the door I thought I was delusional. I smelled steak. Then I heard everyone in the kitchen laughing. I slunk in with my head down to announce the bad news. But when I looked up, there was my grandmother flipping a huge piece of steak, and Courtney and Cheryl mashing potatoes to go with it.

"Congratulations," they yelled.

"But I didn't get the money," I admitted. My grandmother gave me a kiss on the cheek.

"This one's on me," she said.

My grandmother had worked two extra shifts that week to pay for the dinner. She had planned to do it all along.

"I'm very proud of you," she said.

My grandmother had gone all out. There was steak and potatoes and string beans. We had ice cream and homemade pound cake for dessert. None of that Kool-Aid either. That night, we drank Coca-Cola.

It had been a long time since we had enjoyed a good meal together. It reminded me of the Friday-night dinners we had at my grandmother's when we were still living with my mom.

"Mmmmmmmmmmm, this is delicious," we exaggerated with each bite.

My grandmother held up another piece and asked, "But what about this piece?" And we answered in unison, "Oooooooh, yeah. Deeeeeelicious."

"This is even better than fried chicken," joked Courtney. Courtney talked about having steak for every meal. As for me, I didn't want this to be a once-a-year deal. Steak for every meal was a bit much, but I wanted to at least have the option of having it when I wanted it.

Over the weekend, my grandmother explained that big companies often needed time for accounting and it was perfectly normal to wait a week for a paycheck. She told me not to worry about Sauer or Charlie and the others. "Just keep working hard. Treat them the way you want to be treated and everything will work out." I got to work on Monday feeling much better.

When I walked in, I saw Charlie kissing his wife and two daughters good-bye. I would have never imagined that he had a family. It turned out that Scott was still sick, so I continued to pull in his place. The benefits to pulling is that the work is done outside the truck. I liked it because I could see how the operation worked. It wasn't long before my mind started churning out new ideas.

By the end of my shift, I realized that one person could do the work of two people simply by using another "stop bar," a three-by-three-foot piece of plastic that cost about $1.50. The stop bar is placed on the end of each belt to stop packages from falling off. I suggested this to Sauer.

"Do you think it will work?" he asked, excited about the prospect of increasing productivity.

"I know it will," I said.

"I'll tell you what," he said. "Chauncy isn't feeling well. I'm going to let him go home. Why don't we try it."

It worked. It was my first management-type move. Unfortunately, the union members weren't as happy and again, everyone was sore with me. Even Dominic.

"What about when Chauncy comes back?" Dominic said. "He don't have a job now. Your great idea will cost him his job. And it's not that great an idea, anyway."

"Yes it is," I said, defending my idea. "It worked today."

"Well, it was a slow day today," he argued.

"Well, it will work tomorrow," I insisted.

"Don't you care about Chauncy?" Dominic said. "He's your union brother."

I wasn't even in the union yet. But I didn't want to alienate the only person that seemed to be my friend, so we took the stop bar out and went back to business as usual.

In the meantime, Sauer told his supervisors about the idea. They loved it and it became the new procedure—Sauer took the credit, but at least he stopped calling me Carter.

When the other workers realized that the "stop bar" idea made our work easier, they slowly warmed to it. And when they realized that I had other ideas that would make our jobs easier, they warmed to me as well.

After a few months, I became a full-time puller. I continued to be one of the hardest working guys on the belt. If I was caught up, I helped the next person. One day, the next person was Charlie O'Malley. The operation normally shut down from 4:30 to 5:30 for lunch. The way it worked was if someone didn't finish his load, he had to continue to work into the break until he was done. They didn't hold the next load because of one guy. At 4:40 Charlie was still working in his truck. He looked overwhelmed. I saw his wife and kids waiting for him so I went in to help pack up his trailer.

"What are you doing, laddy?" he asked. He was as cranky as ever.

"I was going to give you a hand," I said and started packing boxes. At first he was surly.

"What are you putting that box over there for?" he barked. "You don't know how to load. You're not a loader, you're a puller."

"Well, I'll tell you what," I said. "Why don't you teach me how to load and I'll teach you how to pull." Maybe I felt sorry for him, or maybe I was trying to get him to like me, or maybe I was still worried he was going to "get even," but for some reason I had a soft spot in my heart for Charlie.

"You think I need you to teach me how to pull," he said. "I don't need that. I was pulling trailers before you were born."

I tried another approach. "One of the problems I have is trying to read these packages as fast as they come by," I said. All of a sudden, I had his attention. "So I have a little trick that I use that helps me read quickly."

"What is it?" he said.

"First of all, the majority of the packages are for Brooklyn, because it's such a big place in New York," I explained. "So once you see the letters B-R-O-O-K, you know it's Brooklyn. There's no other option."

"Okay," he said, nodding his head. He was sitting on the edge of a box.

"Most of the packages that go to the right of us are either Syracuse, Buffalo, or Rochester. They all go in the same area. The only place left is Manhattan. So all you have to do is make sure that the Manhattan's are not in there."

I showed him a box that said Manhattan. Then I explained how to double-check with the zip codes.

"Does that really work?" he asked.

"I'll tell you what. Tomorrow, when I come in, I'll load and you pull and we'll see how it works."

"Good," he said. "But let's keep it to ourselves to make sure I can do it."

The next day, halfway through the shift, I told him to start pulling. It was light out, so I could double-check the boxes when they came in the truck.

Charlie was doing pretty good. He made a couple of mistakes, but for the most part, he had got the hang of it. I could see the pride in his face. He started yelling, "Brooklyn one-one-two," and I yelled back, "Right on."

"This is easy," he said. "I like doing this."

Sure enough, over came Sauer to spoil the moment.

"Charlie!" he shrieked. "Jesus H. Christ. What are you doing out here? Oh my god."

He climbed in the trailer. "Carroll, what are you doing?"

"We switched up a little bit," I said.

"He don't know how to read," Sauer yelled loud enough for the rest of the belt to hear.

"Yes, he does," I yelled back louder. "He's been reading them all. I've been checking them while I'm in here to make sure."

"Who told you to check them?" Sauer asked.

"I figured I'd check them just in case he made a mistake," I said. It turned out to be another great idea. Until then, nobody checked the boxes inside the trailer because the light was usually too low. Mistakes cost time and money. Sauer took the idea to management and in a few days, the lights were adjusted inside the truck and they called my new idea the double checker.

Alternating the pullers and the packers was another idea that stuck and it wasn't long before it became standard procedure. At first the pullers grumbled a bit, but after a while, they didn't care. It created teamwork and a better working atmosphere. Before, the pullers were kind of elitist. They put the packages on the rollers and if the packer didn't go fast enough, he placed the next package on the floor. It caused tension on the belt. By alternating, there was more incentive to work together because whatever you did as the puller, the packer could do to you the next day.

Over the next six months, I became a leader on the belt, even though I was one of the youngest. My salary increased to $7.54 an hour, which made me rich in my eyes. I put half of every check in savings. I bought some clothes. I gave my grandmother $10 a week. I gave my brother and sister a few bucks a week. I still took classes at

Temple so I spent the rest on books, food, and having fun. My confidence came back and so did my ambition. After a few more weeks of watching Sauer, I was sure that I could do his job.

"I think I want to be a supervisor," I told him. "How do I do that?"

"It's very hard work," he said. "It's stressful—a lot of responsibility. How old are you? Twenty-one? Yeah, I don't think you can do it. It's too hard."

"What do you mean?" I asked. "What exactly is the job?"

"I can't even explain it," he said. "That's how hard it is. It would take me all day to explain what I do."

Sauer was giving me the runaround, so I asked Al Brown. Although Sauer took credit for most of the improvements around the belt, Al Brown and the other manager knew that I was the one who was responsible.

"You want to be a supervisor?" Mr. Brown asked. "Okay. When there's an opening, I'll see what I can do."

From that day on, if a supervisor called in sick or took a break, they let me run the belt. Normally, the person who covered for the supervisor acted like Sauer. They ordered others around while reading the paper or drinking coffee. When I covered for a supervisor, I worked even harder.

It wasn't long before I figured that the key to becoming a successful supervisor was to know how to motivate the other workers. When I helped Charlie, that sent a message; I was giving up the puller position to help a union brother. That made our job easier and I tried to get others to do the same.

Although we had three belts—California, New York, and New England—the packages didn't come with the same frequency on each. Often, there was zone shipping, which meant one belt got hit with all the packages at one time. While one belt got hammered, the guys on the other two belts relaxed and then, sure enough, a half hour later it was their turn to get hit.

When I saw that one belt was getting hammered, I went to help.

"Hank," I said. "While I'm a little light, I'm going down to help these guys. Wanna give me a hand? Just turn the labels over." Pretty soon, Hank was helping and the next thing you know, we're all helping each other.

I didn't know it at the time, but this was extremely valuable to UPS. It cross-trained the employees. Before, everyone was isolated. Dominic only knew California, Charlie only knew New York. But now, because we were all working together, the employees started to gain more knowledge. So when there was an attendance problem, there were plenty of people to fill the gap.

I suspected that UPS didn't need so many people to work the belts. Normally, UPS staffed for the most volume. So if you needed six people to handle the peak volume, they scheduled six people on each belt. When the volume was not peak, there were six people doing the work of three. Same thing for each area. But because the peaks are never at the same time, twelve people can cover all three belts by moving to meet the heavy volume.

I didn't have the courage to test this theory out. The stop-bar idea taught me that the union frowns on innovations that cut down the number of workers. But once again, a snowstorm came to the rescue. This time it came in October, when nobody was expecting it, so five people in our area, including the supervisor, couldn't come to work. The other areas had the same problem. Management was worried.

"Who's down there?" asked Mr. Brown.

"Rodney Carroll," said Jerry Ball, the manager. "They're never going to make it with five people missing."

Mr. Brown called me into his office and I described my idea.

"Give us a shot," I urged. "I think we can do it."

Mr. Brown reluctantly agreed, although he really had no other choice.

"But we'll be down to check on you later," he warned.

I gathered the twelve employees for a GIT and explained the situation.

"We're going to get some people, right?" asked Malcolm.

"No," I said. "It's like this all over the building so we're going to have to make it with twelve."

"Whooo, we're going under," said Malcolm.

"Malcolm, relax," I said. "We're not going under. We can do it. All we have to do is move to the work. Keep people going."

It's important to note that this is a union company. Union guys get paid the same amount of money whether they load one truck or four trucks. They get paid by the hour not by the truck. It doesn't bring them any more money to work harder. Now they had this twenty-one-year-old punk telling them that twelve people can do the work of eighteen.

"We're going under," Malcolm repeated.

I gave a few more motivational words, trying to convince people that this was a great chance for our area to stand above the rest. Out of twelve people, I might have had three who thought it could work, including me; six who weren't sure; and three who were sure we were going under.

The meeting broke and everyone got in their place. I called down to input to get a heads up of where the volume was going to start and we were off. For four hours, I worked like a man possessed. I loaded packages with Charlie. Read packages with Robert and pulled packages with Dominic. Malcolm worked at his only speed, slow, because he insisted that when there was a lull in his area, he needed to save his energy for when he got hit.

An hour into the shift, Mr. Brown and a couple other managers came on the catwalk to watch. We weren't exactly clean, but we hung in there. It turned out that we were doing better than many of the other areas.

I'm not sure how many people felt as good as I did about what we had accomplished. Malcolm still argued that we went under. But more important, the UPS management saw an area working together with the highest production levels in the operation. When the first opening became available, I was promoted to part-time supervisor.

The part-time supervisors, or "sups" as we were called, were required to attend a one-week workshop to learn how to be a supervisor. From 1:00 P.M. to 6:00 P.M., for five straight days, we learned how to dress, how to fill out time cards, how to keep attendance records, and give Group Instructional Talks, to motivate the employees.

"If someone misses a couple of days," directed the instructor, "say, 'Oh, great, Jake decided to show up today. Maybe he'll even decide to do some work.' Or if misloads become a problem, respond with 'Eric had three misloads in the California trailer yesterday. That's a problem. But you're going to do a better job today, aren't you, Eric?' "

"Isn't that going to embarrass the people?" I asked.

"Yeah," the instructor answered. "But if you embarrass them, they won't let it happen again."

I called this the hammer approach. In every profession, there are supervisors who believe the best way to motivate workers to perform at high levels is to either scare or embarrass them. The hammer goes by the book. There're no exceptions or excuses. If you're late, you're late. If you make a mistake, you're fired.

The hammer approach is usually effective in the short term. No employee wants to be fired so they normally work extra hard to save their jobs. Productivity usually shows an upward curve at first. The problem is that after a while, the hammer approach wears thin. Employees become disgruntled. Morale drops and that effects productivity. Employees look for other opportunities because they don't feel valued and eventually they quit.

The bulk of the training focused on dealing with the workers. In my first seven months on the job, I developed my own leadership style. I tried to inspire my fellow workers to be a team. I believe that many supervisors, in any profession, make the crucial mistake of distancing themselves from their workers. I found that people work harder, and are happier on the job, if they see their supervisor working beside them.

Throughout the week of training, we role-played different scenarios with the instructors. One person acted as the employee and another as the supervisor. The goal was to try to get the employee to make a commitment to change inappropriate behavior. At the end, the instructors analyzed the results and offered strategies on how to improve.

Scenario One: An employee missed seven straight days without calling. He has been suspended before. How do you handle it?

According to the instructors, the correct answer was the hammer approach: "You haven't been in for seven days and frankly I can't do any more for you. Your absence cost the company money and therefore I'm going to suspend you again and you will probably be discharged."

My approach was a little different. I tried to appeal to the employee at a different level. "Didn't you tell me you were trying to save for a car? First of all, you're not here and you're not getting the money in your check. But more important, we need you. You're one of the best pick-off people we got. I had Sam up there the other day and ten boxes got past him. We need you here. What's the problem? Is there anything I can do?"

"No, no," interrupted Al Brown, who was leading the class. "That would never work in real life. This guy has a habitual problem. You have to discharge him."

"What are you trying to do?" the other instructor asked.

"If it were me," I said, and before I got a chance to finish, the instructor responded, "Who told you to think about if it was you?"

I was going to say my grandmother, but instead I answered, "I always do that." As the week progressed, they wore me down. "They'll take advantage of you. You won't earn their respect. It will be out of control."

My approach slowly shifted to the moderate hammer philosophy preached by the instructors. UPS is a hugely successful company and has been for more than eighty years. Who was I to question its policies? I wanted to be successful at UPS and I wasn't sure disagreeing with the instructors on my first week was the best thing for my career.

I finished the week, earning praise from the instructor. I was ready to start in my new area on Monday. When a person is promoted to supervisor, they don't remain in the same area. I was assigned to the "smalls sort" area. Thousands of envelopes and small packages are shipped through UPS every day. These packages go to the smalls sorts. They may get lost in a big trailer, so they are sorted, tagged, and placed in large bags in their own area. Then the bags are tied and placed on the belts where they are packed into trailers like the other boxes.

I arrived to work on Monday afternoon a few minutes early. I was confident. I took diligent notes during the "sups" training and studied every role-playing scenario over the weekend. I grabbed the report from the day before and called everyone over for my first GIT.

"Sharleen. Who's Sharleen?" I yelled, and a woman in overalls with a Phillies hat waved her hand. "Oh, you. Yeah. I understand you had five mistagged bags yesterday, but I know you're not going to have five today." Right by the book. I kept going.

"Jason."

"Here."

"Okay, good to see you here, Jason. I understand you weren't here last Thursday or Friday. I don't know if you had a problem or not, but I'm going to need you here every day. Let's do a good job and make the area proud."

I was too busy straightening my tie and adjusting my clipboard to notice the disgusted expressions. I walked around the area, trying to learn the operation when Jim Sterling grabbed my arm. The chain of command at UPS goes from part-time supervisor to supervisor to area manager to sort manager to division manager. Sterling was a fifteen-year veteran. He was an area manager and all business.

"Do you know that Jason wasn't here last Thursday and Friday?" he asked.

"I know," I answered. "But he's here today."

"Jason has an attendance problem. Here's his record." As I opened the folder, Sterling asked me how I wanted to handle the situation.

"What do you think?" I said, reading through the two pages of absences.

"We ought to bring him in with the shop steward and really rattle his cage," he advised. "Let's rattle everyone else's cage, too, and let these people know you are going to be a no-nonsense supervisor."

"If you say so," I said, following orders.

Sterling made it a big production.

"Jason. Where are you, Jason?" Sterling had his hands cupped over his mouth to amplify his voice. "Alright, we need to have a meeting."

John Manning, the shop steward, heard the request and sprinted to the office to meet us. There are four shop stewards on each shift. They are voted in through the local unions to represent the workers against the management.

"What's the problem?" he yelled, looking right past me at Sterling. "What's this going to be about?"

"Sit down and shut up," ordered Sterling.

"Fuck you," said Manning. I was shocked at how quickly it turned into a screaming match.

"Why don't you take your guy outside and cool off," Sterling instructed. "Maybe you can ask him why he has a problem showing up for work."

Manning and Jason left the office and Sterling shot me a glance as if to say, "Just watch the master."

After a few minutes, Manning and Jason came back.

"Jason's daughter was sick and that's why he had to be home," Manning explained. "His wife was visiting her mother who was also sick. He says it won't happen again."

Sounded good to me. Let's all shake hands and get back to work.

"That's not going to be good enough," Sterling said. "We understand that you have people who are sick in your family, but we're running a business here. You need to be here every day. You need to have another way to watch your daughter because you got a problem. What happened two weeks ago?"

"The heater blew," Jason answered.

"Yeah," Sterling said, riffling through Jason's folder. "And what about the week before that?"

Jason tried to answer, but Sterling wasn't interested. "Look, I don't want to hear all this. These are just excuses. You guys go outside and come in with something else."

When they left the office, Sterling turned to me.

"Are you following this?" he asked. "You can't let them come in with some rinky-dink excuse. They're trying to tell us that it's okay for him to be out when his daughter is sick. If you buy that, his daughter will be sick every week. You know how some of these kids are, they're sickly."

I nodded. I couldn't believe what I was hearing, but I was like a young recruit, trying to learn everything I could.

Ten minutes later, they came back and Jason agreed to be in every day. But still, Jim wouldn't let up.

"Just so you remember this, we're going to put an official warning letter in your file so that you know we mean business. Now get back to work."

During our training, we learned a disciplinary procedure called

LSD, which stood for "letter, suspension, discharge." LSD was the procedure agreed upon by both the union and UPS. Before anyone in the union could be fired, they must have received a warning letter and a suspension.

The next few days I continued to learn. I put the names on the reports with the faces of the workers. I became familiar with how the operation worked. I observed how the conveyers came in to simulate the flow and which shippers had the most smalls so I could prepare for heavy volume. I kept records and made sure the time cards were filled out properly with the correct social security numbers.

Back home, the neighbors were talking about my new job. After class in the morning at Temple, I came home to change into a shirt and tie for work. I didn't have a car so I walked through my neighborhood to the bus with pride. I carried an old beat-up briefcase that my grandmother bought from a thrift store. In it were my notes from the training session, spare time cards, a UPS procedures manual, two blue pens, and two red pens. It was when I first realized the dignity that comes with something as simple as a job.

On Thursday, Jason didn't show. A half hour into every shift, I called in the attendance. Two minutes later, the phone rang.

"Is this true? Jason's not in," barked Jim Sterling. "Oh man. I'm telling you right now, we have to suspend him. You gonna be alright down there?"

"Yeah," I said. "I'll do the best I can."

I walked to the belt and asked three different people to cover for Jason.

"No," they replied. "That's not my job. I do Baltimore. I do D.C. I do Pennsylvania."

"Who's going to do Jason's work?" I asked.

"That's not our problem," they said. "You're the sup."

I called to the tower to request another person for Jason's job. No one was available. In the meantime, Jason's area backed up. This was my chance to show my workers that we are all part of a team. I rolled up my sleeves and started banging out Jason's work. I sorted and bagged and kept the area clean. The other workers didn't appear impressed, but I was patient. I knew it would take some time to fit in.

The next day, John Manning came in the area and asked to see me. He handed me a piece of paper.

"What's this?" I asked.

"It's a grievance," he answered. "Your employees filed a griev-ance against you for doing employee work. Section 1A-2 column B of the union contract clearly states that you can't do union work."

"But the only reason I'm doing it is because Jason's not in," I explained.

"It's still union work," he said. "You're doing union work and we're filing a grievance. We want two hours of pay for the most senior guy on the line." Even though I only worked an hour, they argued that I worked fast enough that I accomplished two hours of work.

I called Jim Sterling and told him what had happened.

"What the fuck? I'll be right down there," he said.

Jim was not going to sneak up on anyone. He came screaming and hollering down the catwalk, yelling at John Manning.

"Fuck you. You can't do this. This is a new supervisor. You're tak-ing advantage of him."

When a grievance is filed, there is a hearing to determine the outcome. The business agent, who acts as the judge, happened to be in the building, so our hearing was scheduled for that afternoon. At 4:30 P.M., the business agent, John Manning, Jim Sterling, Al Brown, a worker from my area named Richie, and I stood outside a small of-fice ready to begin. As everyone walked in, Jim pulled me back.

"Don't admit you were working," he said. "Whatever they say, you were not actually working. You were training, or doing test packs, or testing the system, but you were not actually doing work. You got that?"

"What was that again?" I asked. I was sure I misunderstood.

"You could have been training, or testing the equipment, or mak-ing sure the batteries fit. There are a lot of things you could have been doing, but you weren't actually doing Jason's job."

We walked in and the hearing began. Richie went first. Richie had worked at UPS the longest, making him the senior worker in the area, so if there was any money from the grievance, he got it.

"The supervisor—and I don't even know his name because he never came around to introduce himself—was doing work that a Teamster brother could have been doing."

Cheap shot, I thought. Right away, Jim interrupted.

"Point of order. The supervisor was not doing work. The supervi-sor was testing equipment."

The business agent turned to me. "Is that right, were you testing equipment?" I didn't know what to say.

"I don't really understand the problem," I said. "Jason wasn't in and somebody had to do his work."

"I didn't ask you if Jason was in," the business agent said. It was a contentious atmosphere and he had no patience with filibustering. "I asked you if you were doing work. Were you doing work or not?"

"I'd rather not answer that," I said.

Jim jumped out of his seat. "What? What do you mean you won't answer it? Answer it. Tell him you weren't doing work."

"I was doing whatever Jason would have been doing," I said. I tried to avoid the question as best I could, but I couldn't lie. "That's what I was doing."

"Exactly," said John Manning. "You were doing Jason's work."

"Yeah," I said. "And if Jason had been in, I wouldn't have been doing his work."

That sealed the case, and the business agent ruled for Richie and Manning, although he awarded only one hour's pay, which was about seven bucks.

Everyone filed out except Jim and me.

"First of all," Jim said, "when Jason gets in tomorrow, we'll be right back in here because we're going to fire him. But we'll talk about that tomorrow. Secondly, what the hell were you doing?"

"Jason wasn't in. I called the tower and they said they didn't have anyone at the time. The area was getting backed up and I knew there was going to be a problem."

"You understand that we had to pay them money, don't you?"

Al Brown happened to overhear our conversation.

"Lay off the kid," Mr. Brown said. "He doesn't understand."

"These are our packages, this is our company," said Jim, glaring into my eyes. "These guys work for us. You got a lot to learn. You got an absolute lot to learn. I hope you make it here, pal." And he walked out.

Mr. Brown motioned for me to sit down.

"Why didn't you get the people to chip in like you did in the other area?" he asked.

"They wouldn't chip in," I said. "I guess they don't know me yet."

He instructed me to call him the next time it happened and he'd try to help out. Then he told me there better not be a next time.

"This is not a good day for you. If you have another one, it could be a problem."

I left work on my fourth day as a twenty-one-year-old part-time sup feeling rotten. I was one mistake away from being fired. I got home and went straight to my room. My grandmother came in and asked about my day. I told her the story. Then I told her that my supervisor wanted me to lie.

"But I didn't," I told her.

"Good," she answered back. "You should always stick to your convictions. It's always better to do that than to let someone else lead you." She stood up, smiled, and gave me a kiss on the forehead. "I'm sure you'll do fine tomorrow."

The next day, I went to work with a new attitude. Before the GIT, I approached Jolanda, one of the women who refused to help with Jason's work. Jolanda was a veteran in the area. She was forty years old and had been with UPS for ten years. She weighed around 250 pounds. She usually wore a house dress with some floral design, black work boots, and curlers in her hair.

"Yesterday I asked if you would chip in," I said. "I don't know that it would have been that much harder. Why wouldn't you do it?"

"That's not what we do here," she said. "Everyone watches their own back here. We don't chip in. I get paid the same amount whether I do this amount or that amount."

"How about when you're not feeling well," I said. "Don't you want someone to be there to chip in?"

"Nobody ever does," she responded. "So why am I going to help someone else out."

I said, "Okay," and called everyone over for the GIT. The hammer approach wasn't working for me. I had to ask two or three times before the group stopped talking and even then, I didn't have their full attention.

"Yesterday as you know, one of our key workers, Jason, wasn't here," I said. "And as you know, we weren't able to get anyone to fill in. And as you also probably know, I tried to do his work and someone filed a grievance."

I didn't name names, which got the group's attention. "I'm not upset with the person that filed the grievance, because I guess that's the way things work here. If you're not getting what you want, you file a grievance. But from now on, if I have a problem, I'm not going right to management. I will discuss it with the person first and I'm asking that you do the same. Then if we can't work it out, you can always file a grievance."

That was the end of my GIT. I never talked about the workload. I didn't single anyone out for misloads, although Jolanda had several. I didn't even mention that Jason didn't show up for work again. As the group filed out, I approached Jolanda.

"You want to talk to me about the missed tags I had yesterday?" she said before I could speak.

"Well, if you want to talk about it, sure, but I came over to say thank you for letting me know how things work here. Now I'm better equipped to deal with it."

"You don't want to hammer me about the mistags?" she asked again.

"No," I answered. "I think you know how important it is to put the right tag on the right bag. So what do you want me to tell you?"

"Alright, thanks," she said with a smile. "I guess I was just rushing. It won't happen again."

Jason came back to work the following Monday with a note from the doctor that said he had bronchitis. It wasn't good enough for Jim Sterling. Although Jim was justified to suspend Jason or even fire him, I wanted to try a different approach. I told him that I wanted to talk with Jason, get the whole story, and give him one more chance.

"Maybe we can come up with a solution to fix it."

"No. No," barked Jim. "They see that as weakness. You got to get him, he's been out three of four days and he's got to pay. We need to make an example out of him."

I tried to explain that we could always suspend him the next time, but Jim didn't want to hear it.

"I don't agree with this," I said.

"You don't know what you're doing," Jim replied. "You've only been a supervisor for two weeks. You don't know what the heck you're doing. You got to follow me on this."

Jim brought Jason and Manning into the office and started the onslaught.

"We talked about this last week and obviously it didn't make a difference," Jim bellowed. "I don't want to see these crummy notes. I told you we want you here every day. Now the rookie supervisor here wants to give you a break. That's because he doesn't know you like I know you. I know that you don't really care about this job and that's why you don't come in. He wants to give you a break, but you're not going to get a break. You're going to be suspended for the next three days."

We got back to the area with only a few minutes left in the shift. I gave the group their time cards to punch out. They punched out in order of seniority. Finally I handed Jason his time card and he punched out.

"Thanks for earlier," he said when he returned the card. At first I thought he was being sarcastic.

"For what?" I asked.

"I understand you were trying to give me a break even though old man Sterling didn't want to."

"I felt like we should talk about it and see what we could do to help," I said.

"I'm not sure there is anything you could do to help, but thanks anyway." Jason informed the other workers about what I had done and slowly things started to change for the better.

Instead of recognizing people for what they did wrong in the GIT, I congratulated them on their successes. Pete went eight days in a row without a missort. At the end of each GIT, I updated Pete's progress. As Pete got to eleven days, then twelve days and thirteen straight days, people rooted for him to increase the streak. Others started their own streaks.

"How about me? I went three days now."

"Three days for Coleta," I announced.

Pete's record kept climbing and so did the productivity in our area. There are thousands of small packages that are sorted each day. The average person goes a couple of days without a missort. Pete was at fifteen days and there were a half-dozen others right on his heels. Even when a missort was made, they were anxious to start another streak.

I received recognition at the supervisor's meetings. I was nervous at first because I led the area with my own approach, but management focuses on results.

"Rodney Carroll is a guy to be on the lookout for," announced Al Brown at one of the meetings. "His area is now in third place as far as service records."

At the GIT that afternoon, I informed the group of two points. First, Pete's streak ended at eighteen. "Yup," Pete admitted. "I had a Reading package in a Tamaqua bag. I don't know how it happened."

Normally the workers don't talk at the GITs. It's supposed to be supervisors only. "This is your time," they taught us. "They're on the clock. You talk, they listen."

Everyone was supportive of Pete and he vowed to beat the record with ease.

"I'm sure you will, Pete," I said. "But I have another announcement. We are now the third-best area in the building as far as service."

"Get out," Jolanda yelled. "Who's second?"

"MG2," I said.

"My friend, Kevin, works in MG2," yelled Jason. "We're definitely better than them."

"And South Load Two is first," I said.

"Oooh, we're probably not better than them," said Pete. "But we can come in number two." Everyone agreed.

The group focused as a team. Every week, they asked about the number-two area. I even got into the spirit with the other sups. It was at a time when Muhammad Ali was making one of his many comebacks, and I talked trash and danced around impersonating Ali. "We're gonna get you," I chanted, pointing at Sal Germana, the sup at MG2. "We're coming for you. We're the greatest of all time."

Each day I arrived thirty minutes early to collect the reports. There was an operation report, a service report, and an attendance report. I immediately flipped to the service report. Meanwhile, the employees mulled around the time clock waiting anxiously for the GIT. They couldn't wait to hear how we ranked.

A few weeks passed without gaining ground until we realized a problem. Newtown Square and Newtown were both cities in Pennsylvania, but went into separate bags. The mistakes were in Mo's area, a five-year worker who worked hard and kept to himself. Mo averaged seven missorts a day—not bad considering he worked one of the most difficult regions to sort.

"If we could get Mo down to four missorts a day, we'll be there," suggested Jolanda.

"The problem is Newtown and Newtown Square," Mo said defensively. "This used to be twenty missorts a day. I'm down to seven and that's great." I agreed with Mo. "You don't need to worry about my area," Mo said. "You worry about your side. I'll keep mine at seven and then we'll catch them."

Finally, Richie stood up to speak. "Look, Mo. Before you load Newtown and Newtown Square, leave your bags on the floor. I'll double-check the bags to make sure that you don't have any missorts." Richie was the only one that could get away with this because he was the senior guy and everyone looked up to him. Mo reluctantly agreed. The problem was that Richie needed extra time to check the bags. At the end of the day, I paid Richie fifteen minutes more to look through these bags.

Jim Sterling was quick to notice the overtime.

"How come Richie Allen isn't punching out until 4:45?" he asked. "Is he getting you? Is he going to the bathroom? Walking around? What's going on?"

"No," I replied. "He's actually checking bags."

"His own bags," asked Al Brown.

"No. He's checking another person's bags."

"Who told him to do that?" said Sterling.

"It was his idea," I said.

"Aha," said Sterling. "Yeah, it was his idea, because he wants more time."

"Actually we're trying to reduce our missorts so we can become the number-two area."

The next day Richie found five packages that were missorted. After further investigation by the group, we discovered that Newtown Square's zip code ended in 190, while Newtown ended in 189, which made it easier to distinguish. The next day we had four missorts.

We continued to investigate the Newtown situation. The group was obsessed. They learned that one company shipped packages almost every day to Newtown Square.

"And every day they put Newtown on the label," revealed Jolanda.

We contacted customer service and they contacted the customer. That did it. We went from third place to the number-one area in the building. The atmosphere in the sort became lighthearted. The team had fun and it showed in their work. In return, I was flexible in my management style. If they needed to come in late or leave early, I helped when I could. They continued to work hard to keep us on top. I got a twenty-five-dollar-a-month raise. When Richie wasn't there the next senior person checked bags to make extra money. They appreciated the extra income and took pride in our area. Sure enough we began to develop teamwork.

=

Any successful business must find a balance between keeping costs low and maintaining high service. My area was running well in terms of service—we had few missorts and no mistags—but the strategies I implemented cost UPS extra money in wages, putting us near the bottom in terms of operations.

Jim Sterling was the manager of operations and Mike Shivers was the manager in charge of service. While I received accolades from Shivers, I heard nothing but criticism from Sterling. At one point, Sterling sent me a memo that reported my area running third from the bottom in terms of operations. "Last year the area was running at 81 percent efficiency and since Rodney Carroll started, it's down to 59 percent."

UPS is extremely technical in terms of measuring efficiency, and that is one of the reasons it is so successful. The amount of time a worker should spend on any given task is estimated according to a formula the company calls Master Standard Data. MSD is based on the belief that there is an appropriate amount of time used for every task in the operation. Everything is measured in Time Measurement Units. So grabbing a box, reading it, and placing it on the rollers should take 150 TMUs; sorting an envelope takes twenty TMUs; running a package from the truck to the front door takes four hundred TMUs. Thousands of hours of data are used to establish the appropriate TMU for each action. Once the times are established, a manager can estimate that loading one thousand medium-sized boxes should take four hours. If it takes four hours and fifteen minutes, production is too slow.

UPS had this down to a science. Every variable was factored in from the weight of the average box to the amount of traffic on the average delivery. There is always some unexpected factor; a box is warped or there is a parade in town, but for the most part, there is so much data used that the averages usually play out accurately.

I didn't know anything about MSD or TMUs as a part-time sup. But Sterling reminded me every week that according to the MSD for our area, we were running hours behind. He strongly urged me to fix the problem and I did. I cut hours. It was a classic rookie move. I focused all my attention on production and ignored service.

"What are you doing?" I said to Richie one day.

"I'm double-checking this bag."

"Don't worry about it," I told him. "Put it back on the belt. Let's go. It'll be alright." In a week and a half, we were in the top three production areas but our service status fell.

"Good job," said Sterling. "Keep up the good work."

"Four missorts to Newtown?" asked Shivers. "I thought you guys had a program for that?"

I couldn't win. For three months, our area went back and forth. When service was up, production was down. Second in production, third from the bottom in service. The workers felt that I didn't know what I was doing. And they were right. I continued to overcompensate, hoping that the problem would work itself out.

Finally, thanks to a veteran worker named Steve, who wanted to go home early one day, I discovered the secret to balance.

"What about checking your bags?" I asked him.

"I don't need to check my bags," he insisted. "I never get any missorts in my area."

"Okay. Get out of here," I said. I was always willing to cut hours for the sake of production.

But Steve made me think. Maybe we didn't need to check all the bags. After the shift, I stayed late to look over the reports for the last ninety days. I got a cheese steak and a Dr Pepper from Tony Luke's across the street. I camped out in a side office and charted the sections that had the most missorts. Steve was right about his area. He rarely had a missort that wasn't caught in the Baltimore hub. Even so, he did so much volume—a couple thousand packages and letters a day—that a few missorts didn't affect our service frequency. There were only a few hundred packages to Newtown and Newtown Square, however, so every missort was costly.

After three hours of looking through graphs and reports and eating one more cheese steak, I developed a chart that ranked the sections in my area according to frequency, which was defined as missorts divided by volume. Then I allocated the quality checks to the areas with the highest frequency. It was a simple concept. A few weeks later, my area struck an effective balance of service and productivity that made us the overall best area in the operation.

Supervisors at UPS were treated differently depending on where they ranked in production and service. If you were one of the worst, every part of your operation was scrutinized until it improved. If you were one of the best, every part of your operation was analyzed so it could be duplicated in other areas. If there was a problem in the operation, the management asked the best supervisors to solve it. Or if there was a staffing problem, the managers took workers from the best areas to help out. The middle-ranking sups didn't get much recognition or criticism and consequently most people like to be in the middle of the pack.

I loved the limelight. I loved the recognition. I loved the pressure of being number one and then trying to stay at number one the next week. Mike Shivers used to say, "Rodney Carroll, his area is bad," meaning that I was one of the top areas in the operation. Then he'd add, "But I am the original badness." Shivers was an older guy, but always seemed to be enthusiastic on the job. Occasionally, he ran the input area and put us to the test.

"Hold on to your socks," he warned. "We're going to blow you guys away."

"Bring it on," I shouted back. "Our guys can handle it."

I knew my area was in sync one day when Shivers dumped an extra heavy load on us. Afterward, he watched from the catwalk, and when my team saw him, they pumped their fists in the air and yelled, "Yeah, yeah, keep it coming."

It was the kind of atmosphere that I thrived in. I was ready to move up the ranks to full-time supervisor. I spoke about my ambition with Al Brown. He agreed that I had the ability. But he told me that every supervisor had to be a driver. Even Jim Kelly, the CEO, experienced a stint as a driver. For me, driving was a problem for two reasons. First, I didn't have my license. But more important, I was still in school. I couldn't be a driver and take classes full-time. Earning my degree was extremely important to my grandmother and me. I had two more years left before I graduated from Temple.

I decided not to pursue the full-time position until after graduation. In the meantime, I could learn to drive and then when I graduated I'd have my degree and a great job making an impressive salary for a reputable company.

I was living a pretty good life. I was twenty-two years old. I made $560 a month. I was in college and getting good grades. Although I still lived with my grandmother, it was convenient because Temple was only a few blocks away and I could walk to school. I didn't spend much time at home. I slept there, but I was up early and was in the library by 8:00. After class, I went to work, then grabbed a bite to eat and went home. I enjoyed dating and spending time with my friends.

My job and lifestyle also seemed to earn me a sense of respect among the adults in the neighborhood. One day, Mrs. Davis, a woman who lived on the 2400 block of Gratz, called me over as I was walking to the bus. Mrs. Davis had a daughter named Sharon, who was a couple of years younger than me.

"You seem like a nice guy," she said. "Where do you work?" I told her.

"Oh, good company," she said. "Do you have a girlfriend?"

"Why do you ask?" I said.

"Do you think my daughter, Sharon, is pretty?" she asked. Sharon was an attractive young lady, but it was well known throughout the neighborhood that she dated a tough guy named Slice. I don't have to tell you what kind of guy Slice was.

"Doesn't she go out with Slice?" I asked.

"Yeah," said Mrs. Davis. "But he's no good. He's not going to do anything. She needs to go out with a nice guy like you."

I told Mrs. Davis that I appreciated the compliment, but I didn't want any problems with Slice. The incident reinforced the fact that I was on the right path. I wasn't on the corner drinking or doing drugs every night like many of the neighborhood kids. I wasn't in fights. I didn't have a criminal background. I didn't fall into any of the traps that typically caught kids in my neighborhood.

I focused on school and work. I even got my driver's license to prepare for the time that I would drive for UPS. My girlfriend, Joan, taught me how to drive in her mother's Chrysler New Yorker. When I finally got my license, we drove down to surprise my grandmother. I told my grandmother we would drive her to church. When we picked her up, I was in the driver's seat.

"What are you doing?" she said. I showed her my driver's license. "Well, let's go."

That afternoon, my grandmother told me that she had been saving for the day when I got my license. She had $750 for a down payment on a used car. All she asked in return was a ride to church every Sunday.

We had no experience buying a car but the next weekend we were off to the used-car lots. At the first one, the salesman shot us a grin as if to say that he knew he had a couple of live ones.

"Oh, what a nice family," he said, shaking my hand before he kissed my grandmother on the cheek. He was a classic used-car salesman. He wore a polyester suit and a white Kangol hat. "You guys just looking or are you here to buy?"

"We're here to buy," I said.

The salesman licked his chops. He pointed to a 1973 Buick Electra 225 with forty-one thousand miles on it. It was canary yellow with a black, vinyl interior. "This baby here is a runner," he said. He called it a luxury car because it had four doors and power windows. The sticker read $1,995.00.

"Can we get a good deal?" I asked innocently.

"Don't worry about the money. We can work that out," he said with his arm around my shoulder. "More important, can't you see your girl looking at you pulling up in this baby, you roll down the window," he rolled down the windows, *bzzzzzzzzzzzz*, " 'Hey, how you doing?' you'll ask. 'Want a ride?' "

He was right, I could see it. He encouraged us to take a test drive.

"I'll tell you what I'll do," he said. "You're a good family. You got your beautiful grandmother here. Now I don't know if I can get this done, but I'll go talk to my manager and see if I can talk him into it. How about $1,795? You're a good family, friendly. Good people."

Sold.

I found out later the car was probably worth around $1,295. My grandmother paid the down payment and I paid eighty-nine dollars a month for two years. I was surprised that the financing was not a problem. In fact, they were impressed that I worked at UPS.

"This way you can establish credit," my grandmother explained. I felt like I had accomplished something that was a big deal. I had purchased a car, established credit, and paid for car insurance.

We were thrilled driving home. I drove extra slow because I didn't want to get in an accident. I asked my grandmother if she ever thought she would own a car.

"It's your car," she said. "I'm just along for the ride."

As we drove down the street, the whole neighborhood "oohed" and "ahhed." I parked in the first spot on the corner in front of Mrs. Poindexter's house. I didn't want to risk nicking a bumper by parallel parking. The spot was under a streetlight so I could see it from my bedroom window. I must have checked on that car twenty times that night.

The next day, I drove to work and parked in the employee parking lot.

"Hey, nice car," Dominic said. I quickly learned that my car was a gas guzzler. I could actually hear the gas going from the tank to the engine. I even turned off the radio, because I thought it might help conserve gas. But I didn't mind.

I got the car on Tuesday after work and on Sunday morning, as my grandmother and I left the house to go to church, we noticed one of the back windows was broken. I didn't have anything valuable to steal inside the car—they even left the AM/FM radio. But I was devastated. We called the police, but they were no help.

"Well, you know, that kind of stuff happens," the lieutenant said. He meant that this kind of stuff happened in the area we lived in.

At church, my grandmother thanked God for the car. I was still fuming about the break-in. After church we decided to get a car alarm. On Monday morning before school, I brought the car to Pep

Boys, an automotive store in my area. They fixed the window and installed an alarm. The new window was seventy-five dollars and the alarm was one hundred dollars.

The alarm was an effective deterrent for a couple months. Then one Friday night, someone managed to snip the alarm. I came out Saturday morning and my entire car was on crates. All four wheels were stolen. It was right around the corner from my house. Again, the police were no help. I asked everyone in the neighborhood, hoping to find a lead. I was so angry, I was ready to hurt someone, or get hurt trying. But no one was talking.

I sat on the corner across from the abandoned beauty salon.

"This is the type of environment I live in," I said to myself. "It does no good to try to get anything because someone will just take it away. I've got to get out of here."

I called AAA. They brought two back tires and towed the car back to Pep Boys. The entire process, including the tires, rims, and wheel locks cost five hundred dollars. I didn't even know there was such a thing as wheel locks. But I did know that my savings account was going in the wrong direction.

As frustrated as I was by my car problems, my grandmother reminded me that I still had a good job and I was still in college.

"The best way to get even is to better yourself," she advised. "Make sure your spirit stays alive."

"I have to get out of here," I told her. "It's only a matter of time before something serious happens."

A few months went by. I was still a top part-time sup at UPS, my grades were still good, and for the most part, my car stayed clear of the Pep Boys. One Thursday during my shift at work, Tom Morino, the sort manager, called me into his office. Tom Morino was only five-foot-five, but he acted like he was seven feet tall.

"Today is your lucky day," he said. "Your ship has come in."

"What is it?" I asked.

"United Parcel Service has decided to give you a chance of a lifetime," he said. "You're going to become a full-time supervisor and because you're taking architecture classes, we're going to put you in the industrial engineering department."

"Wow," I said. "Great."

"Monday, you need to be at the regional offices down by the airport for orientation."

"What Monday?" I asked. It never occurred to me that he meant I was going to be promoted right away. It took most guys at least ten years to become full-time sups. I started in February of 1978, was promoted to part-time sup that November, and this was May of 1980. So in just over two years, I was being promoted to full-time sup.

"I have class on Monday," I explained.

"Well then you have to decide what you want to do," he said. "You have to decide if you want to take this opportunity or not."

"Wow, I guess I have to think about it," I said.

Morino couldn't believe my indecision.

"Don't you see, opportunity is knocking," he said and pounded on the desk. "It's knocking at the door. Aren't you going to open the door? Let me explain something to you." He told me about the benefits and the opportunity for stock options. Then he said something that caught my attention.

"What are you making now?" he asked. I was making $690 a month. "How does triple your salary sound?" I did the math in my head but before I could carry the two, he said, "We're planning on starting you off at nineteen hundred dollars a month."

"When?" I asked in shock. I had no real concept of how much money that was, but I knew it was more than I had imagined earning at age twenty-three.

"Monday!" he said. "That's what I'm trying to tell you. You will begin as a full-time supervisor at nineteen hundred dollars a month. Do you know how many people would love to be sitting where you're sitting? Do you know how many people have been here much longer than you and still aren't where you are? How many people are out there who can't feed their families adequately? You're not even married. You're going to be a young, single guy, making over twenty thousand dollars a year plus benefits. And eventually you're going to own stock. If you take this promotion, you're going to be a rich man. You may have hundreds of thousands of dollars in stock one day. And you live with your grandmother. Your grandmother is going to be so proud of you. I know you live in North Philly and I know it's a tough neighborhood. You'll be able to move out of the area."

He said the magic words.

"I'll tell you what I'll do," he continued. "I'm going to tell my boss that we weren't able to talk today, but I left a message and we're going to talk tomorrow. So you got just one night to think about this. When you come in tomorrow, I got to tell him yes or no."

I left his office in a fog. I didn't remember working the rest of my shift but at this point my area was almost running itself. I drove home and I sat down with my grandmother.

"Guess what?" I said. "UPS offered me a full-time supervisor position."

"Oh my lord." Tears streamed down her face. She stood up to get a handkerchief.

"Why are you crying?" I asked.

"I've been praying for this day for years and years."

"But you don't even know all the details," I said.

"I know them in my heart," she said.

I told her about the stock, the benefits, and the engineering department. With every detail, she cried a little harder. Even I became teary.

"You won't believe the salary I'm going to get—nineteen hundred dollars a month."

"Ooohh," she said. Making eighteen dollars a day, plus bus fare, gave her a clear perspective of how nineteen hundred dollars a month could change my life.

Then I said, "There's one problem with this. They want me to start this Monday and I have class on Monday."

"Did you tell them that?" she asked.

"Yeah," I said. "But they said that this is such an incredible opportunity I had to make a decision by tomorrow morning."

"What do you mean?" she said. "Drop out of school?"

"They're saying either take it or leave it," I explained.

"You don't want to leave school," my grandmother said. I agreed.

We talked for several hours, debating the pros and cons of each decision. We broke for dinner—Beefaroni and Kool-Aid—and then continued to discuss the different options. It was a sleepless night. The next morning, my grandmother asked me if I had made a decision.

"I don't know what to do," I said. "What do you think I should do?"

"You're a man now," she answered. "You have to make the decision, because whatever decision you make, you're going to have to live with it." I was afraid she would say that.

I took a deep breath. "I'm going to take the job," I told her. I was nervous about my decision. Especially because I knew how much my grandmother wanted me to get my degree. I was afraid she was disappointed in me. That was the last thing I wanted.

My grandmother walked me out of the house and down the block. She stopped me at the corner. "God has put you in a position to take this job," she said. And she kissed me good-bye.

8. The Sunshine Club

The defining moment in any supervisor's career is how they handle their first formal disciplinary action. It establishes your reputation with the union, with the management, and with your workers. There are guidelines for when to warn, when to suspend, and when to discharge an employee, which makes it easy for some supervisors. But for me, I often saw room for interpretation in a dispute and so I tried to remain flexible.

As a full-time sup, I was in charge of five areas instead of one. That meant five part-time sups reporting to me, five times the paperwork, five times the staffing changes, and five times the disciplinary problems. My first disciplinary case centered around Hank Worthy. Hank was one of the hardest workers in my area, but he was always late. Every afternoon, he came flying in the door at 2:15, fifteen minutes late for the two o'clock start. He received a warning letter before I started and now we were scheduled to have a hearing to determine if Hank was going to be suspended.

I set up a meeting with Hank and John Manning, who was still the shop steward, to try to avoid the formal hearing. After only a month as a full-time sup, Manning and I had developed a decent working relationship. He didn't come into my office cursing and I didn't disrespect his employees.

Manning agreed to the meeting and he and Hank were scheduled to meet in my office at 2:00. At 2:15, Hank burst through the door, huffing and puffing. He apologized, caught his breath, and took a seat next to Manning.

"What's up, man? You're late three days a week," I said, cutting to the chase.

Being the diligent union rep, Manning didn't let Hank speak.

"He's doing the best he can," Manning said. "Isn't he a good worker when he gets here? Doesn't he catch right up?"

"Yeah, he does," I agreed. "But that's not the problem. The problem is he's late almost every day and we have to fix it."

"I don't want to be suspended," Hank said. "I can't afford to lose days and I don't want it on my record."

"Alright," I said calmly. "Well, what can we do to remedy the situation?"

Manning raised his voice. "Why don't you cut him a break." Manning argued that because Hank was a good worker and held seniority, he should be paid starting at 2:00 even though he didn't come in until 2:15.

"No, I can't do that, John," I said. Then I turned to Hank. "Tell me, Hank, exactly what do you do before you get here."

"It's none of your business," interrupted Manning. "You don't have any right to know what this guy does before he gets here. This is his personal life."

Manning was a union guy, right down to the Teamster jacket and hat that he wore every day. He saw his job as making sure that the union never gave up any rights. He was the kind of guy who wouldn't pick up a piece of paper a minute before his shift started. Everything by the book. And I respected him for it. I believed that a union made a company stronger because without it, you tend to take shortcuts.

In this case, however, Manning didn't realize that Hank didn't have a leg to stand on. His record was well documented and technically he should have been suspended. Hank didn't mind sharing his trials.

"I work a job down on the dock in the morning before I come here," he explained.

"What time do you get out?" I asked.

"I get out at 1:30," he said.

"One-thirty! You get all the way from over there to over here by two-fifteen?" I said. "God bless you. I'm surprised you get here that fast."

"Well, sometimes I ask if they can let me out early, that way I get here on time," he said. "But if they need me to unload trucks, I have to work until one-thirty."

It was a reasonable excuse to me. Hank had a family to support and I knew it must have been difficult to juggle two jobs. I was glad we decided to talk about it, because I had a simple solution.

"Why don't we change your start time to two-fifteen?" I said.

Hank was one of the most senior guys on the staff. The privilege of seniority is that Hank could punch in first and punch out first. First in, first out was the coveted assignment because the setup was the lightest amount of work. But technically, the privilege of seniority was first preference on start times. Hank had the ability to change to 2:15 and the next senior person could start at 2:00.

"No, no," Manning interrupted. "This is the third-senior guy on the wall. He gets the first start time."

But Hank was interested in what I had to say.

"I need to make four hours a day," he said.

"Well, you can be the cleanup guy," I suggested. "You'll be the top senior guy at the end of the day so you can leave last if you want to. The option is yours."

"So that means if I wanted to get out early, I can leave at my normal time, but if I wanted to work late, I can be the last to go?" Hank asked in wonderment.

"Yeah," I said. "Because you'll be the top senior guy."

"Okay. Change my start time," he said.

For nine months in my new job, the area ran smoothly. I was at or near the top in service and production and I had earned a reputation with the union as a fair-minded sup. Outside of work, my energy was spent finding a new place to live. I checked in the paper and met with real estate agents. I dragged Karl and Herb with me on weekends. I didn't see those guys as much anymore. Karl was traveling back and forth to Michigan for an electrical engineering program at General Motors and Herb was still taking classes at Temple to earn his CPA certificate.

At first I decided to rent a place, but my grandmother suggested that I buy instead. I had no idea that I was capable of buying a place. I thought that in order to buy, you needed all the money at once. The house that I eventually purchased cost thirty-nine thousand dollars. I thought that I had to have forty thousand dollars cash to buy the thing.

"By the time I have forty thousand dollars I'm going to be an old man," I told my grandmother.

My grandmother explained that I didn't need all the money at once. She told me that when you own your house, no one can tell you how to live.

"It's always better to own than rent," she said.

I finally settled on a duplex near West Oak Lane, the area that my mother and stepfather used to live in. The advantage of a duplex was I could rent half of it to help pay the mortgage.

It was three months from the time I made an offer until closing. My family knew that it was only a matter of time before I moved, but now it was definite. Cheryl didn't seem too upset—her main concern was that she could have my room and stereo. Although my grandmother was sad to see me go, she said it was for the best. I was twenty-three years old. I made my own money and "it's time to be your own man," she told me. "You need to focus on your own career. Don't worry about us."

But I was still torn. All my life I had dreamed of moving away and I was thrilled that it was finally happening. But I felt awkward about leaving my family behind—Courtney was only sixteen.

On the first night in my new place, I slept on the floor—I had new, thick carpet and it was a couple of weeks before I accumulated any furniture. I laid on my back and stared at the ceiling.

I escaped before something terrible happened, I thought to myself.

I felt a big weight lift off my shoulders. It was the deepest sleep I've ever had.

I moved into my new place on a Thursday and on Monday morning Morino called me into his office.

"I have good news for you," he said. "Next Monday, you don't have to get your car all dirty by coming down to South Philadelphia. You're going out to paradise, son. You're going out to Doylestown."

Morino explained that in order for me to advance in the company, I had to understand other areas of the operation and that meant driving.

"You're going to be the driver's sup," he said.

I had no idea where Doylestown was, so that weekend I made a dry run to figure out exactly where I was going on Monday. After an hour in the car, I reached the outskirts of Doylestown. Morino was right. It was a beautiful town located in an affluent suburb of Philadelphia. It reminded me of Mayberry. In one block, there was a fishing pond, an old-fashioned barber shop, and a farmer's market.

I followed the directions to a small mechanics shop on the corner of Main and Court.

I came back to the same place Monday morning and walked into the shop.

"I'm looking for Doylestown," I said.

"You got it," a short, balding man said. Gary Pincus was the center manager.

Pincus was famous in the company for being hard-nosed and unforgiving. One time, the workers walked out on a little wildcat strike. Pincus didn't give in to their demands. It cost the company money, but it solidified Pincus's stature in the company.

"You better get back in here or we're going to get some scab drivers," threatened Pincus. After thirty minutes, they came back and went to work.

As Pincus introduced me to the group, I felt uncomfortable. Not only had I never delivered a package, but I didn't know how to drive a truck. I didn't even know how to drive a standard stick shift. I was the youngest person in the group. These people had been with UPS for seventeen years and more. They were a close-knit group called the Sunshine Club. They even created a Sunshine fund, where everyone chipped in a couple bucks a week to help out in case of emergencies.

I don't know how they got the name Sunshine Club, because to me, they seemed old and crotchety and they clearly had no patience for a young rookie sup who was going to tell them how to do their jobs.

"Let me tell you something," said Bob Wenton, an old, scraggly guy who was the leader of the group. "I was here before you came, I'll be here while you're here, and I'll be here after you go."

My first role as supervisor was to ride with drivers to get an idea of what the job entailed. "I know I'm the new guy," I told everyone. "I want you to do your normal day's work. I'm not trying to get in your way. I'm just trying to observe what you're doing."

After a week, I learned that the group was taking me for a ride in more ways than one. According to the Master Standard Data for the Doylestown area, a day of pickups and deliveries is an eight and a half hour job. The goal is to do a "scratch job," which meant that the day took exactly eight and a half hours. If it took eight hours and fifteen minutes that was great, if it took eight hours forty-five minutes it was bad, but not a disaster. The problems began when it took more than nine hours because it meant the drivers weren't working hard enough. There was an incentive for the drivers to work longer hours because they could earn as much as thirty dollars an hour in overtime.

I started on Monday with John Matthews. We had a great time. We chatted. I asked about his family, he told me about his four children. We pulled into the hub in nine hours and ten minutes. Pincus gave me a dirty look. Tuesday, I learned all about Jim Pappert. Jim was like Spanky from "Our Gang." He was a little guy who always had a smart comment. We had a long lunch, took the scenic route, and pulled into the station in nine hours, two minutes. Pincus urged me to speed things up. And I did on Wednesday with Elenor "my friends call me Ely," Lawrence. Only eight hours fifty-eight minutes. It was not the improvement Pincus had in mind and he let me know. After three days, Pincus already considered me a cancer on the operation.

On Thursday, I rode with Darwin Bishop, one of the older and most experienced drivers. Darwin hated his first name so everyone called him Bish. He delivered in the rural areas and had for twenty years. The houses on his route had no addresses and neither did the packages. They simply read: Mable Stollins, Quakertown, PA.

"Oh, Mable," Bish said, checking the label. "This is going to be a while."

Bish described what was ahead of us: Mable lived ten miles through the main town, over a ridge to a right at the fork in the road, over a rickety bridge, down an unmarked dirt road one hundred yards past the red barn to a farmhouse. Mable lived behind the farmhouse in a modern, two-story Victorian home. Thirty minutes later, Bish backed down the driveway, parked the truck, and led me five hundred yards over a narrow bridge to Mable's front door.

"Man, this takes a long time," I said.

"Yeah," he answered. "But that's what you have to do out here."

Naturally, Mable wasn't home.

"We'll have to come back again later," said Bish, with a sly grin on his face.

The day with Bish was a new record for Doylestown: nine hours, thirty-eight minutes.

"What happened out there?" Pincus yelled as we walked in. "You only had eighty stops. You should have been in here at 4 o'clock."

"Long day," answered Bish. "Ask the new sup. It was just a long day."

Pincus was merciless with me. Every day he threatened my job and now he was angrier than ever. "I don't know if you can cut it here," he said.

My four days in Doylestown seemed like a year. I left my house at 6:15 in the morning and got home at 8:30 at night. I felt like a fraud because I didn't know how to drive and I had no idea what Pincus expected. If Mable wasn't home, we couldn't deliver the package. What was I supposed to do?

I learned why Pincus thought I was a joke on Friday when I rode with Ron Gerhart, a young man in his late twenties. Riding with him was like a culture shock. He worked me to death. He drove fast, ran to the door, "UPS, I got four packages for you, okay, got to go, got to go," and ran back to the car. We stopped for lunch but organized the truck while we were eating. He parked the truck as close as possible for each delivery, so the walk was shorter.

"What are you doing?" I asked.

"This is the job," he said. "This is what you got to do."

The other drivers walked from house to house, had long lunches, and took forever to find the packages in the back of the truck, especially after a pickup. They were obviously taking advantage of me, but I didn't know any better. Ron and I finished in eight hours eighteen minutes. When we got back to the shop, I checked the records for the last month. The longest shift was eight hours thirty-eight minutes and that was because of a parade. I felt like a fool.

I didn't play the radio during the drive home that night. Instead, I grew more and more incensed. Did they really think they could take advantage of me like that? Did they think I wasn't smart enough?

Over the weekend, I decided to try a different method. In the

Philadelphia hub, the workers were my own age and from a similar background and I knew the job inside and out. In Doylestown, I supervised drivers who were old enough to be my parents. I couldn't be Mr. Nice Guy because it was obvious they weren't going to accept me just because I gave a speech about teamwork.

After my regular Saturday basketball game, I picked up a book called *340 Methods*, a UPS guide that describes 340 tricks to be a better driver. By Monday, I memorized about 320 of the methods and was armed for my day with Dawn Stevens.

Dawn was a crabby older women, whose faced looked like a sharpei. To make matters worse, Pincus warned, "You better not come in here late again, or you're not going to be coming in here at all."

Pincus didn't have to worry. I wasn't going to be late.

"How you doing?" Dawn said innocently to the first customer.

"Great," the customer answered. "You coming to the county fair next week?"

"Yeah, I'm going. What are you going to make?" Dawn asked.

"I'm not sure yet, how about you?" The conversation lasted five minutes. A week earlier I would have considered it good customer relations, but now, I was convinced it was a calculated attempt to steal time from the company.

"Listen, Dawn," I said when we got back to the car. "We don't have time for all this talking. Say, 'hello and good-bye.' Be polite and let's go."

"But I've known her for years," she said.

"I understand," I said. "But we don't have time to talk, let's go."

A couple of stops later, there was another conversation. This time I interrupted.

"Sorry, sir, we don't have time to talk, let's go, Dawn."

Now Dawn was angry.

As we drove to the next house, Dawn stopped short at a yellow light.

"You couldn't make that light?" I asked.

"I didn't want to chance it," she said.

"Look," I said. "You better drive aggressively." By lunch, Dawn was actually frightened of me. And I didn't let up. If she carried two boxes, I challenged her to carry three. I dared her to take more than one hour for lunch and I pushed her to run to each house.

"Can't you back this truck up any faster?" I griped as she backed into a driveway.

"You want to back it up?" she barked back.

"No I don't want to do that," I said. "That's what I pay you to do."

When we got back into the building I walked Dawn into the office and we sat down.

"Let me tell you something," I said. "You walk too slow. You write too slow. You talk too much." I listed the ways she deviated from the method book. "When we went to Acme you took the long way around. You didn't think I saw that. I saw that. You went to the bathroom four times, eighteen times you dropped your pen. Your key wasn't ready seventeen times."

She tried to defend herself, but I wouldn't let her.

"You don't talk," I yelled. "You just listen to what I got to say."

Her eyes watered, but I showed no mercy. I was prepared to make her pay for the way the whole group treated me.

"What are you crying for? You think you're going to take advantage of me? I'm going out in the car with you again tomorrow," I said. "We're going to get this right tomorrow."

I unloaded all the anger and frustration and humiliation of the first week on Dawn.

The next day, we met at 8:30 sharp. I wore a UPS baseball hat and glasses. I looked like a state trooper. I was prepared to battle Dawn again all day, but it wasn't necessary. Dawn was a machine. Her key was always ready. She ran to every door, "Good morning, UPS, I have two packages for you. Sign here. Thank you, have a good day." Next stop. "Hi, how you doing? Yeah, I'll see you at the fair. Gotta run. Have a good day." She was perfect.

We did a scratch job. At the end of the day, we talked in the office.

"Great job," I said. "Today, twenty-two times you had your pen ready to get the signature first. I like the way you drove aggressively but not too aggressive. I liked the way you parked. I think you did an outstanding job."

I was complimentary. But it was too late. My reputation had spread throughout the Sunshine Club. I was a hammer. I got results, but at what price? Two mornings later, my reputation got worse. I was coming back from lunch when a mechanic asked me to move a truck into one of the garages. I feared this day would come, but I climbed into the driver's seat with confidence. I turned the ignition, let the clutch out slowly, and started to move forward.

All of a sudden, my foot slipped off the clutch and the truck stalled. Naturally, the entire area was outside watching. I tried again, but this time, I let the clutch out too fast and it stalled again.

"This guy can't even drive. Jesus Christ," said Pappert. "And you think you're gonna tell us how to drive?"

I was thoroughly embarrassed.

Every weekend for the next month, I drove to Doylestown and signed out a truck. At first, I just drove around the property. Then, when I was comfortable enough, I drove around town. The hardest part of driving a truck is backing it up. In a car you can turn your head around, but the mirrors are the only way to see in a truck. So I pretended to deliver packages by backing into a driveway. I practiced three-point turns and parallel parking and any other skill a good UPS driver needed.

One Saturday, I backed out of a driveway to find three cop cars with lights flashing and sirens blaring blocking the street.

"This is the police. Come out of the car, put your hands on top of the truck."

Apparently a black driver in an all-white neighborhood maneuvering in and out of driveways on Saturday with a UPS truck was a suspicious sight and one of the neighbors had called the police. They thought I had stolen the truck and was looking for a house to break into.

My UPS identification stopped the sheriff from cuffing me and a call to Pincus stopped him from charging me with theft. The next Monday Pincus called me into his office and told me he was sorry that I was hassled. He was impressed that I had learned to drive on my own time.

Over the next month, I learned the job inside and out. And slowly I became more successful as a supervisor. Now that I knew the job, I used the experience to help the drivers succeed.

"This is Rick L-O-Y Loy. I'm heavy out here," said Rick Loy. Rick always spelled his last name. "I'm probably going to be in late."

"How much do you have left?" I said.

"I haven't even been into the Cherry Blossom section and there's at least thirty-five stops there."

"Have you made the pick up at Kmart?"

"No."

"Okay, I'll get someone to cover the Kmart pickup, you do the Cherry Blossom section. Will that help?"

"Good. Now they'll come right off and I won't have to fight the pickups. I'll make it."

I studied maps and routes of who picked up in what areas. John Matthews always struggled around five, because he had a pickup at Jones Electric. There were so many packages that it blew out his truck and he could barely move. Bob Wenton's route passed by Jones Electric at 4:30 so I asked him to stop by and pick up fifty packages to make the load easier for Matthews.

The Sunshine Club told me that small trucks were easier for residential and rural areas and big trucks were easier for business areas. So I made sure to assign the most appropriate truck for the route. The ideas weren't revolutionary, but they made the job easier for the drivers.

Slowly the Sunshine Club accepted me. I continued to ride with the drivers from time to time to make sure I understood what they went through.

"Hey, Bish," I said on Wednesday afternoon. "I need a relaxing day. I'm coming with you tomorrow."

Thursday morning, I rode the same route with Bish that I had three months earlier. This time it was different. His wife had made lunch for both of us. He brought homemade bread. A big thermos of lemonade, chocolate chip cookies, and three turkey sandwiches.

"He's a big, young guy so here's an extra sandwich for Rodney," Bish's wife said.

Our first package was addressed to Mable.

"With the rain we've been having," Bish said, "I'd hate to test that rickety bridge. What's today? Thursday. Mable is probably getting her hair done. We can catch her in town."

We drove through town and sure enough, there was Mable with curlers in her hair, in the beauty salon on Main Street.

"We have a package for you," Bish mouthed through the window, pointing to the box.

"Put it in my car," Mable mouthed back.

Bish was a master. He put the package in the backseat of the car, I got the signature, and we were off. We saved at least thirty minutes by avoiding the dirt road, the rickety bridge, narrow driveway, and the walk around the farmhouse.

We finished the route in eight hours and twelve minutes, almost ninety minutes faster than the first time. We saved time, we saved gas, we saved tire wear. I came to appreciate those salty, crotchety old-timers, who reminded me of sea captains. Pincus liked the young guys that ran around dripping sweat and skipping their lunch, and they were good workers.

But Bish was too old to run. He made up the time because he was smart. He had the trust of the people. He had the alarm codes or keys to the house. Instead of waiting around and having to come back, he arranged to put the packages in the garage or in the basement or in the kitchen.

The more time I spent with the drivers, the more they warmed up to me and the more I warmed up to them. For Christmas I bought everyone insulated socks. I wrapped each box individually with a note. By this time, I could joke around: "Dawn, this probably won't put a smile on your face, but at least it will keep your feet warm." It was the first time anyone gave them Christmas gifts. Pincus couldn't believe it. "What are you doing? Buying gifts? Who are you, Santa Claus?"

But it wasn't until Elenor was caught stealing from the company that the Sunshine Club fully accepted me. Elenor was a single mother of two children and popular among the drivers, but she was fired on the spot for stealing. The next morning I gave the PCM—at this point, GITs were renamed Prework Communications Meetings. Most of the workers understood the firing, but they were still sad because she was like part of the family.

PCMs are supposed to last three minutes. That day, mine lasted ten.

"When I was a kid, I had many opportunities to steal," I said to start my speech. "And I want you to understand, I was poor. I was hungry. I had shoes on that had holes. I needed money." The place went silent.

"And what's worse is that everyone expected me to steal—everyone in the neighborhood, in the school, and the police. Probably only my grandmother would have been surprised. Everyone thought, 'Sure, look at him, he's going to steal.' But I didn't.

"I guess we all need money. As UPS employees, the best is expected of us. But we're human. Sometimes, we don't give our best. But that doesn't mean we shouldn't try. Even though one of us made a mistake, I know that you guys are still the best and we should never give in to what we know is wrong."

In June we had moved into a building in Willow Grove with several other areas. By the end of my speech, there were probably fifty drivers, including managers and other sups listening. Even Pincus, who was usually working in his office, saw the crowd grow and listened from the side.

Most of these people had never been to the inner city. They didn't know anything about my upbringing. They came expecting to hear the usual lecture: "Unfortunately, we have a problem here, but we have our standards and we better not forget that. It is regrettable that one of our drivers abused that trust but let it be a lesson to all of you."

Jim Casey, the founder of UPS, had said, "When people see that what you are trying to do for them comes from a sincere heart, they'll believe you, they'll do what you ask them to do, and they'll keep on doing it as long as you ask."

I wasn't planning on making a personal statement. It just happened and I guess it hit a nerve with the audience. From that day on, the drivers would do anything for me. We became a bonus center, which meant our area was running better than expected and the drivers made extra money. Times were good and there was talk about promoting me to manager in the new Willow Grove hub.

Bill Richards was the division manager and Pincus's boss. He ran the whole building. He was a big, chubby guy who loved sports. He agreed to have me promoted.

When it got around that I was leaving, the Sunshine Club protested. They petitioned Richards to let me stay. "The area is running better than it has for twenty years. Let's not break up a winning team," read the petition, signed by all twenty drivers.

Once a month on Saturday mornings, we met for a meeting called Challenge of the '80s to discuss UPS's competition. One meeting we were discussing Federal Express, which had just started, when Rick L-O-Y Loy said:

"Yeah, but what about Rodney Carroll leaving? That's what we need to talk about."

"If that happens," said Richards, "it will be because Rodney does such a good job and he deserves to get promoted. Don't you think he deserves to get promoted?"

Then Dawn stood up. "Why can't we promote him right here? Pincus has been around long enough."

The day I was promoted to manager of the Willow Grove hub, I apologized to Dawn for berating her on our first ride together. She apologized for trying to take advantage of my inexperience. The Sunshine Club isn't together anymore. Most of them have retired. Dawn helps organize the county fair. Bish and his wife restored an old farmhouse across the bridge, down the dirt road, and right on the first unmarked road after the big willow tree.

9. My Brother's Keeper

Courtney and I slowly drifted apart when I started working at UPS. To this day, it is one of my biggest regrets. I was so concerned about my career, that I didn't have time for anything else. Or anyone else. When Courtney and I did talk, it was mostly small talk about Mom Mom or the Eagles. One time he called me at work because he was trying out for his high school football team and he wanted advice. Courtney dreamed of being a professional football player. When he was younger, he couldn't wait to play pickup games on our block.

Finally, when Courtney was twelve, we needed an extra player against our arch rivals on Garnet Street and Courtney finally got his chance.

We played tackle without pads and although Courtney was undersized, he tried harder than anyone on the field. He never stopped running and he even made a couple of tackles that helped us win. More than anything else, he loved being included.

"Make sure you're aggressive during tryouts," I said, throwing out a random cliché—I didn't have too much time to talk. "Bring your maximum effort the entire time."

"Okay, Rodney," he answered. He sensed I was distracted. "Thanks for your time."

Courtney was crushed when he didn't make the team. I was disappointed, too.

I felt responsible. After playing high school football for four years, and experiencing the tryout process, I understood how to impress coaches. I could have showed Courtney some basic techniques—how to keep his balance in a three-point stance, how to use proper tackling technique, how to catch the ball and pull it into your chest, how to keep your head up at all times. I could have done it all in a single afternoon, but I didn't.

Sports can be the greatest thing and the worst thing. Many aspects of professional sports are obviously out of control, but in it's purest sense, sports are great. They help build confidence and self-esteem. Sports offer a sense of purpose and belonging. Perhaps most important to a kid in the inner city, sports simply gives you something to do after school.

From the time Courtney was little, he craved acceptance. Courtney finished school at 3:00 P.M. and my grandmother didn't get home from work until 6:00. That's three hours of free time. It was those three hours that accounted for the majority of the trouble. My old neighborhood was deteriorating at a fast rate. In my day, most kids hanging out after school were either drinking or smoking. If they experimented with drugs it was marijuana. Cocaine was mostly an upper-class drug. Nobody in my neighborhood could afford it. But in the early '80s, all that changed when crack found its way into our neighborhood. Crack was basically cheap cocaine. So if you could afford marijuana, you could afford crack. Crack was much more powerful and addictive.

Suddenly, there was more theft and violence. There were more drug wars, which led to more shootings. People walked around strung out of their minds, looking for crack houses. Drug dealers recruited anyone hanging around the street.

"Have you ever tried crack?" a drug dealer would ask an unsuspecting kid in the neighborhood. "Come down to 1402 Woodstock Street. Make sure you come around the back and I'll give you a taste for free. What else do you have to do?"

But if you're playing a sport, you have practice every day. You have a sense of pride about your body and an obligation to your teammates that makes you want to avoid other distractions. After practice, you're so dead tired that the only thing you want to do is go home and get some sleep.

When Karl's brother, Bruce, was cut from the tenth grade team at Franklyn High School, he was devastated. His life spiraled down quickly. He went from a decent kid to one that pierced his ear, branded his arm, and started hanging out on the corner after school.

When I heard the news about Courtney, I was worried the same thing might happen to him.

I called him at home during one of my breaks.

"Don't sweat it," I told him. "We can work together during the summer and you can try out again next year."

"Yeah," he answered. "Sounds good."

If I had been more sensitive, I probably would have noticed the distant tone in Courtney's voice. He probably knew we weren't going to work out together during the summer—and we didn't. Courtney never made the football team, but he continued to seek acceptance.

I saw Courtney almost every week for the next several years. I went by every Sunday to take my grandmother to church, and Courtney usually joined us. A few times, I pulled up to see him standing on the corner with a bunch of guys I didn't recognize.

"Hey. What's up?" I said as I walked by. Courtney usually mumbled a quick response.

"Who are those guys?" I would ask when Courtney came in the house.

"Oh nobody, just some guys I hang out with."

After a while, I stopped asking.

One day, I spotted Courtney walking by himself with a brown bag in his left hand. He tried to avoid me.

"Hey," I yelled, rolling down my window. "Wait up."

Courtney reeked of alcohol. I could smell it even before he stuck his head in the car. His clothes were disheveled and he looked like he hadn't showered in days.

"Take a ride with me," I said and pulled him into the car. I knew Courtney was struggling, but I didn't know how badly—or maybe I didn't want to know.

"Get in the car."

"I'm not drunk," he protested.

"Come on, give me a break, I can smell it all over you."

"Well, I had one drink," he conceded.

"One drink is one too many. That's how it starts. What are you, stupid?"

"You're not my father, you don't tell me what to do. You're just making a big deal out of nothing." I had little patience for Courtney. I was still working long and crazy hours. Courtney knew better than this.

"It is a big deal, because you're messing up your life," I said. "What else has to happen in your life for you to know that alcohol is no good?" I was so frustrated, that I didn't wait for a response.

"You're going to end up just like mom. You're going to grow up and your kids are not going to like you."

He started crying. That was a taboo subject for Courtney. He knew that she had had an alcohol problem, but he had been too young to understand its severity.

"I can't believe you said that," he cried. "That's something that a son shouldn't say about his mother. Who do you think you are? Mom did the best she could. You don't know the pressure she was under trying to raise us. Sometimes you need to have a drink. If you were worried about someone else but yourself, maybe you would under-stand that she was doing the best she could. She never wanted to hurt us. I'm tired of you and Cheryl talking about Mom like that. All I know is she loved us."

Before I could apologize, Courtney calmed down, wiped his eyes, and said, "Okay. I won't drink again."

I'd like to think that he meant it at the time.

I saw Courtney only sporadically after that day. He graduated from high school and was planning to attend a vocational college to become a machinist. At twenty-one, he was still on welfare and living at home to take care of our grandmother who was now eighty-one and retired.

He came to Sunday church less and less.

"I'll meet you guys up there," he'd say, then he wouldn't show. I told myself that he was fine. I told myself that he was just look-ing for a break. He took care of my grandmother full-time and if he wanted to do something else on Sunday, what's the harm? I'm sure that if I had looked for signs of drinking, I would have found them, but I wasn't. I didn't have time for those distractions in my life. So if Courtney was still drinking, he had no problem hiding it from me.

Until one Wednesday evening when I made an unscheduled visit to my grandmother's house. Things were going well at work, and I wanted to surprise my grandmother and Courtney with steak and chicken for dinner.

It was six o'clock and my grandmother was alone. The lightbulbs outside the front door were broken. The house appeared unkempt. Unopened mail was piled at the door.

"Where's Courtney?" I asked.

"I don't know," my grandmother said. "I haven't seen him in a while."

"Well, I guess we'll have to start without him."

My grandmother and I prepared the food and had a nice dinner together. When I finished the dishes, Courtney still wasn't home. It was 8:30.

"What time does Courtney usually get in?" I asked.

"Well, it varies," said Mom Mom.

"What do you mean 'it varies'?"

"Well, sometimes he comes in at 9:00. He could come in right now. Or sometimes he may not come in till late."

"What do you mean, late?" I asked.

"He might not come in until the next day."

"So you mean he stays out all night?" I had no idea.

"He's not like you, Rodney," my grandmother said in a calming tone. "He's not responsible, like you. He's too influenced by other people. I try to tell him not to listen to those people, but he listens to them anyway."

"That's not the point," I said. "The point is that he's not supposed to be out all night. He's supposed to be here with you." I waited for him to come home. I waited and waited and waited. My grandmother tried to calm me down, but she soon realized it was no use and she went to bed around 11:00. Midnight came, then 1:00 A.M., then 2:00 A.M. No sign of Courtney. I grew angrier and angrier. I knew I had been conned.

"You staying in a good crowd?" I would ask him.

"Oh, yeah, Rodney."

"Are you a leader or follower?"

"I'm a leader," he answered proudly.

All lies. I should have known. You don't just go from not drinking to staying out all night. It's a long progression. Courtney must have thought I was the one who was stupid. Finally, I left because I was unsure what I would do to him if he walked through the door.

I got home at around 2:30 A.M. I called to see if Courtney was home yet. My grandmother answered.

"Go to sleep Rodney," she said. "He's not here."

The next evening, I went back again and this time Courtney was home.

He had the routine down to a science.

"Hey, Rodney, how you doing? I'm just making some food for me and Mom Mom."

My grandmother hadn't told him I had been there the previous night.

"Let's talk for a second," I said.

"Sure, Rodney, what's up?"

I started setting him up.

"It's great to see you today. Are you usually here around this time?"

"Oh, yeah," he said. "I'm usually here. I get here right around 6:00 or 6:30 at the latest every day."

"Good, cause I'd hate to see Mom Mom here by herself."

"Oh, she's never home by herself," he said. "I'm here. I either bring dinner or I make dinner or we're having leftovers."

"Is that right?" I said. "So it's fair to say that you never stay out late?"

My grandmother knew what I was doing and tried to intervene.

"Oh yes," she said, putting her hands around both of us. "Two brothers talking. What a blessed sight."

My grandmother hated to see my brother and me argue, so I escorted Courtney outside and got right to the point.

"I was here last night," I said, staring him in the eye.

Immediately, Courtney got angry.

"Man, you were setting me up. Who do you think you are? I didn't say I was here every night."

"What time did you get home last night?"

"Why do you ask me that? What time did you leave?"

"Just answer the question."

"Well, it was late."

"What time?"

"Could have been 9:00 or 10:00, I didn't look at a clock. Why, what time did you leave?"

"I left before you got home. And it was well after 9:00 or 10:00." We were playing this cat-and-mouse game until finally Courtney had had enough.

"You can't tell me what to do. You come down here once a week. You're not doing nothing. I'm here all the time. I need to have my own time. I have a social life. I got things to do."

"A social life is one thing," I yelled back. "But staying out all night is another."

This was going nowhere. Finally, I said softly, "Why don't you just come clean with me. We don't need this. Just tell me straight what's going on and we'll go from there."

Courtney calmed down as well. "I like to hang out with my friends," he said.

"So what are you doing, drinking?" my voice went up a couple of notches.

"What makes you think I'm drinkin'?"

"What else are you doing, talking?"

"Yeah, we talk, every once in a while I have a drink. I can have a drink if I want to, can't I?"

"I thought you were never going to drink again?" We were now yelling again.

"I said I was never going to get drunk again. I didn't say I wasn't going to have a drink."

"No, you said you weren't going to have a drink."

"I never said that." Again, we went back and forth.

"You know you're heading for trouble?" I warned. "What about our pact."

"Forget that stupid pact," he yelled. "This is ridiculous. Just about everybody drinks. Bank presidents drink, ministers drink, cops drink. People drink. Just because you don't drink, you're the odd one, everyone else drinks."

"The problem is that not all these people have moms—"

He cut me off. "Now you're back on Mom again."

"No, I'm just saying you know what can happen. Not everyone has the same situation."

I didn't have the energy for this and it was obvious that I was making matters worse by preaching. "You know something Courtney? You're right. You are old enough to make some decisions. So go ahead and drink. But the problem I have now is that I want to be sure Mom Mom is being taken care of properly."

"No problem," he said, rubbing his hands together. "Anytime you want to come take care of her, let me know, I'm out of here. Until then, I'm doing the best I can."

He waited for a response, but I had none. He was absolutely right. I was with my grandmother even less than he was. I came down once a week, but I didn't wash clothes or make dinner. So even though he was slowly deteriorating, he still did more than me. And we both knew it.

"That's what I thought," he said and walked away.

It wasn't until recently that I heard Courtney's story of how he became caught up in drugs and alcohol. He told me that during the summer before his senior year at high school, he had rebelled against the strict rules of my grandmother. His friends stayed out late and partied. He was embarrassed to have to ask my grandmother's permission to go downtown or stay out past 9:00 P.M.—and most of the time, my grandmother's answer was, No.

"I wanted to be accepted so much, I guess I couldn't handle it," Courtney confessed.

So Courtney did what millions of other teenagers of all classes do every day—he gave in to peer pressure. He started with beer.

"Let's go get some forties," his friends suggested, and Courtney didn't need much persuasion. For years he had seen my mom and many of our other relatives drink. To him it seemed natural. But what he didn't know was that with his biological makeup, he couldn't drink just one beer.

"I might as well just drink a case," he said. "Because I couldn't get enough of it. At first, it just made me laugh and it was fun. It was fun for quite a while in the beginning and then things turned dark."

Courtney's so-called friends hung out later and later, having contests as to who could drink the fastest. And Courtney usually won.

"I was good at it," he said. "It was bad for me, but I was good at it. I just always wanted more. I wanted more and more. I could never just have one beer. My system was just greedy for it."

And it escalated. His friends experimented with drugs and Courtney was quick to follow. He smoked marijuana, then snorted crack cocaine, and often did something called Black Beauties. To this day, I still don't know what Black Beauties are.

I was shocked to learn that Courtney had started drinking with my mother before she passed away. She moved back to North Philadelphia and he saw her from time to time. Eventually he went to visit her and they did the only thing they still had in common, drink.

When they drank, they mostly talked about my grandmother. They groused about how strict she was. Our mother blamed Mom Mom for her problems. She once told Courtney that the man that he knew as his father, wasn't his father. She tried to get Courtney to forgive her for the way she treated him. I can't imagine how difficult those conversations must have been for him.

But as Courtney said, "Our minds were in a stupored state." He said that he drank with my mom because he felt a connection. "It was a sick connection really," he said. "But I was willing to continue drinking with her just to have that connection with her."

Things got worse for Courtney. His drinking binges became more frequent. Most of the time he took real good care of our grandmother. He loved her very much. He called her the angel that God had sent to rescue us. My grandmother, for her part, tried to rescue Courtney from alcohol. "You need to leave this foolishness alone," she told him. She tried to get his focus back on the church. But it didn't work. Courtney started avoiding those conversations. At first, Courtney was able to care for my grandmother despite his addiction. He could step out of his partying world and jump into his domestic world. But other times, he neglected her.

After my run-in with Courtney, I made sure my grandmother was taken care of. My grandmother was relatively healthy and usually insisted on looking after herself. Nonetheless, I hired a nurse to come in once a day to check on her and we had Meals-On-Wheels bring by lunch and dinner.

Unfortunately, this had an adverse affect on Courtney. He spent even less time at home. The guilt of letting Mom Mom down tore away at Courtney.

The guilt turned to self-pity, something I understood all too well. "Why can't I have a family with a mother and a father. With peace and love," he said. I had often wondered the same thing.

Courtney told me that ever since we were children, he had craved my approval and he knew that I would be disappointed with him. "I didn't want you to think I was a failure," he said.

As angry as I was with Courtney, my grandmother was understanding.

"He's got that disease," she told me. "He's just like his mother. Why don't you spend some time with him. Don't try to change him or lecture him. Just spend some time with him. You know how much he looks up to you."

"Okay, Mom Mom."

After that, I came down a few times a week just to see Courtney and he was receptive. We went to Jim's for cheese steaks. We played basketball. I brought him back to my house to watch the Eagles game. I gave him my old car—the Buick.

Things were going well. I knew I wasn't going to change him, but at least if he was with me, he wasn't drinking. Then after a few months, he started showing up late or simply didn't show up at all. He always called the next day with an excuse, but I knew he was drinking. I knew he couldn't get himself together by the time I picked him up, which meant the disease had gotten worse.

"This isn't working," I confessed to my grandmother. But she was still optimistic.

"Don't get discouraged," my grandmother told me. "You are making a difference. Just keep at it. Don't give up on him."

The next weekend, I got two tickets on the forty-yard line to an Eagles game against Miami. Courtney is the biggest Eagles fan I know. He still is. He would never miss that game.

"I'll pick you up at 2:00," I told him.

"I'll be waiting, Rodney," he said. "And Rodney. Thanks."

The game wasn't until 4:00, so we planned to get there early, do some tailgating, catch the warm-ups, and then settle in for the game.

I wore my Reggie White jersey and even brought a Randell Cunningham jersey for Courtney. At the game, I was going to surprise him by buying a Wes Hopkins jersey—his favorite player. Although things had been strained between us, I didn't hold anything against him and I didn't think he held anything against me either. He was still my brother and I knew he was trying.

It was going to be a good big brother–little brother outing. I had figured when we got to the game, we could talk about how things were going and see where I could help. I pulled up about ten minutes early, but Courtney was nowhere to be found. Two-fifteen, no Courtney. Then three, then four.

I turned on the game in my grandmother's house.

"I'm sure he'll be here any minute," she tried to reassure me.

"I'm sure he'll be here any minute," my grandmother repeated twenty minutes later.

"No," I answered quietly. "He's not coming. Tell him that I came by." I put the tickets on the table and left.

As much as he tried, Courtney couldn't take care of his alcohol and drug problems by himself and in June of 1992, he hit bottom—for the first time. He fell into a deep depression.

"I knew that I was failing everybody," he said. "I felt like a total loser. I might as well have just died. I was just making things worse in life. I felt worthless."

My brother checked himself into a long-term rehab program called The Firehouse. He lived there for six and a half months. He graduated the program and got a good job at Episcopal Hospital. Within two weeks he was abusing alcohol again.

"I was weak," he said. "Even though I was clean for six and a half months, the disease was still calling me. I was too weak to overcome it. I gave in."

He tried fighting the addiction on his own but had numerous relapses. He tried another rehab program called Eagleville—the same one our mom went to years before. After that program, he stayed sober for eight months before another relapse.

For my part, I spent less time in North Philadelphia. I guess I didn't want to be reminded of Courtney. I never saw Courtney as a failure. I saw a little boy who grew up without a father. A child who was emotionally abused by his mother to the point where he had to cry himself to sleep—quietly. I saw a boy with a huge heart who loved to laugh and joke and eat fried chicken. I saw a youngster who desperately wanted to be included and loved. I didn't think about it then, but now I sometimes wonder if he wasn't also a boy who had been let down by his older brother.

10. Jimmy Little

At twenty-seven, I was one of the youngest managers at UPS—eleven years younger than the company average. I earned three thousand dollars a month, plus stock options. I still lived in the bottom apartment of the duplex. One night I heard a fight at the end of the street. Two gunshots were fired. The next weekend, I started looking at houses in the suburbs. I bought a five-bedroom, two-and-a-half-bath house built in Bensalem, Pennsylvania, ten miles outside the city. The house had a big yard, a garage, a basement, a deck, and most important, an environment free of violence.

To me it was success.

After nine years at UPS, I understood the UPS hierarchy well enough to know that a critical step in my career was advancing to division manager. A division manager's job in UPS culture was similar to a junior vice president's. There is a large salary increase, the stock options double, and you even get your own office. Once you make division manager, your future is secure.

I also knew that the best way to earn a promotion to division manager was to prove myself as the midnight sort manager in the Willow Grove building. The eyes of the company were on the sort manager because the overnight service from New York to Washington was a huge moneymaker for UPS.

The operation ran from 11:00 P.M. to 3:00 A.M. The challenge was organizing the operation and motivating the workers so that the packages were sorted, loaded, and sent out without delays or mistakes. It was also difficult to find dedicated employees for the shift. UPS believed in hiring college kids, but how many college kids want to spend their nights loading trucks? Manager after manager tried to master the sort, but had failed.

I knew I could do the job; I just needed a chance. For three years I hounded Frank Ryan to promote me to sort manager. Finally, when Ken Abbott's team delayed trucks for the third straight night, Ryan gave me the chance I was waiting for.

"Remember, this job is the stepping-stone for division manager," Ryan reminded me as if I didn't know. "If you do well here, you are set. Just don't screw up."

I left his office prepared to conquer the sort. The thing that made other sort managers nervous about the job was what I liked best: I was accountable for everything and everyone. Everyone that worked in the building reported to me. I supervised three area managers, six full-time supervisors, an industrial engineer supervisor, a human resources supervisor, a security supervisor, and two hundred hourly employees.

The sort schedule was basically the same every night. Trucks from New York arrived first with the Maryland, Virginia, and D.C. packages. Thirty minutes later the Maryland, Virginia, and D.C. trucks arrived with packages headed for Philadelphia, New York, and New Jersey. Trucks from both directions arrived intermittently throughout the rest of the evening. The trucks needed to be unloaded, sorted, repacked, and ready to move by 2:30 A.M.

My first night on the job, I walked into the sort meeting and introduced myself. The sort meetings started four hours before the sort. The managers and full-time supervisors gathered to plan the operations for the evening.

"We're going to have one hundred fifty thousand packages tonight," said the industrial engineer.

"I-95 has construction through Baltimore so I expect some late arrivals there," added the trailers supervisor.

"We got buried again last night. We need more workers," said Brendan, the area manager of the New York side.

"Well, don't take them from us," replied Collins, the area manager from the D.C. side.

"We have eleven people starting in orientation. We'll put three people in New York, four in smalls sort, and four in D.C," said the human resources manager.

"We had an injury last night; part of the problem was that too many plastic bags were left on the floor and people were slipping," explained the safety supervisor.

"Some of the workers were late because they got stuck at the guard shack without identification. Let your people know that we're not letting anyone in unless they have an I.D.," explained security.

"Okay," I said after all the reports. "Let's all work together and do our best. Have a good night."

I spent my first week saying very little. I had learned in my stint in Doylestown that it was dangerous to start making changes before I understood the operation completely. Each night I walked throughout the operation observing as much as I could. I watched the workers unload the trucks. I noticed the sorters placing the packages on the belt. I inspected the loaders stacking the packages in the trucks. I observed the smalls sort area. I noted the interaction between the managers and supervisors. I studied the energy of the part-time sups and the passion of the hourly workers.

One day, an industrial engineer tapped me on the shoulder.

"Hey, Rodney," he said. "I'll give you the same advice I gave the others. All you need to worry about is finishing the sort. We make so much money on this that even if you don't run as productive as possible, it will be fine."

I shook my head.

At the end of the week, I evaluated the production and the service. It wasn't long before I realized that the problems on the midnight sort were the same problems I faced in my other positions at UPS: there was a lack of teamwork within the building. There was tension between the management and the union employees.

"All I have to do is learn from what I did before," I told myself on the drive home after the Friday night sort. "It worked before, it should work again."

I routinely put in sixty-five-hour weeks and on my days off I wanted nothing more than sleep. My routine was to go to bed on Saturday night at 5:00 P.M. and not wake up until Monday.

I kept to my routine that weekend and on Monday, I came to work ready to implement the strategies that worked so well in the past. I knew that teamwork takes time to develop, so I started with more concrete changes. First I made sure that everyone was retrained on the proper way to do their jobs.

I didn't like what that industrial engineer had told me. Not only because I had higher expectations for the area, but because when you settle for less than your best, you get sloppy.

I had learned that lesson from Bish. Bish never ran around dripping sweat like the younger guys at the hub. He didn't have to because he knew his job. He had twenty-one years of safe driving. He never had an accident. Bishop wrote neat, so it wasn't a problem to trace a package. The other guys raced around, constantly backing over a mailbox or running over a rosebush. They wrote sloppy so it was difficult to trace their deliveries. They hustled but only because they were always behind. Bish did the job the way it was supposed to be done and in the long run he was more valuable to the company.

When the job is done correctly, there are less injuries, work is more enjoyable, there is less wasted time and not as much panic during stressful times. I made sure we did the little things right: place the packages on the belt with the labels up, don't touch the packages that are coming off their belts, constant cleanup, no packages on the floor. I insisted that the area was run spotless. I called it, "inspection ready."

Next I convinced the area managers to move the workers to where the load is the heaviest. Dave Collins's area was doing nothing while Brendan's was getting hit at the beginning of the night, so I asked Collins to send help for the first thirty minutes on the New York trucks. He reluctantly agreed.

My next operational change was inspired from my days as part-time sup in the smalls sort. When a truck entered the hub in Willow Grove, the large packages were unloaded onto a belt. The small packages either went on the belt as well or were sent to smalls sort. If they went to smalls sort, they were contained in bags—twenty packages to a bag—and the bag was placed back on the belt. In the past, when things were heavy, there were less packages sent to smalls sort because the manager moved people from smalls sort to the heavy area.

I changed all that. My theory was that we wanted the least amount of packages coming across the belt as possible. So when things were heavy, I moved more people to smalls sorts so more packages could be consolidated into bags. Our smalls sorts volume jumped from 15 percent to as much as 30 percent. Consequently,

even when we were hit hard, the belt didn't become too heavy because a third of the packages were going to smalls sort. And smalls
sort was prepared to handle it.

The idea also saved on travel time. The Willow Grove hub is a
huge building—there's a fifteen-minute walk from the New York
trailers to the D.C. trailers. But the smalls sort areas were in the same
place. So if the people on the New York sort needed help, the D.C.
sort was only a few feet away.

At every sort meeting, I asked the industrial engineer to create a
sort-planning worksheet. It took the anticipated number of packages
and divided it into percentages, so human resources knew what areas
needed workers.

"Forty-seven percent of the volume is going to the New York side
of the building," said the industrial engineer. That translated into
seventy-two people during peak hours.

"Brendan. How many do you have?" I asked.

"I got seventy-three people," he answered.

"Last night you planned seventy-three people and you only had
seventy-two. What was the problem?" I asked.

"Joe McCardy called off again," he replied.

"Well, what are you going to do about it?" I asked.

"We're going to suspend him," Brendan said.

"What's that gonna do?" I asked. "Now you're not going to have
him for three more days. Is suspending him going to make him come
in on time?"

"No," said Brendan. "But I'm tired of talking to him."

"I understand that," I said. I told him the Hank Worthy story.
"But if you don't keep trying, he doesn't come in and you're going to
have a problem. So we need to find a way to get him in."

My systems were slowly working—production and service were
up and injuries were down—but there was still room for improvement in the teamwork area.

Friday nights were less pressure than the rest of the week because the packages didn't have to be delivered until Monday morning.
Monday through Thursday, the trailers left at 2:30 A.M. without exception. On Friday night, they could leave at three o'clock and it
wouldn't be a disaster.

So during our sort meetings on Fridays, I spent more time addressing behavioral issues. The first one was on teamwork.

"I've been observing things for a couple of months now; I think the reason we don't work like a team is because we don't trust each other," I said. "The first thing you have to do is admit you don't trust."

"I'll admit it," said Dave Collins. "I don't trust Brendan."

That was easy enough.

"Why not?" I asked.

"Because every time I ask him to send a guy down to help, he sends Jimmy Little."

Jimmy Little was about five-foot-three and weighed no more than 130 pounds. He was one of the worst employees in the building. He was slow. Everyone knew he was no help.

Of course, that made Brendan defensive.

"Well, I'm not going to send my best guy down there," he said.

"Why not?" I asked. "Does Jimmy Little actually help Dave Collins?"

"It's better than nothing," said Brendan.

"I'd rather have nothing," interrupted Collins. "Because now I got Jimmy Little's hours and my production goes down."

"I guess you want Paul Pride?" yelled Brendan. Pride was one of the best workers in the operation.

"Yeah, if I got Paul Pride for one hour, I could send him back to you, instead of having Jimmy Little for the rest of the night," said Collins.

"I'm not going to send Paul Pride," insisted Brendan.

"Why not?" I asked.

"Because he's not going to send him back."

"Bingo," I said. "No trust. The only reason you send someone is because I asked you to and you send the worst person you have. What we need you to do is send someone that will actually help. Maybe you don't send Paul Pride. Maybe you could send Wayne Stewart." Stewart was a solid worker. "You keep your best, but send someone who can help."

"Well, who's he going to send me when I need help?" asked Brendan. "He's going to send Martha Mahoney." Martha Mahoney was a classic prima donna. She dressed like she didn't have a nickel to her name, but her nails were always done professionally and she reeked of cheap perfume. She refused to be a packer because "the trailers were dirty."

"I suppose you want me to send Robert Shellingburger when you send me Jimmy Little," said Collins. "If I send you Bob Shellingburger then my area goes down and I'll never get him back."

"That's why I don't send you Paul Pride," retorted Brendan.

We went round and round like that for twenty minutes.

"Now you guys understand what's going on," I said. "There is no trust, therefore, there is no teamwork. Real teamwork is when you want to do something that is actually going to help the person. Why don't we start tonight," I suggested. "Brendan, you send Wayne Stewart; and, Collins, you send someone besides Martha Mahoney."

Two hours into the shift Brendan's voice came through the walkie-talkie.

"I'm sending Wayne Stewart to the east end to help out," he said. "It is now one o'clock in the morning. I expect to have him back in my area by 2:00. I repeat, Wayne Stewart is coming down."

"Copy," said Collins.

I immediately called Collins. "I don't care what you do, make sure you get that guy back there by 2:00."

At 1:58 Wayne Stewart was in Brendan's sight on his way back.

The next night Brendan needed help. Collins was at lunch so Ray Largomicino, the full-time sup, took the call and sent Martha Mahoney. Immediately Brendan called me. He was livid.

"I can't believe he sent me Martha Mahoney," said Brendan. "Did I not send him Wayne Stewart last night? Oh my god. I told you he was going to jerk me around."

I called Collins.

"What's the problem?" I said. "Why'd you send Martha Mohoney?"

"I didn't send Martha Mahoney."

"Well, somebody did."

Collins felt horrible. To make up for it he sent four people to help. After that night Brendan and Collins made a pact that Martha Mahoney and Jimmy Little would never leave their designated areas. Slowly Brendan and Collins earned each other's trust.

"Tell you what I'm going to do," Brendan said over the walkie-talkie. "I'm running so good that I'll send you Paul Pride and Wayne Stewart to come clean your whole area."

"Thanks," Collins answered back. "But I don't need those two guys. I'm alright. As a matter of fact, send Jimmy Little down here and we'll teach him how to load."

More and more people started coming to my Friday "fireside chats," as they were called.

One Friday I talked about support: Many people try to advance themselves by lowering someone else. As a driver supervisor, I tried to make myself feel better by slamming the people around me. But what I needed to do was make myself better by making everyone else better.

The next week I talked about positive feedback; your workers want to know how they're doing. There is no such thing as saying, "Good job," too many times. There's lots of different ways to say it.

I talked about self-fulfilling prophecies. If you constantly tell a person, "you're bad, you're no good," they will end up behaving that way. But if you believe in someone, many times it will help them believe in themselves.

Each week we grew closer as the operation ran better. Finally one night I shared my vision for the future of the hub.

"You guys are the best, the absolute best at UPS," I said. "The only problem is that UPS doesn't know it. They don't realize that the best management team in the entire country is sitting right in this room." I looked around at each of them and continued. "They don't realize it. And you know what's worse? You don't realize it. Not even the people here realize how good you are."

"I realize it," said Frank Santos, a full-time sup.

"You do?" I asked. "What makes you realize it?"

"I think I'm pretty good," he said.

"I didn't say, 'pretty good.' I said 'the best.' There's a difference between pretty good and the best. A lot of people can be pretty good. But very few are the best or want to be the best. Does anyone here know what the best operation is in our region? It's New Stanton. Let's try to be the best operation in the region. Let's go for it. Let's be the best."

That night every manager, every supervisor, committed to being the best. Again, I used techniques that had worked in the past to motivate the supervisors. We kept track of productivity at the sort meeting.

"The smalls sort did twenty-eight percent of the packages last night," said Joe O'Hara, the smalls sort manager. "A new sort record."

"We have another new record," O'Hara said the next night. "The record has jumped to thirty percent." And just like in Philadelphia, it started to catch on.

"I ran seventy-two percent effective," said Collins. "A new North American record."

In turn, the managers and supervisors developed ways to motivate their workers. We started an 0-fer club, which meant that each time a sorter or packer had a truck without a missort, they earned 0-fer points. If the truck had 1,500 packages, they earned 1,500 0-fer points. We gave away T-shirts for the 15,000 club, hats for the 20,000 club, and pizza parties for the 25,000 club.

We had certain people that were consistent workers and did a good job every day. Other people had to constantly be motivated, encouraged, or disciplined.

At the sort meetings, we targeted people that needed more motivation than others.

"Did you say, 'good job,' to Sam last night?" Brendan asked Collins. We were looking out for each other and chasing the same goal.

That encouragement and attention began a ripple effect down from the area managers, to the full-time sups, to the part-time sups, to the hourly employees. Everyone was aware of what we were trying to do as an operation. Instead of the supervisors directing workers from area to area, the workers moved by themselves. "I'm running a little light here," said Paul Pride. "I'm going to run to the other side of the building to check out doors seventy-two and seventy-four. I'll be back."

There was almost no need for managers. Dave Collins, Brendan, and I pretended to inspect the operation.

"This is CEO Oz Nelson. This is Senior Vice President Jim Kelly," I said, pointing to Brendan and Collins. "Show us what you got." And the part-time sups illustrated how the area ran perfectly.

But it wasn't until we converted Matt Cappazoli from part-time sup to quality manager that our operation soared. Cappazoli was a law student at Temple. He didn't care about UPS. He was trying to get through law school. He was in classes all day and he had home-work at night. He worked at UPS because he had a wife and kids and he needed benefits. Cappazoli ended up graduating from law school and is now one of UPS's top attorneys.

But back then, it appeared like his days at UPS were numbered. His law school commitment kept Cappazoli from preparing for his shift. He was a good motivator and his people liked him. But they didn't like waiting for their time cards every night or losing vacation time because he forgot to apply for it.

One night I brought him into the office.

"I want you to be a lawyer," I said as I closed the door. "I know that your primary reason to be here is law school and that's what you want to do. The problem is that you're not doing a good job as a part-time sup."

Cappazoli sat up in his chair and trotted out a few excuses.

"I understand why, I know why," I said, cutting him off. "But when you're here, we need you to do a good job. So I have an idea. You can motivate people. That's your strength. I want you to be in charge of quality. Make sure that we have the top quality going out in the area. Is that something you feel you can do?"

"Definitely," he assured me. This was ten years before UPS created a full-time position called quality manager.

From that night forward we had an injured employee handle Cappazoli's paperwork, two other part-time sups oversaw his area, and Cappazoli focused his time on quality. He made sure the trailers were loaded properly. He checked that the packages were stacked with the labels up. He made sure that there were no loose boxes around and that the floors were spotless.

He made sure the workers double-checked the labels by placing mock packages down the wrong rollers.

"Are you checking the boxes?" Cappazoli asked in his best cross-examination skills.

"Yeah, I'm checking them."

"What about this one right here?" Cappazoli said as he pulled out the missort.

Thanks to Cappazoli, our quality numbers soared and in no time, we were the absolute best operation in the UPS system. We ran production numbers that shocked the company. The goal was to run two hundred packages an hour. We were running 220. Before I started, the operation ran 180. An increase of forty packages an hour means big-time money.

We ran on all cylinders like a souped-up sports car. Everyone knew that the sort manager job was a stepping-stone to division manager. It was just a matter of time before I was promoted.

District Manager John Morrisey was a stocky, six-foot-four, friendly, Irish guy who looked like a descendant of W.C. Fields. He was a drinker and his workers loved him because he took everyone out for cocktails after the shift. His usual was a shot of Johnny Walker Red and a beer.

"Keep 'em coming?" the waitresses asked at the start of every happy hour.

"That's right," he replied. "Man can't walk on one leg."

His philosophy was that a few drinks were all you needed to solve your problems. If you were sick, you drank. If you had a bad night at the hub, you drank. Marriage problems? Have a drink.

I didn't drink and at first it caused some tension between us.

"What are you doing? Drinking Coke all night?" he said. He believed that because I drank only Coke, I never got my problems solved. After a while, he respected my decision.

"Rodney's here," he said. "You know he's not going to drink but he don't have any problems anyway."

One night a few days before Christmas, Morrisey took me out for a Coke.

"You're doing a hell of a job up there," he said, as he sipped his whiskey. "A hell of a job. You're even surprising Frank Ryan, and Frank Ryan likes you like a son." Frank Ryan was the division manager of the Willow Grove building. He relished collecting the plaques for high productivity and service during the regional meetings. "You're single-handedly decorating his office," said Morrisey. "You're doing an outstanding job. What do you want to do next?"

"Of course I'd like to advance and be a division manager," I answered.

"Are you flexible to move?" he asked like he had a position in mind.

"Yeah," I said. "I'm flexible to move."

"We'll work something out," he said. "We have a lot of things going on, a lot of opportunities. A young man like yourself is going to go far."

I left the bar feeling validated. My hard work and dedication were going to be recognized. I told my grandmother that it wouldn't be long before I was promoted.

After the holidays, Morrisey called me back into his office and told me that the $300 million air hub in Philadelphia was under way. He said the planning team was choosing people for positions, "as we speak," and it was only a matter of time before I got my promotion.

At a meeting later that day, Ken Abbott—the same Ken Abbott that failed miserably at the Willow Grove night hub—was named air hub division manager. Abbott was a fine manager and a good friend, he was just a lousy hub guy. Abbott told Morrisey that he would only take the position if I were his sort manager.

"Yeah, but that's not a promotion for Rodney," said Morrisey. "We're planning on promoting him to division manager. There is a feeder division manager position that I'm recommending Carroll for."

"Listen," said Abbott. "I can't do the job without Rodney."

While Morrisey and Abbott talked, another manager chimed in.

"I have a guy that's been around much longer than Carroll," he said. "He should be the feeder division manager. Carroll's only been around a short time. His career is still ahead of him. It's my guy's last chance to get promoted."

They agreed.

I learned all this when Abbott called me later that night.

"We just came from a meeting," he said.

"Yeah, what happened?" I asked, anticipating good news.

"They're going to make me the hub division manager," he said. Abbott had turned down a job for hub division manager in Richmond, Virginia, three months earlier because he had recently adopted a child, so I was happy that he got a second chance.

"Great. Congratulations," I said, waiting to hear the news about me.

"It turns out they want you to be my sort manager," he said. "Well, actually, I want you to be the sort manager." He explained what happened.

"Ken, what's the deal here?" I asked in shock. "Why didn't you tell them you couldn't do the job?"

"I did," he said. "But Morrisey wanted me to be promoted and they all felt you were the number-one candidate of the future."

I was not sympathetic to Abbott's problem. "Well, Ken, I appreciate that," I said. "But this is ridiculous. I'll tell you, this is not right."

I hung up and called Morrisey at his office. He told me the same story.

"There are going to be a lot of jobs, Rodney," he said. "It's going to happen. Just relax. I'll put you on the planning team. Don't worry, everything is fine. You're our number-one candidate."

If I've learned one thing through my experience at UPS, it is that I never want to be the number-one candidate again. Two days later, I got an official letter saying I had been named sort manager for Ken Abbott.

I tried to maintain a positive attitude on the planning team. I trusted Morrisey and his promise to promote me as soon as possible. I believed in UPS. I believed that they treated me fairly. I figured that since I had done so well in the past they had no choice but to promote me.

Around Christmas, I learned differently. I was transferred from the planning team to the Philadelphia pre-load site. Everyone else from the planning team was promoted, but this was a lateral move for me—at best.

At Willow Grove I ran the entire operation in a brand-new building. Now I was just an area manager in a building that was old and dirty. It was quite a change.

The Philadelphia pre-load is one of the toughest jobs in the country for a manager. It is the final sort before the packages are delivered to UPS customers. The sort is organized by street addresses—200 to 250 Broad Street, for example, is on one shelf, 251 to 259 is on another shelf, and so on. The shift starts at 10:30 P.M. and ends at 11:30 A.M. the next morning. There are full-timers who have been there twenty-five years. Half of the employees seem to work in slow motion. The operation constantly broke down, and I didn't appreciate the transfer at all. I spent most of my nights sitting in the office or roaming around aimlessly, wondering how this could have happened.

I knew one thing for sure: I wasn't going to kill myself anymore for UPS. I was disappointed and hurt, and to some extent, I was immature. My attitude was, "I'll show you. You think I'm going to come in here and clean up another operation so someone else can get promoted?"

I was also embarrassed.

"How come Abbott was promoted before you?" my friends asked after every passing promotion.

"Ken Abbott's been around a long time," I said. "I'm just waiting for it to happen. It should happen any time."

But it didn't happen, and after a while, it wore on me. I decided to simply do my job—nothing more. I considered going back to school. I thought about being a lawyer. I thought about all kinds of things other than working at UPS.

And in some ways, life was easier. People who want to be the best are consumed by their passion every minute of the day. Hall of Fame running back Walter Payton didn't just show up at training camp before the season and say, "Okay, I'm here, I'm ready to be the best." He worked out every day during the off-season—running up hills, lifting weights, watching game film—so he could be the best.

If you're content with mediocrity, however, then you can go home and relax. And that's what I did. I didn't want to lose my job so I made sure my operation didn't slide. I didn't want to do anything where they could say, "Yeah, we were going to promote you but you did a terrible job." I just maintained. For a year, I was miserable at work.

All the while Morrisey reassured me that my promotion was coming.

"Don't worry, don't worry," he said. "You're the number-one candidate."

In February 1992, Christine Owens was promoted from the Lawnside hub in New Jersey, which left an opening for a division manager. When I heard the news, I was sure the job was mine. The decisions are usually made within twenty-four hours, so after my preload shift, I hung around waiting for the call.

No call.

I went home and stayed awake next to the phone.

No call.

I fell asleep in my chair and when I awoke I rushed to the answering machine to check for the call.

No call.

When I returned to work that night, I heard Tom Hulliger had been promoted to division manager in the Lawnside hub in New Jersey. Tom Hulliger had worked at the pre-load with me. He did a nice job running his package center, but he had never worked in a hub. He had never been an hourly worker, a part-time sup, a full-time sup, or an area manager.

The next morning, I went to Morrisey's office to get an explanation. When I got there, the office was filled with boxes.

"What the heck is going on?" I asked the guy in the office next door.

"Didn't you hear?" he responded. "John Morrisey resigned."

I was livid. The last thing Morrisey did before he resigned was promote Tom Hulliger and this was the way I found out? I tracked down Morrisey's home telephone number.

"Hey, Rodney, how you doing?" The tone in his voice suggested that he had no idea I was upset.

"I was surprised to learn that you had resigned," I said.

"Yeah, you know, I worked thirty years. It was time to go," he explained. "You and I should get together and get a drink sometime."

"Sure, I'd love to get a drink," I said. "I'd also like to figure out what the plan is for me."

"I'm telling you, Rod. You're an up-and-coming star."

"Yeah," I said. "You keep telling me that. But I'll be honest with you. I was a little puzzled by Tom Hulliger's promotion."

"Tom's a good man," Morrisey said.

"I'm not saying he's not a good man," I responded. "I'm just wondering what happened."

"That Lawnside hub is too small for you," Morrisey explained. "You need to run a bigger operation. Like when you ran Willow Grove."

"But it's still a promotion," I explained. "I'm not running a big operation now."

"People know what you can do, Rod," he said. "Don't worry. You'll be fine."

That was the last time I spoke with John Morrisey. Suddenly, I wasn't so sure about my chances for promotion.

I became even less sure when I met Morrisey's successor, Ron Clever. In all the time I knew Clever, I never saw him smile. If you said, "How you doing, Ron?" he just stared. He was six-foot-five and could have passed for Clint Eastwood's brother. He was mean and seemed to enjoy terrorizing the other managers.

"I know you guys are all in shock about John Morrisey," said Clever after he was introduced. "I'll tell you right now, there's going to be some changes in Philly. It's not going to be business as usual anymore. So the train is leaving now, if you want to get on board."

Clever was hired to make the company money. He didn't care about Rodney Carroll or about anybody else. In no time, people started retiring, quitting, transferring, or getting demoted. At first, I wasn't nervous because I knew I was good at my job. But I noticed that he was giving very few promotions. In fact, the division manager positions were decreasing. In Clever's mind, there were too many division managers. He believed that one person could do the job of two positions.

Clever's style was much like Jim Sterling, from my days as a part-time sup; Gary Pincus, from Doylestown; and a million other managers in companies throughout the country. He was the classic hammer. He believed the best way to get results was to intimidate.

Three weeks after Clever started, I pulled out of the parking lot and I saw Clever walking to the street.

"Hey, Ron," I yelled. "Can I give you a ride somewhere?"

"You don't think I got a car?" he yelled back.

"Well, maybe you do have a car," I responded. "I'm just asking if you need a ride."

"If you think I have a car, why would I need a ride?" he said. And he kept walking.

Like most hammers, Clever's style led to short-term results, and that was why managers like him survived. Twice a year there was a meeting where all the managers in the district reported on the productivity of their operation over the last six months. In the past, it was an informal gathering to discuss managing techniques and build teamwork. Clever changed all that.

In the opening session, Bill Osbourn was the first to report. Osbourn was a jolly, big, fat guy, who reminded me of Frosty the Snowman. He smoked a cigar, didn't work real hard, but was funny and people liked him. Osbourn was famous for his reports. They were like two-minute stand-up comedy routines.

"My production is not going the way it should, but neither is my waistline," he said to start his report. Everyone in the audience laughed. He showed some charts, gave some numbers, and finished by saying, "So that's my report. We're going to have a good Christmas year like we did last year. Drivers will be happy, the customers will be happy, and most important, I'll be happy." And he sat down.

The next report was from Bob Bean. But as Bean started speaking, Clever interrupted.

"Excuse me, Bob, I'm not finished with Mr. Osbourn. Will you have a seat?" said Clever. "Mr. Osbourn, will you stand back up there again and put that graph back up? Now I appreciate the entertainment, but we're not here to be entertained. We're running a business. You understand that?"

"Yeah, I understand that," said Osbourn.

"I don't see anything to laugh about," said Clever. "As a matter of fact, there are a lot of people in here laughing. I don't think that's funny. You're costing us money, Mr. Osbourn."

Osbourn tried to defend himself, but Clever wouldn't let him. "Why are stops on road down from 14.2 to 13.2? Something to do with your waistline?" Stops on road are the number of stops a driver makes per road hour.

"No," said Osbourn. "I was just trying to be . . ."

"You were trying to be funny?" asked Clever, rhetorically. "Again, I don't think it's funny. Now maybe if you think it's funny we can get you a job out in California. Maybe you can tell jokes. But right now, you're running a package center, is that right? At least trying to run it. How about the injuries? You got four injuries compared to two at the same time last year. Did someone slip on a banana peel?"

There were a few chuckles from the audience and Clever was right on it.

"I don't see anything funny here," he said and stared down the perpetrators. "I'll tell you what, we're going to have this same meeting here in six months. Mr. Osbourn, take that graph and turn it ninety degrees. That's how this graph better be when you come back six months from now. Am I making myself clear?"

"Yeah," said Osbourn.

"Okay, now take your seat. Mr. Bean, you ready? What are you going to do, a song and dance?"

Bean couldn't speak. He stuttered for a few minutes before he finally said, "I'm doing a very bad job. We had a really bad second quarter."

"I'll say so," agreed Clever. "Why don't you put it up there so everyone can see how bad it was. Do you want to explain this to us? Why are you getting these results?"

"I have no explanation," said Bean.

"I'm going to give you six months to get an explanation," said Clever. "Now take your seat. Next."

Manager after manager tried to report only to be publicly humiliated and belittled. Before the meeting, I had resigned myself to passively give my report and blend back into the crowd. But Clever lit my fire. When it was my turn, I walked onstage and placed my graph on the easel.

"I'm Rodney Carroll from the Philadelphia pre-load," I said calmly. I was not intimidated by Clever. "I see a lot of pre-load alumni out there. As you can see, we've been able to maintain over the last six months. Based on the reports before me, I imagine that I should feel pretty good about this because at least we didn't digress. But I'll tell you what, I don't feel good at all. I'll tell you the truth, I don't enjoy that pre-load every night because I go to the pre-load and I just try to maintain. And I can maintain. But in my opinion—I'm pretty sure I can back this up—I'm one of the best managers in the company. And these results don't show that I'm one of the best managers in this company. So I'm going to tell you right now. When I get back here in six months, this sixty packages per hour will be no less that eighty-five packages per hour. That's all I got to say." And I sat down.

I had no idea how Clever was going to react. There was a moment of uncomfortable silence.

"Finally, we have someone that gets it," said Clever. "How many of you people want to make the same amount of money you made last year? Anybody? That's right. Well, you got to do better. You can't do the same. And for crying out loud, you can't do worse. 'Cause if you do worse you're going to get less money. That's how it is."

From that point on, everyone who spoke made a commitment for the next six months. Some were modest—Jimmy Douglas committed to going from 15.1 stops on the road to 15.2. Some were outlandish—Robin Forbes promised no injuries or car accidents for the next six months. But they all made commitments, and that's what Clever wanted because then he could hold people accountable. If my sort didn't do eighty-five packages an hour, or Robin had a driver who scraped an elbow, he could hold us accountable.

I left the meeting thinking, what the heck did I get myself into? I pulled eighty-five packages an hour out of thin air. If I were thinking clearly, I would have said seventy.

"I'll tell you right now, I don't know how you're going to do it without smoke and mirrors," said Dan Roblisky, the industrial engineer manager. "Because there ain't no way that sort is going to run eighty-five packages an hour."

The only thing I had going for me was that the building was going to be expanded and a new sort was going to be installed. We were pulling out the antiquated carousel and replacing it with motorized belts similar to the ones at the Willow Grove building.

"I need to plan the new sort," I told Dan.

Dan made sure I was on the planning team. I knew exactly what needed to be done and now I was in a position to make it happen. I installed belts with dual motors so that during heavy times, the belt could be reversed, and we included a return chute so that missort didn't have to be rolled back in a hand truck.

My ideas were not groundbreaking. They were a lot of little changes that added up to big improvements. Before the new sort was installed, my area still hovered around sixty packages per hour—and Clever was quick to point it out every time I saw him. Following the new sort, my area was up to ninety-one packages an hour.

At the managers meeting six months later, Clever was even more ruthless than before. Thanks to me, he had specific commitments to hold the managers accountable for and he was relentless during the reports.

"Okay, Bob, you said you were going to be at 13.9 stops on road hour—up from 13.7, which was down from 13.8. Where are you?"

"13.6," Bob said, expecting to be lambasted.

"13.6? What kind of excuse do you have for me?" said Clever.

"I don't have any excuse."

"What kind of reason do you have?"

"There is no reason."

"Do you understand? You get paid to get results," barked Clever. "This company has made it because we get results. I want to hear results. Did you not say you would get 13.9?"

"Yes, I did," Bob said meekly.

"I can't hear you," yelled Clever. It was agonizing to watch.

"Yes, I did."

"Well then, what is your area doing? You don't know how to do your job, is that what you're saying? Sit down. Who's next? Jim Lewis?"

Lewis slinked to the hot seat.

"I guess you're going to tell me that the construction down by the casinos is slowing your drivers up?" said Clever.

"Well, it is slowing them up a little bit," answered Lewis, taking the bait.

"So I guess I'm supposed to tell my customers that their packages are arriving late because you can't find a better way to get them there. Is that what you want me to do? Do you want me to get on the phone and start calling customers up?"

Lewis started to panic under the pressure.

"I don't want you to call the customers," he said, his voice cracking.

"Are you going to call the customers?" asked Clever.

"I'll call them," said Lewis.

"No," yelled Clever, rolling his eyes. "Don't call the customers, just get the job done. I need a break."

I was the next guy to report after the break.

"I guess you can't wait to get up there? Can you, Rod?" he said, knowing my results.

"You know, Ron, you're right, I can't wait to get up here. I can't wait to put this graph down because I'm running ninety-one packages per hour."

There was only one other manager who exceeded his commitment. Instead of congratulating us, Clever used our success to criticize the others.

"So you actually exceeded what you said you were going to do. Is that right?"

"That's right," I said.

"I'll bet you think you're pretty special? Don't you, Rod?" Clever said. "You should think you're special because you are. Out of all you guys, only two exceeded their commitment. If I were the rest of you, I wouldn't spend a lot of money in the next couple of months."

After the session, I ran into Clever in the hospitality center.

"I guess you want me to congratulate you," he said. "I'm not going to congratulate you. That's what we pay you to do. You understand. You did what we pay you to do. I'm not congratulating you."

"I didn't ask for any congratulations," I said. And I kept walking.

11. Unload Lynch Mob 82, Airsort Renegades 75

It was four more years before I finally got the promotion John Morrisey had told me I deserved back in January of 1987. In that time, my attitude slowly moved from enthusiastic to apathetic. I moved quietly from assignment to assignment, caring less about being the best and feeling more like I was being mistreated and unappreciated.

I felt my career at UPS was finished. The work I had done at the Willow Grove hub was ancient history. The person that was going to promote me was two district managers ago and the current manager didn't exactly view me as the number-one candidate.

After a one-year stint in Grand Rapids, working on an automated sort, I reached an all-time low when I was transferred back to Philadelphia to work for Brendan, whom I had hired in 1980. In fact, I fought to make sure that Brendan kept his job when Bob Berry, an area manager, wanted to fire him for being a wise guy. I also gave Brendan his first chance as manager when I was running the Willow Grove hub.

"I'm going to get you the promotion you deserve," he told me on my first day.

"Just forget it," I said. "I'm tired of this promotion stuff. I'll do a good job, but I don't care about any promotion."

To make matters worse, my job was center manager—the same job I'd done in Doylestown, eight years earlier. It was official; my career was moving backward. I fulfilled my promise to Brendan and did a decent job. Again, I made some modest changes that helped productivity. Things were going so well that in four months we had no lost-time injuries—an incredible accomplishment.

"I told Bob Lekites what you're doing down here," Brendan said, referring to our new district manager. "He says to keep up the good work."

"Yeah, yeah, yeah," I said. "Well, you tell Bob that I'm not doing it to get promoted. I'm doing it because there's a better way to do stuff and I'm just trying to help the drivers."

One day, Bob Lekites and Chris Mahoney, a senior vice president, asked to see me. There aren't many reasons for the district manager and senior vice president to want to see you. Could this be my promotion?

I put my jacket on, straightened my tie, and headed upstairs.

"How's it going?" Bob asked and offered me a seat.

"Good," I said. "We're reducing claims, educating the drivers, and working well together."

They asked me specific questions about the operation. They asked how I handled certain situations. Finally Mahoney said, "The reason we called you here is because we're going to use your operation as a pilot center for reduction of claims."

"That's what you called me up for?" I asked.

"That's it," Lekites answered. "This has been very helpful. Thanks for your time."

Another month passed and my operation continued to thrive. On October 11, 1994, Lekites called me back to his office. I didn't bring my jacket, my sleeves were rolled up, my tie undone. When I walked in, Mahoney was there as well. Again, they offered me a seat.

"Do you have any idea what this is about?" asked Lekites.

"I'm assuming that you want an update on the claims picture and I'm more than ready to update you. As a matter of fact . . ."

"Whoa, whoa," said Mahoney. "We know you're doing well. But we want to talk to you about the Lawnside hub in New Jersey."

Ever since Hellinger took over the site, it had turned into a disaster. The current manager was Stan—who used to work for me as a part-time sup. Stan was a great guy with a huge heart. To this day, he's one of my good friends. But he's not the kind of guy who can turn an operation around. And that's what the New Jersey hub needed.

I can't believe this, I thought to myself. These guys want me to go work for Stan and bail him out.

"What about the Lawnside hub?" I asked in a less than overjoyed tone.

"That's my point," Mahoney said. "Do you know how bad that hub's going?"

I was losing my patience. "No, but I'm sure you're going to tell me."

Lekites, who was aware of my history with UPS, sensed my hostility. "The hub is going down the drain. Service is down, production is down, staffing is down. It's an eyesore in the region as far as hubs go. That's why we brought you here. We'd like you to go to the Lawnside hub."

I knew it.

"Okay, when do I start?" I asked without hesitating.

"Monday," Lekites answered.

"Okay, I'll be there Monday." And I got up to leave.

But before I reached the door, Mahoney stopped me.

"Whoa, whoa, whoa," he said. "I realize you're dedicated to what you're doing, but let's talk about it for a few minutes. What do you think about your new assignment?"

"It's nothing I haven't done before," I said.

Mahoney and Lekites glanced at each other.

"You've been a division manager before?" Mahoney asked.

"Yeah," I answered, not even listening to what he said. "I've been a division . . ." Then I caught on. "What did you say?" I asked.

"What do you think about your new assignment as division manager for the Lawnside hub?" he repeated.

"What did you think we wanted you to do," asked Mahoney. I told him. I told him the whole story, including all my frustrations.

"You mean you would have just gone over there and helped out," he said.

"I've always tried to do whatever the company asked me to do," I answered.

"Well, there's no question in my mind that we promoted the right person this time," Mahoney said. "Welcome aboard."

Everyone who worked for UPS knew about the New Jersey Lawnside hub. As Mahoney said, it was an eyesore. The biggest problem was that employee morale was extremely low. But thanks to a local YMCA, that all started to change.

To motivate the workers we organized a basketball league. We rented the gym after the twilight sort and played games three days a week from 9:30 to 11:00 P.M.

Each area in the hub was a team. The part-time sups played with their area. I played on the full-time managers team. There were twenty teams in all.

Originally, there was some concern about injuries but the opposite turned out to be true. At the hub, if someone sprained an ankle or jammed a finger, they went home or to the hospital and submitted an accident report. If they did the same during basketball, their team-mates yelled, "Walk it off, walk it off." Without fail, they came out of the game, got some water, and returned to the court ten minutes later.

We allowed the people to invite family and friends to watch so we had as many as two hundred people in the stands. We used referees who needed to earn hours to get certified for high school competition. We had a scoreboard and kept statistics. We awarded trophies for sportsmanship, MVPs, and voted on all-stars.

In order to participate, the employees could not be late or absent to work. They had to be in good standing. They could not be out on injury and, of course, the sort had to be finished on time. It was amazing to see workers hustle to finish a sort, or find people with long-term back injuries all of a sudden back to work.

There was something for everyone. The teams were co-ed and most everybody played, but the few that weren't athletic designed a sports page with articles about the game:

Lamont "hard to guard" Wilson scores 27 points
as the Unload Lynch Mob beat the Airsort Renegades, 82–75

And as I had hoped, teamwork on the court translated into team-work at the hub. During the work sort, instead of the employees re-ferring to me as Mr. Carroll, I heard shouts like, "Hey Rod, we got you guys Thursday night. You better watch out." We experienced vir-tually no turnover. In fact, some people worked simply to play in the league.

By November of 1995, the New Jersey Lawnside hub was a showcase for the entire country. We sported a big sign that read, "Welcome to Lawnside hub—a total quality hub." Pictures of the employees covered the walls next to posters measuring consecutive workdays without an injury and packages sorted without damage.

UPS conducts a computer-based, anonymous survey, twice a year, called the Employee Relations Index or ERI. It asks employees to rate the operation by answering questions like: I can trust my supervisor, or UPS is a good place to work. Employees circle five for always, one for never, or somewhere in between. UPS considers 67 percent favorable a positive score. When UPS took the survey at the Lawnside hub, we received 91 percent favorable.

All of a sudden, my enthusiasm for my job was back. I enjoyed coming to work every day. I believed in the people I worked with. My hoop game had never been better.

Following peak season the next year, I began to hear rumors that I might be transferred down to the Philadelphia air hub. This was the same air hub that I helped plan, so I had a good idea of the size and scope of the operation. It was the third largest hub in the country with 3,200 employees and 125 management people. Every package was labeled as high priority. The packages traveled by plane and weather problems in Philadelphia or Boston or Chicago consistently caused the operation to run late, so there was a lot of stress.

The hub was always staffed for peak times, so during down hours the employees caused trouble. There was cursing and screaming and fights and thefts. There were gangs, lawsuits, sexual harassment, racial discrimination, and age discrimination claims. It was a nightmare for whoever was in charge. And I didn't want any part of it.

I wasn't interested in promotions anymore. I wanted peace and stability and I had both at the New Jersey Lawnside hub. When I first heard the rumors about my transfer, I immediately called Mike Issac, the operation manager.

"Mike, get someone else for this," I pleaded. "Make sure you understand this, I do not want to go to the Philadelphia air hub."

Two weeks later, I was assigned to the Philadelphia air hub. I had known Mike Issac for years, and if he believed I was the best person for the job, a simple phone call would not change his decision.

I spent my first week in Philadelphia walking around shaking as many hands as I could. I spent the next month in focus groups, allowing the employees to voice their concerns and complaints.

"Hi, my name is Rodney Carroll. This is your chance to tell me anything that is on your mind."

At first nobody spoke.

"Now if you don't have anything to say, we'll sit here for thirty minutes and then you can go back to work."

"Well, nothing is going to happen anyway," said a young man wearing a Pearl Jam T-shirt.

"You're right," I answered. "If you don't say anything, nothing is going to happen. But if you say something, there is a possibility something may happen."

Eventually, they began to talk.

"There's no soap in the bathroom."

"The women's bathroom has had a broken mirror for eight months."

"The lockers are damaged and we can't lock them."

"The cafeteria doesn't have all-beef hot dogs."

"When it rains, the trucks make puddles and it gets slippery. We need a mop."

"We need hooks for our coats at the end of the belt."

I wrote everything down. "Anything else?" I asked.

"Yeah, UPS doesn't care about us."

I heard it from every group. "UPS doesn't care about us."

That particular complaint stuck with me. I knew how horrible it was to come to work when you don't feel appreciated, so I became obsessed with showing the employees that, in fact, UPS *did* care.

I organized a team of the most vocal people from each focus group and formed a committee called the "We Care Team."

"Because UPS does care about you," I told the group. "The problem is that sometimes we're so busy running a business that we don't show it. So your job will be to make sure that people understand that UPS does care about every one of them."

Nan Myland was in charge of the We Care Room. I had known her when she was a part-time sup at Willow Grove. She was clever. She was a hard worker who cared about people.

Nan and I armed each "We Care Team" member with T-shirts

with a bold, "We Care Team," across the front and we scheduled monthly meetings, where participants could make suggestions for improving morale at the hub. We turned an empty room in the center of the hub next to the cafeteria into a game room where employees could relax before and after work. It had a pool table, pinball machines, a Ping-Pong table, and four big televisions perfect for watching sports. On the nights the Philadelphia Eagles played Monday Night Football, the hub normally experienced a steep rise in absentee rates. The first night after the game room opened, we had standing room only for the Eagles/Cowboys game.

Day by day, we made progress. When a major snowstorm was predicted for the Philadelphia area, Joel Goldman, the industrial engineering regional manager, was concerned snow would keep employees away.

"How many people do you think will be in?" Goldman asked Gary Ford, our industrial engineering manager, during a conference call. By then, we were down to two thousand employees.

"Probably around five hundred."

"What?" shrieked Goldman

"You don't know this place," Ford said.

The storm came as expected. As each person walked in the door covered in snow, the We Care Team greeted them with a cup of hot chocolate.

At first, people hesitated.

"How much is it going to cost?"

"It's free."

"What's the catch?"

"Just put the cup in the trash when you're done."

"Can I have two cups?"

"Here, have a second cup."

We gave 850 people hot chocolate.

Then I sent every person a thank-you letter on official UPS stationery.

The hot chocolate and the thank-you notes made an impression both on those who had come in despite the snow and those who hadn't come in because of it.

A couple of weeks later, another snowstorm was forecast. On the conference call, I said I expected 95 percent attendance.

"Get outta here," said Goldman.

"I'm telling you right now," I said, "they'll be in."

The snowstorm hit and again we met the employees at the door with hot chocolate. We even had hot tea because a few people didn't like chocolate. The management team couldn't believe their eyes. That day, we handed out hot chocolate or hot tea to 90 percent of our workforce.

=

Strange as it may sound, gangs at the Philadelphia air hub were not uncommon. They sprouted because of the demand for workers. A person who was hired brought a friend and he another friend, and before you knew it, there was a gang in smalls sort. Left Eye, Jose, and Big Ty were the leaders of the three gangs in the Philadelphia air hub.

Left Eye was a gang leader in input. He earned his name because he had a lazy left eye, although he was sensitive about anyone staring at it or talking about it. He wasn't big or anything, but he exuded toughness. He had at least ten tattoos, including one of a long snake that twisted around his right arm from wrist to shoulder. I never saw him fight, but it seemed like he could knuckle pretty well.

Unlike Left Eye, Big Ty was huge. He ruled the outbound area with a six-foot-four, three-hundred-pound frame that burst through his overalls. His head was always covered by a bandanna and he had scars over three-quarters of his face.

Jose was the pretty boy. Although he worked in the trailers all day, he seldom wore a T-shirt, choosing instead a collared or button-down shirt. His hair was always slicked back. He had a neatly trimmed mustache and a goatee and carried about two pounds of gold jewelry around his neck.

Left Eye, Big Ty, and Jose made developing teamwork at the hub next to impossible because the workers were afraid to enter the other areas. Every so often, there was a fight in the cafeteria or a skirmish in the bathroom.

I always arrived after it had happened, when it was impossible to hold anyone accountable because no one would talk.

"What happened?" I'd ask the worker who had blood dripping from his face.

"Nothing."

"What do you mean nothing, how'd your face get that way?"

"I walked into a door. I'm alright."

"Come on now, we know someone beat you up," I said.

"Don't worry, I'll take care of it."

"Take care of what?"

"Nothing."

These were young kids in their late teens or early twenties. They were just like my friends growing up. Kids who made bad decisions and were now paying the price. I hated it.

Finally, I'd had enough. I called Left Eye, Big Ty, and Jose to the conference room. I asked Randy Maier, my sort manager, to join us.

"You guys know what I want to talk about?" I asked.

"Yeah," said Left Eye. "You want to talk about why I have to be up here with this smelly Puerto Rican. That's what you want to talk about."

"I got your Puerto Rican right here," snapped Jose as he threw a pen across the table. Before I knew it, Jose and Left Eye were wrestling on the conference table. Randy and I broke up the fight. Big Ty just watched.

"What you got?" Big Ty asked after the dust settled. "I ain't got time for this kind of stuff. I got stuff to do."

"What do you have to do?" I asked.

"I got to walk around and check some things out," said Big Ty.

"Look, Big Ty," I said. "Things are going to change, starting now. We're not paying you to walk around anymore."

"Look, just because you're the boss here, don't mean that nothing can't happen to you," threatened Big Ty. "I'd hate for something to happen to your pretty car."

I sat back and thought for a second.

"Well, Big Ty," I said quietly, looking him right in the eye. "First, let me tell you something. I grew up in North Philly at Nineteenth and Dauphin. I've been dealing with guys like you for the last twenty years. And let me tell you something else. If anything ever happens to my car, do you know who I'm going to come looking for? You. I don't even care if it is these two guys here who do something to my car—I'm still coming for you. You got that?"

Big Ty tried to back off. "I just made a statement. You can't blame it on me."

"Listen," I said, looking at all three. "This gang stuff is not going to happen around here anymore."

"Look," answered Left Eye. "I got to protect my turf."

"No," I answered. "The problem is your turf ain't here. Your turf is somewhere in Southwest Philly. This is UPS turf."

"Well, if a guy comes over to input, and he don't act right, then we're going to have to take care of business. You know what I'm saying?"

"We can do this a couple of ways," I said. "One, I can take all three of you out, and that way, we won't have to worry about this anymore. Or, you guys can stay here and do some honest work."

"What do you mean, take me out?" yelled Jose. "You threatening me? You can't threaten me!"

"Fire you, Jose. I will fire you." I pulled out three folders. "I have your attendance records right here and they're less than terrific. We need a truce while you're at UPS. You guys want to cause trouble when you're outside of here, that's fine, but when you're on UPS's ground, there's no fighting, and no threatening, or you guys are out."

"I'm going to think about it; I'll get back to you," said Big Ty.

"You do that," I answered. "In the meantime, make sure nothing happens to my car."

The reason most people are in gangs is that they want respect. They don't necessarily deserve respect, but that is what they're after. By calling Left Eye, Jose, and Big Ty into a private meeting, I was hoping it would show that at least I respected their authority over their gangs.

A week later we had another meeting. They all agreed to the truce, with one catch.

"We need to take care of Clyde Johnson because he beat up Shorty," said Jose. "This is the only place we can get to him. After we take care of him, we will join the truce."

"You can't fight here." I was firm. "If you fight here, you're going to get fired."

Jose shook his head. It was obvious he was going to get revenge. After the meeting I alerted the managers to keep an eye on Clyde. I knew it was only a matter of time. We knew where he worked, we knew where the hit would likely happen. We put video cameras in the bathroom near his work space. We needed proof, or like always, the union would try to protect Jose's job.

The next day, a manager saw Clyde enter the bathroom. Three members of Jose's gang followed. They blindsided Clyde and unmercifully pummeled him.

After I was paged, I arrived at the office to find two managers watching the fight on closed-circuit television.

"Is anyone going to break this up?" I asked.

I ran down to the bathroom to find Clyde lying in a pool of blood with a broken arm.

"What happened?" I asked.

"I tripped in the bathroom." It was like some code of secrecy.

"Come on now, we saw the whole thing," I said.

"Nothing happened."

"Look," I said. "We got you on tape. Just tell us who beat you up and we'll take care of it."

"Nobody beat me up. You guys are crazy. I fell down and broke my arm."

We grabbed the three goons in the video and questioned them in separate rooms. We showed them the tape. All three said the same thing. "That's not me on tape. That guy just looks like me."

We fired all of them, including Jose, for instigating the fight. It was a critical step. Now we were down to the two gangs who'd stuck by their promise of a truce. I declared a new policy: Fighting for any reason would result in termination.

I left that night feeling good about the way we had dealt with the case. But as I walked past the security gate, the guard told me that a suspicious-looking person had been hanging around near my car. I sprinted through the parking lot.

"What are you doing here?" I yelled.

"Who are you?" he answered, not the least bit intimidated.

"Never mind who I am," I said. "Who are you and what are you doing near my car?"

"Is this your car?" he asked.

"Yes."

"Oh," he said. "Big Ty told me to watch it and make sure nothing happened to it."

12. No Place Like Home

In 1992, my grandmother had a stroke. The doctor called it slight because it didn't kill her, but it did make her right leg extremely weak.
After she returned from the hospital, she spent most of her time in
the house. She couldn't walk on her own and relied on a wheelchair.
Leaving the house was such an ordeal that my grandmother rarely
even attended church on Sundays.

My grandmother had friends in the community who rallied
around her. The deacons from her church came by at least once a
week to read the Bible and pray with her. Friends and neighbors
brought food. Cheryl, Courtney, and I kept her company and kept
the house clean. But at nightfall, my eighty-eight-year-old grandmother was alone.

One day I went by after work. I went to her room and found her
sitting on the floor next to her bed. The room was dark.

"What are you doing on the floor?" I asked as I helped her up.

"Oh, I was looking for something," she said casually as if nothing
was out of the ordinary.

"What were you looking for?" I asked.

"Oh, uh, I dropped my money," she answered.

"What do you mean, you dropped your money? Where?" I
started looking around although I knew she was trying to hide something. "You fell out of the bed, didn't you?" I said moments later.

"No I didn't fall out of the bed," she answered, mocking my tone.
"I was trying to get down and then my leg—" She stopped. "You
know it's not as strong as it used to be. It needed some rest, so rather
than get into bed right away, I figured I'd rest here for a while."

I looked at my grandmother.

She was sitting on the floor with her right leg stretched out and her left leg bent behind her. She was leaning against the bed and appeared winded like she had just tried to get up.

"Look, Mom Mom. I'm really worried about you," I said softly.

"Now, Rodney, I can take care of myself. You just go on and take care of your own business. You got places to go, and a lot of responsibility. Don't worry about me."

"I am afraid that you're going to be in trouble and I'm not going to be able to get here in time. If there were ever a serious problem there will be nobody here to help you. I really think that you need help."

"Absolutely not," said my grandmother.

Over the past few months, I had sporadically spoken with Cheryl about finding a nursing home for my grandmother. Cheryl graduated from high school and taught a basic computer course at the computer-learning center. She enjoyed teaching and was good at it. Cheryl had gotten married and had four children. She lived not too far from my grandmother in a safer area of northeast Philadelphia.

The thought of putting our grandmother in a nursing home hurt us both, but we knew she needed twenty-four-hour care. I visited several nursing homes in Philadelphia and with each one, my horror increased. Without exception, the homes were sterile and lifeless. They were like museums. The residents were like zombies. Although my grandmother was unable to walk, she was still mentally strong. I couldn't imagine her spending her last days in such a place, and I abandoned the idea. But apparently, Cheryl discussed it with my grandmother.

"Absolutely not. I'm not going into a nursing home. I'd rather die in my own house."

My grandmother's perception of a nursing home was similar to what I had seen, only she was prepared with documented evidence. She opened the drawer to her nightstand, pulled out an article from the *Philadelphia Inquirer*, and handed it to me. The headline read: NURSING HOMES: NO PLACE LIKE HOME. The article described the nursing home situation in North Philadelphia: the lack of trained health-care professionals, the antiquated facilities, the lack of security, and statistics that basically implied that once you entered a nursing home, you were as good as dead.

"They die of sadness," my grandmother explained. "No visitors. No privacy. No respect."

"I agree with you," I told her. "But still. You're here alone, and what if something were to happen?"

"I've been here for sixty years and I've survived," she said.

"Mom Mom, I think I'll cut back on my hours so I can—" My grandmother cut me off.

"Don't even think of jeopardizing your job," she ordered. "You continue to work hard. Make me proud. Don't worry about me."

"But now you can't even get around by yourself."

"No problem," she said. "I'll just have to work on this leg and get the other leg stronger." She kicked a few times. "See? It's getting a little stronger already."

"There was a fire over on Cleveland Street last week," I continued, trying to build my case. "When I heard about it on the radio I was a nervous wreck."

"Yeah, well they were probably smoking," she explained. "I don't smoke."

"But this house is old," I countered. "There could be an electrical fire." She rolled her eyes.

"Look, it just comes down to the fact that you need more help than we can provide. You need twenty-four-hour attention and I can't do that for you." I paused. It was obvious that I was not going to change my grandmother's mind. I didn't know what else to say. I shouldn't have said anything but I did. "I'll try to come visit you more often."

As soon as that sentence left my mouth, I wanted it back. My grandmother looked up. The one thing my grandmother made perfectly clear all the time was that she never wanted to be a burden to anybody. That's why it hurt so badly when she said, "If you don't want to care for me, if I'm too much of a bother, I will understand. But I don't want to go into a nursing home."

I gulped. What could I say?

I helped my grandmother into the living room. I turned on the television. We watched *Sanford and Son*. I made her some coffee. We shared some butter pecan ice cream. We watched television in silence. I felt horrible.

I thought back to when the situation was reversed. When the state wanted to put Courtney, Cheryl, and me in foster homes.

"Well, I'm not going to take you kids," my grandmother could have said. "I've already raised my children. What you really need is a younger parent to take care of you and someone who can help you with your homework. You need to live in a better neighborhood and you need both a mom and a dad. But don't worry, I'll come visit you."

An hour passed and my grandmother was clearly tired. I helped her back into her room and tucked her into bed. Before I left, I stuck my head under the bed.

"What are you looking for?" she said.

"I'm looking to see if I could find that money."

"What money?" she said. We smiled.

I didn't sleep that night. Regardless of my guilt about suggesting a nursing home, I knew that my grandmother needed more care than she was getting. Maybe if I came down every day? I thought. Maybe twice a day—before and after work? I could move her in with me. Or maybe I could just move back in with her. I pulled out a pad of paper and wrote down my work schedule. Many of my hours were at night and I was traveling a few times a month. Even when I worked normal hours, they were ten-hour days. I wrote down the number of hours I needed to sleep. I wrote down seven, then crossed it off and made it five. Still it was fifteen hours a day that I couldn't be there for her.

On my way to work the next morning I stopped by the Philadelphia Corporation for the Aging. Cheryl had recommended it.

I described the situation to a counselor. When I finished, the counselor looked at me like I was a monster.

"And she's living alone?" she asked in amazement. "Listen, Mr. Carroll. If you really care for your grandmother, you'll put her in a nursing home."

"But she refuses to go. And I don't blame her after seeing some of the nursing homes around here."

She was familiar with the newspaper article. She assured me that not all nursing homes were like that. Then she said, "Look, we deal with this kind of thing a lot over here. What you need to do is to find a better reason for your grandmother to enter a nursing home, something other than her health."

"Thanks for your time," I said. "I'll give it some thought."

As I drove home, I passed by North Penn Baptist church.

"That's it," I said to myself. "That's the answer."

Until my grandmother's stroke, she had attended the same church for fifty-six years. Surely there had to be people from her church that were now in nursing homes.

I stopped at the church and spoke to Reverend Berry. After hearing my story, he reassured me that I was making the right decision and told me that three of my grandmother's closest friends, Mrs. Roundtree, Mrs. Long, and Mrs. Battle all lived at Cedarbrook Nursing Home right here in North Philadelphia.

"I'm actually doing the service there in a few weeks," he said. Apparently, ministers from the local churches took turns visiting the nursing home on Sundays.

I knew all three women from my days visiting my grandmother on weekends. Mrs. Long and Mrs. Roundtree were my Sunday-school teachers. But my favorite was Mrs. Battle. She was the organist at the church. She bragged about never having a lesson in her life and it showed. She could mess up "Chopsticks." She played either too fast or too slow, and she played in more keys than a locksmith. But everybody loved her.

The next day during my lunch hour, I drove down to Cedarbrook to investigate. My own prejudices kept me from being too optimistic.

"There's nothing good in North Philly," I said to myself.

Although it was in a rough neighborhood, the actual nursing home looked modern. It was ten years old. The floors were waxed and clean. It even had an enclosed garden area in the back.

I picked up a brochure on my way in and learned that they had nurses on duty twenty-four hours a day. There was an area for therapy and stretching. The rooms were not private, but they had large showers, where my grandmother could bathe sitting down until her leg got stronger.

I walked to the front desk and asked to see Mrs. Battle.

"She's not here," said the woman behind the desk.

"How about Mrs. Roundtree or Mrs. Long," I asked.

"There not here either," she responded. "They're on a bus trip."

"What do you mean a bus trip?" I asked.

"They went to the museum today," she replied matter-of-factly.

I shook my head and said, "Okay."

I came back two days later.

"Not here," the same woman said. "They went bowling."

"Bowling?" I responded. "They're ninety-year-old women."

My vision of the nursing home was of everyone sitting around watching television.

"When's a good time to come back?" I asked.

"You have to catch them early," she said. "They usually leave by ten o'clock and come back around 6:00 or 6:30. But visiting hours are over at 8:00." She suggested that I come back on Sunday morning for the church service.

I walked in on Sunday morning to the unmistakable sound of Mrs. Battle on the organ. There was no doubt in my mind. She was playing "This Little Light of Mine," or rather her version of it.

I recognized Mrs. Long sitting near the back and I sat down a few seats away. At the conclusion of the service, I approached her.

"Hey, it's Mrs. Lucas's grandson," she yelled. She couldn't remember my name. "Hey, how you doing?" She called over to Mrs. Battle before I had a chance to answer.

"Myrtle, look who it is."

"Oh, yeah," Mrs. Battle answered. "Mrs. Lucus's grandson. How is Lula doing?"

"She's doing alright," I said. "She's hangin' in there."

"Tell her to come by and see us," said Mrs. Long, who nudged her way over.

"You guys are hardly ever around," I said.

"Yeah, yeah," Mrs. Roundtree said. "We keep busy."

"Next week we're going on a shopping trip to New York," interjected Mrs. Long.

"I'm not going on that," said Mrs. Battle. "I'm going to be rehearsing for a concert." There was an awkward silence after that statement, but nobody said a word.

We spoke for about fifteen minutes longer and they described how much they enjoyed living at Cedarbrook. It was exactly what I wanted to hear.

I went to my grandmother's directly from the service. She was lying in bed. She looked tired.

"Guess who I saw?" I asked after I inquired about her health.

"Who?"

"Well, I saw Mrs. Long, Mrs. Roundtree, and Mrs. Battle."

Immediately, my grandmother knew where I had been.

"I told you if you don't want to care for me, fine. But I don't want to go into a nursing home."

I didn't push it.

"They just told me to say hi. They wanted to know how you were doing. I told them you were fine."

I was surprised and encouraged when my grandmother didn't change the subject. "How are they doing?"

"Oh, they're doing great," I said enthusiastically. "Fantastic. They are active. They have a lot of friends."

"Great," said my grandmother.

"Hey," I said, seemingly changing the subject. "Why don't I pick you up next Sunday and take you to church. Reverend Berry will be there and you can get out and get some fresh air."

"Great," she said.

When I picked up my grandmother, she was wearing her favorite dress and still deciding between two hats. It was the first time I had seen her out of her housedress since the stroke. She finally decided on the blue hat with the red bow. I helped her to the car, put her wheelchair in the trunk, and headed to Cedarbrook.

"What's this?" said my grandmother as we pulled up to the building.

"They're having the church here today," I answered.

"What kind of place is this?" she asked suspiciously.

"You'll see when you get in."

I helped her from the car to her wheelchair and rolled her down the hallway. Sure enough we heard the organ playing "Amazing Grace."

"Myrtle," my grandmother said immediately. "Boy, she still can't play."

When she heard Mrs. Battle playing, she knew where we were. "You brought me to this nursing home," she said.

"This is where they are having the church this week," I said innocently.

Before she could respond, Reverend Berry walked by.

"Mrs. Lucas," he said. "It's so good to see you."

"Good to see you, Reverend," she said. "I'm glad I could be here with you today."

One by one, the rest of the congregation came by to say hi to my grandmother. My grandmother started crying. I suppose she realized how much she missed being with her friends.

As the service progressed, my grandmother's smile grew bigger and brighter. She sang the songs. She joined in the worship service. She participated in the testimonials.

"I thought I was down to my last dime. I didn't know how I was going to buy food. As I was cleaning I found twenty dollars in my pants pocket," said one man.

"I went to the hospital because I thought I had a heart attack, but the doctor told me it was only heartburn," said another.

When it was my grandmother's turn, she stood up without any assistance for the first time since the stroke.

"Even though I had a slight stroke," she said, "and my leg is not as strong as it used to be, I'll be walking around in no time. I'm happy that I'm in my right mind and am able to recognize all the people who greeted me today. I'm thankful that my grandson Rodney brought me here today. And for all this, I thank God."

The final song of the morning was "Glad to Be Back in the Service." It couldn't have been more appropriate for my grandmother.

A few days later I broached the notion of a nursing home once again with my grandmother.

"I think we should talk about the nursing home. I think the nursing home with Mrs. Battle, and Mrs. Long, and Mrs. Roundtree is a good one." I handed her the brochure. "They have a lot of activities. They have the church services every week and sometimes they have them during the week. And you can be around your friends and there is good care if you need it."

"It must cost a lot of money," she said, glancing over the brochure.

I explained to her that the government had programs set up for older women like her. "I applied already, and they will pay for it," I said.

"Are they going to take all my social security?" she asked. My grandmother received her social security check on the sixth of every month. It was for $316.57. It was barely enough to get by on, but she loved getting it.

"They'll take some of it," I admitted. "But you'll still get one hundred dollars a month for spending money. It will go into a bank account for you."

The money was important to my grandmother. Not so much for herself, although she liked to get her hair done for five dollars or go to the flea markets. But mostly because she loved to buy us presents. Christmas was her favorite time of year.

Of course, we never wanted anything from my grandmother, but she insisted. She got such joy from giving us the perfect gift. Months ahead of the event, she'd start investigating what to buy.

"So those are nice blue socks," she'd say. "I bet you don't have any black socks do you?"

I caught on quickly. "Yeah, you know my black socks have holes in them. I could use some black socks."

My grandmother couldn't keep a secret, so by the time Christmas rolled around she had already revealed the identity of all her gifts. But when she handed us our gifts, we still played along.

"Oh, my," I'd say, shaking the present. "What could this be?" I really hammed it up and my grandmother got a kick out of it. "I can't believe it. Two pairs of black socks." So it was important for my grandmother to have control of her own money and when I assured her that she would, she agreed to give the nursing home a try.

"I'll go for two months," she insisted. "But if I don't like it, you have to come and get me and take me back here."

"You got a deal," I said. We hugged on it.

It didn't take long to move my grandmother into her new room. We unpacked her bags and hung some pictures, including a collage that Courtney, Cheryl, and I made out of some old photos we had found while cleaning out the house. We took a walk in the courtyard. Finally, she took my hand.

"It's alright," she said. "You can leave. I'll be okay here."

After the first month, my grandmother was having a great time. She had already been to the zoo, the art museum, and a 76ers game. She went to the eye doctor for new glasses.

"They had to put more medicine in the glasses," is the way she put it.

They even took her to the dentist because she complained that her tooth was sore. The dentist fixed it and the pain was gone. She'd been complaining about that tooth since I was ten. Her favorite event was a trip to a secondhand store on Susquehanna Avenue where she bought on old patchwork quilt for $1.50.

"It's the best deal I've gotten in twenty years," she said.

Her only complaint was a big one. The cooks prepared only healthful food. My grandmother had an incredible sweet tooth. Her favorite sweet was glazed donuts with extra glaze and a cup of coffee. My grandmother also liked good old soul food—fried chicken, mashed potatoes with butter, gravy, and collared greens cooked in bacon fat.

These delicacies were not on the menu at Cedarbrook. They didn't let my grandmother eat many sweets. They didn't have any food with salt in it. Everything was bland. The chicken was baked or broiled—not fried. The vegetables were steamed and the coffee was decaffeinated.

"I've eaten these things for eighty-eight years and now all of a sudden I'm supposed to start eating carrots and stop drinking coffee? What's it going to do, make me live another couple of days?"

A few weeks later, I went to visit with a box of Krispy Kreme donuts hidden under my jacket. I walked into the TV lounge to find Mrs. Long, Mrs. Roundtree, and my grandmother holding hands and crying. Mrs. Battle had died of pneumonia. At the service that Sunday, there was a new organist—a trained pianist. The songs were on key and at the right tempo. But to everyone who knew Mrs. Battle, the music didn't sound as good.

My grandmother's two-month anniversary came around during Thanksgiving time. Courtney, Cheryl, and I agreed never to let my grandmother spend a holiday alone. Since this was the first one since she entered the nursing home, we decided to get together with her to celebrate.

We cooked a big turkey dinner with all my grandmother's favorite foods. We had macaroni and cheese, collard greens, sweet potato pie, homemade biscuits, cranberry sauce, and I put four glazed donuts on a little plate in the middle of the table.

Before the meal, we went around the table so everyone could say what they were thankful for, just like we did when we were kids. Courtney hated this part. He said it was unfair to have all the food sitting in front of him and then have to wait. Consequently, his turn was always quick and to the point.

"I am thankful for these great sweet potatoes, the plump turkey, and I can't forget the cranberry sauce." He smelled the food. "Mmm-mmm good."

The rest of us didn't disagree. Cheryl went next.

"I'm very thankful for Mom Mom and that we are all here together as a family."

My grandmother paused for almost a minute before she spoke.

"Dear God," she said, "I'm thankful for so much. I'm thankful for my family and I'm thankful that I can breathe." She spoke slowly and deliberately. "I'm thankful that my roommate at the nursing home doesn't get on my nerves anymore. I'm thankful that my teeth don't hurt. I'm thankful that I now have one hundred seventy-two dollars and fifty-seven cents saved in my bank account." She picked her head up and glanced at us. "I'm thankful for Rodney and Cheryl and Courtney. I'm thankful that Courtney seems to be doing well and staying out of trouble the best he can. I'm thankful for the quilt that is at the bottom of my bed and I hope it's there when I get back. I'm thankful for my pictures. I'm thankful for my glasses." She sensed that Courtney was going to make a break for the turkey so she finished by saying, "I'm thankful that I have lived a long and healthy life. It's all that I could have asked for."

13. Those People

While the Philadelphia air hub continued to improve in terms of service and productivity, we still faced one major problem: Finding and keeping good employees. UPS is one of the most efficiently run companies in the world, but like many businesses facing low unemployment and a growing economy, we had difficulty recruiting, hiring, and keeping reliable workers.

There are several expenses that go into hiring an employee at UPS. We spend money on advertising, recruiting, application costs, materials, and training. We even pay for the cost assessed to the diminished production during training. In all, UPS spends nearly seven hundred dollars on every new employee hired.

When an employee stays and advances with the company, this money is well spent. But again, like many businesses, hiring and training costs add up quickly if you can't keep people on the job.

Before I started in the Philadelphia air hub, we hired fifty people a week. Of those fifty, only twenty stayed on the job for at least six weeks—the required time to join the union. Some quit. Some were fired. Some who quit were rehired, but quit again.

Historically, UPS looked to college campuses to find new workers. In Philadelphia, UPS combed local colleges like Temple, Drexel, Philadelphia Community College, and assorted technical schools to find college students who needed extra money.

UPS also filled positions with moonlighters. These were people who held full-time jobs during the day and worked at UPS at night and on weekends to earn extra money.

Either way, the results were frustrating. College kids rarely keep the same job for more than a couple of months. Classes and socializing are their first priorities and anytime a job gets in the way, they quit. Moonlighters work full-time jobs during the day and are exhausted by the night shift. They are notoriously unmotivated and don't last long.

UPS tried several gimmicks to encourage workers to stay on the job. They paid bonuses in addition to a regular salary if an employee stayed for more than three months. We instituted a referral program, offering a two-hundred-dollar bonus if the referral stayed on the job for six months. During our September hiring period, we offered a two-hundred-dollar bonus if an employee stayed through December— our busiest time of the year. But, most often, the workers stayed until they got their bonus and then left.

Through all the time and energy spent on finding and keeping workers, our recruiting efforts—as well as most businesses across the country—ignored a section of the population that I knew very well. A group of people that I knew would cherish the opportunity to work and earn a paycheck.

"Why don't we hire people who really need jobs?" I asked at the next planning meeting.

Half a dozen managers gave me a double take. Al Palmer, the district human resource manager, then said what everyone was thinking, "Who do you think we're hiring now?"

I ignored the sarcasm and continued. "We need to hire people who must have jobs to survive. People who are barely making it."

"Like who?" he said.

"Like people from welfare."

The backlash from my suggestion was immediate and uncensored. I felt like a chair umpire on center court at Wimbledon. My head swung from left to right, from person to person, as they shouted all the reasons why it couldn't and wouldn't work.

"They don't have any education."

"We need people who can read and write."

"They're lazy."

"They have too many children to work a job."

"Once they get their first check, they'll quit."

"They can be out all week with a sick kid and never have the same kid sick for more than one day."

"If you think the landscapers are lazy, wait until you see welfare recipients."

"As soon as there's a good television program on, they won't come to work."

I didn't realize so many people had such strong opinions about people on welfare. Half of me wanted to shut them up by revealing that I was once on welfare, but the other half was too embarrassed. When the meeting ended, Rich Hallman, an employment manager who lived in New Jersey, approached me.

"What is it, Rich?" I said, my patience wearing thin.

"I'd like to talk about your idea," he responded. "I read about a program in Camden, New Jersey, that trained welfare recipients for work. If you're serious about hiring them, let's check it out."

Later that week, Al, Rich, and I spent the day at the New Jersey Department of Health and Human Services. Camden County had turned an old warehouse into a training facility for welfare recipients. It wasn't the nicest training facility—there were cracked tiles on the floor and duct tape held together many of the desks—but it served its purpose.

There were computers and printers for résumé writing. The walls were covered with posters portraying different jobs such as machinist or bus driver or crossing guard. There were grease boards with job leads and contact names. There was even a success board with pictures of former welfare recipients who had jobs.

Even with the run-down decor, I felt sort of energized in the room. It was a whole new way to see welfare recipients. They had hope. They weren't home waiting for a check from the government. They were learning computer skills, writing résumés, scheduling interviews, and practicing their interview techniques. They appeared rejuvenated by the process.

After we toured the facility and met several of the welfare recipients, we agreed the idea could work.

"When can they start?" asked Al.

"Two weeks," Peter Stevens, the representative from Camden County HHS replied.

"Great," said Al. "We'll have spots for them at the Philadelphia air hub in two weeks."

We turned to leave, basking in the sense of accomplishment, when Peter asked, "Philadelphia? How are they going to get to Philadelphia?"

That's when we realized this was not as simple as an afternoon road trip across state lines. This was a challenge. We had welfare recipients who wanted to work and jobs available at UPS in Philadelphia, but there was no public transportation to the air hub.

"Well," said Al, shrugging off the experience as a nice try, "I guess that ends that." And we left.

On the way home, Rich and I racked our brains for a way to make it work.

"Maybe we could hire them at Lawnside," Rich suggested. But Lawnside wasn't large enough to hire more than one or two.

"Maybe we can use the existing transportation system," I suggested. But we quickly figured that the welfare recipients would have to take a bus to the bridge, take the train over the bridge, take the subway to the airport, and then walk two miles to the hub.

"That will take two hours, and they will have no way to get home during the night shift," Rich said.

"We tried," Rich conceded, "but we can't make it work."

During the final fifteen minutes of the drive we were silent.

I returned to my office to find a voice mail from Chuck Thomas, a division manager who handled the international operation. Chuck and I had known each other for ten years—we had worked up the ranks at UPS together. I returned his call and we agreed to meet in the cafeteria.

"I understand you went to Jersey?" he said over coffee and Danish. He looked serious.

"Yeah."

"I don't want to say anything, but you guys aren't really going to hire those people, are you?" he asked. Even today, the word "those" sticks out in my mind.

"What do you mean 'those' people?" I asked calmly. "Who are 'those' people?"

"People from welfare," he said. He lowered his voice. "I just want to let you know: it's a bad idea. A real bad idea."

"Why is that, Chuck?" I said. The angrier I got, the calmer I tried to appear.

"You know, you're going to have problems," he said. "Listen, Rod, you're doing good here. Lawnside did well, now the air hub is starting to turn around for the better. Why do you want to mess it up by hiring people from welfare? You know what they're like. They're going to be lazy. You're going to have injury problems. I'll tell you right now, don't do it. I know how hard you worked to get here. I know how long it took. You're going to throw it all away if you try this. Take my advice. This is not a fight you need to take on. Just let it go."

Again, part of me wanted to respond in outrage, "Do you know that I was on welfare? Do you know that some of the smartest, most loyal people I know were on welfare?" But I said nothing.

I thanked Chuck for the advice and returned to my office. When I arrived, there was an e-mail from another manager basically saying the same thing. Then another and another and another. I printed the e-mails, opened the top right-hand drawer on my desk, put the letters in it, and closed the drawer.

The irony was that until the meeting with Chuck and the ensuing e-mails, I had resigned myself to the fact that the idea was dead. We couldn't get the workers from Camden to Philadelphia. Al, Rich, and I agreed, the idea wouldn't work. So why did I feel like a heavy-weight boxer who had taken a dive in the third round?

After work I went back to the old neighborhood. I hadn't been back in a while. On the way home, I thought about what Chuck had said. It infuriated me. But deep inside I realized that he had only said what I was secretly feeling: becoming division manager had consumed my life for the past twelve years. I had finally created a secure future. Why throw it away?

I parked my BMW on the corner in front of Mrs. Poindexter's house. The same place I had parked my first car—the canary yellow 1973 Buick Electra 225—that my grandmother and I had bought seventeen years earlier. The neighborhood looked worse than I remembered. The beauty parlor had boards covering the windows. There was still graffiti on the walls. There were no flowers or trees— I assumed the neighborhood meetings to improve the block were over. It was a perfect spring day, but there were no children playing in the streets. The neighborhood seemed lifeless and forgotten.

As I double-checked to make sure my car was locked, Mrs. Poindexter opened her front door and yelled from behind the screen door.

"Are you from the city?" She didn't recognize me in my navy

blue suit. She must have thought I was looking to knock down the building.

"Who are you?" she repeated. She was wearing a red flowered housedress and blue slippers.

"You don't know who I am?" I asked.

She opened the screen door and looked me over from head to toe.

"Nope," she answered. "Who are you?"

"I'm Rodney Carroll, Mrs. Poindexter," I said. A wry smile came over her face.

"Rodney," she said. "How are you doing?"

"I'm doing okay, Mrs. Poindexter. Thanks."

"Well, tell your grandmother I said, 'hello.' " Then she went back inside and closed the door.

I got back into my car and drove to my grandmother's nursing home. When I got to her room, the door was open and she was sitting at a table next to an empty seat. She had a serious look on her face.

"How you doing?" I asked.

My grandmother didn't move. She sat still in her chair. She didn't say a word. Then, she sat up in her chair and took my hand.

"Do you think about Dr. King much anymore?" she asked. I wondered why my grandmother would ask about Dr. King. The truth was that I hadn't thought about anything but my career in a long time.

"A little," I said.

"I think about him every day," my grandmother continued. "And do you know what I think about?"

Then it hit me. My grandmother gets the same pensive tone in her voice only once a year. I looked at the date on my watch, it was April 4. It was the twenty-eighth anniversary of Dr. Martin Luther King Jr.'s death.

"What are you thinking about, Mom Mom?" I said.

"I ask myself, 'why?' "

"Why, what?"

"Dr. King was not a poor man," my grandmother said. "He won the Noble Peace Prize and could have lived a pretty comfortable life. He had four children and a beautiful wife. He taught at universities. He was prominent in the black community and he also had a large white following so he could have gone into politics.

"He touched millions of people and forced the country to consider race issues like they never did before. So, why? Why didn't he just stop after he received threats on his life? Why did he have to die?"

My grandmother was crying. Big tears poured down her cheeks. She put her face in her hands.

At first I didn't know if my grandmother was looking for an answer. But I felt like I had one.

"Because he believed he could still make it better," I said softly. "Dr. King couldn't have stopped if he wanted to. You know that. Remember those Saturday afternoons when you told us that we always wanted to help people like Dr. King? And you said that the reason he was so special was because he was willing to die for what he believed in. He believed that everyone had the right to be treated equally. He believed that everyone deserved the same opportunities for a better life. And he believed that he could make it happen."

My grandmother lifted her head. I gave her a hug. She tightened her arms around me harder than ever before. Then she pulled away. There was a long silence.

I thought about Dr. Martin Luther King Jr. and John F. Kennedy and Abraham Lincoln. Then I thought about Robert Speaks and Lucky. Finally I thought about my brother and how I hadn't been there to help him. It still haunted me. I stood up and kissed my grandmother good-bye.

"Where are you going?" she asked.

"I'm going to make an impact."

14. Secondary Five

I knew what it was like to be a welfare recipient looking for a chance and I knew what it was like to be part of a business looking for good workers.

When I got back to my office, I opened the top left-hand drawer of my desk and pulled out the e-mails.

I'll show them, I thought to myself. And I got to work.

I felt like I didn't stop working for two months.

"Okay," I said to myself. "Transportation."

We had people in Camden who needed jobs and a facility in Philadelphia that needed good workers. I was not going to let a little thing like a lack of transportation stand in our way.

I went back to the office and called the New Jersey Transit Authority.

"No way," they said. "We can't go across state lines."

I called the Southeastern Pennsylvania Transit Authority. They cited union problems. Neither place would budge. Finally I decided to try UPS. I called Bill Riggans, District Manager. I told him that I had an idea to solve our staffing problems. I explained the situation, including the transportation hassle, and suggested a solution.

"Why don't we charter a bus to pick them up," I said.

"Who's going to pay for that?" asked Riggans.

"Well, the welfare recipients don't have the money to pay for it," I said. "I was thinking that UPS could pay."

"You're very generous with UPS's money," he said. "But what's in it for UPS?"

A great question. Even today as I travel across the county speaking to companies about the value of welfare-to-work hiring programs, I bring this up because corporate America always wants to know,

"What's in it for us?" And they are right. They have a responsibility to the shareholders. As nice as it would be to help people in need, businesses can't start programs that don't make good sense. They have to be able to say, "This is a sound investment."

"I think it could be extremely profitable for UPS," I said.

"I'm listening."

"People on welfare are hungry. They want to work and I believe that if we train them properly, they will have higher retention rates than our other workers. They'll stay around longer and that will turn into positive UPS dollars."

Riggans wasn't a champion of welfare-to-work as much as he liked the idea of doing things that were noteworthy. And transporting people on welfare across state lines to available jobs was most definitely noteworthy. "Alright," Riggans said. "I'll tell you what. We'll try it for three months, and after three months if it's not working, it's gone. So tell them up front, we're only doing this for three months."

"Done," I said.

The next day, Al, Rich, and I headed back to the facility in Camden.

"Did you solve the transportation problem?" Peter asked.

"We took care of it," I said, and explained the arrangement.

"Great," said Peter. "Our next responsibility is to get them jobs."

A week later we came back with human resource representatives to interview the candidates. During the interviews, I noticed a tall, straggly-looking man standing off to one side. His battered construction boots had no laces. He wore ripped and tattered overalls, and even though it was a warm day, he wore a flannel shirt. I saw old punctures on his arms that were unmistakably from drugs. He had an unkempt mustache and his long, stringy hair covered most of his face. He was watching us.

"Hi," I said, sticking out my hand. "My name's Rodney."

"Billy," he answered.

"We're from UPS."

"I didn't see any UPS trucks outside," he said. I chuckled although I wasn't sure he was joking.

"We hear you guys are looking for jobs."

"Is that right?" he said, his voice rising.

"Do you think you would be a good candidate to work at UPS?" I always asked that question in interviews and usually got the same answer: "There's nobody better than me."

But Billy was different.

"To be honest," he said. "I have no idea why you would hire me."

With his hands in his pockets, he told me he was sure that there were people with a better education. He told me that he had to drop out of high school when he was sixteen to support his family—although he made sure to mention that he received his GED. He told me that he was embarrassed to be on welfare.

"But at thirty years old, I need to be a man again," he said. Then he picked up his head and looked me in the eye.

"I'm not the smartest guy you're going to hire, Mr. Carroll. But because I'm not as smart, I'm going to work twice as hard. I'm just hoping that somehow I'll get a chance to prove I'm worth something, not only to myself but to my family and my children. If I had an opportunity, I know I would make the best of it."

Billy reaffirmed my belief in the human spirit. He sincerely wanted to work and that meant more to me than a college degree or work history. That is why I strongly object when some welfare recipients are called the "hardest to place." We sometimes fall into the trap of profiling people. The social scientists do it when they refer to people with specific skill levels or educational backgrounds. They give names for these categories, including the "hardest to place," meaning the background prohibits a person from becoming a successful employee. This usually includes people who use drugs and alcohol, women who are victims of spousal abuse, and ex-felons.

Chris Wilcox and Gale Hagan are two classic examples of what social scientists call the "hardest to place." For years Chris had a drug problem. His three children suffered from the instability of their parents and the limitations of welfare.

Finally, Chris got "sick and tired of being sick and tired." Fortunately for Chris, Cessna Aircraft Company in Wichita, Kansas is another company that believes everyone has the potential to be a good employee—regardless of past mistakes. One of the workers at the KanWorks program, the welfare program in Kansas, introduced Chris to Cessna's 21st Street Facility, a program designed to train welfare recipients for jobs at Cessna Aircraft Company.

The 21st Street program was started in 1990 in a single building, which was eleven thousand square feet. Seven years later, Cessna had added a fifty-eight thousand square-foot learning center, including five thousand feet for day care. They built safe housing, where trainees could temporarily live to avoid dangerous circumstances at home.

The 21st Street program has provided more than two hundred loyal and dedicated employees who have a higher retention rate than more traditionally hired employees.

"We have found that there are an awful lot of people who have led their life in a particular way for a number of years, but who are willing and want very badly to lead the rest of their life differently," said John Moore, senior vice president of human resources.

Chris Wilcox is one of those people. Today, Chris is the final assembly mechanic on the Citation 750 line at Cessna Aircraft. He has already been promoted and is now trusted with building Cessna's most advanced aircraft. But most important, Chris has custody of his three children. They have a safe, stable home with a father who loves and supports them.

"To me, every day that I wake up and am able to breathe is a good day, from where I came from," said Chris. "It's pretty neat to be able to say to my kids, 'There's one of the planes that I built.' Now when somebody asks, 'Where's your dad work?,' they've got an answer. 'At Cessna.'"

Gail Hagan was a victim of domestic violence and she now works for Salomon Smith Barney, a subsidiary of CitiGroup. For two years, Gail had struggled with an alcohol problem. After almost losing her daughter to social services, Gail decided to turn her life around.

She entered a program at Wildcat Services, a nonprofit service provider that trains welfare recipients for jobs. Wildcat is one of the best service providers in the country.

"We're in the business of training people who others thought were untrainable, and making them into good citizens who will do well at their jobs," said Amalia Betanzos, president of the Wildcat Service Corporation.

The best part of the partnership is that Wildcat knows exactly what skills the trainees need to succeed at Salomon Smith Barney and they tailor their training program accordingly. After a sixteen-week training program, trainees are guaranteed an opportunity for work. It took Gail only eight weeks before she graduated to an internship in the financial services industry at Salomon Smith Barney. After two more months, she had a full-time job.

Now Gail, someone who most companies wouldn't have even considered because of her background, works for a company that pays her more than thirty thousand dollars a year. She's earning stock options and has a 401(k). One day, Gail is waiting by her mailbox for a welfare check, four months later she's waiting for her retirement statements.

"This is not charity," said Michael Schlein, the director of corporate affairs at CitiGroup. "Gail is working for a living. She's getting paid, and she deserves to be well paid. We give a lot of people an opportunity, but people like Gail are the ones who are making the most of that opportunity."

As more and more people like Chris and Gail succeed, more and more business leaders are willing to look beyond the stereotypes of people with substance-abuse problems and criminal records, to see people who have made mistakes and now want to change their lives. Most drug addicts or criminals were like Courtney at one point. Not all of them, but most of them were nice kids who tried to do the right thing before getting overwhelmed by societal pressures.

It's not up to corporate America to help welfare recipients. As I learned through Courtney, that's a job that only they could do for themselves. But if a person can break an addiction or climb out of welfare, then they can do anything.

"These are exactly the type of people we're looking for," I told Al and Rich on the drive home. "People who have something to prove."

Like everyone else at UPS, Al had his own theories on why retention was low. He believed that the five-day training program was insufficient for employees to learn the many intricacies of the job.

"This will be a good opportunity to revamp the program," he told me.

"I was thinking the same thing," I responded.

Over lunch, we discussed how to change the program. Then, unilaterally, we agreed to extend it from five days to six weeks. Al and I believed that six weeks gave us enough time to thoroughly teach the trainees the job. We also knew that by working six weeks, employees were eligible to join the union—an important benefit to working at

UPS. I knew many good people who would still be working at UPS today, if they could have just made it into the union.

"Six weeks it is," said Al, as he wiped his mouth and prepared to leave.

"Just one more thing," I said. "We need to create some demand for the jobs at UPS. Instead of hiring fifty employees a week, we are only going to hire forty to fifty employees every six weeks."

Al knew how hard I was working on the program. And he knew that, at this point, I wasn't going to compromise. I would have a tough enough time convincing the other managers to reduce hiring so drastically, so Al didn't respond.

"Thanks for the lunch, Rodney," he said and, as usual, left the check to me.

At the next employment meeting, Al and I made our case for a six-week training course. It was well received. When we were done, I kept the floor.

"For the last several years, people thought they could get a job at UPS anytime they wanted," I said. "Therefore the value of a job at UPS diminished. We have to create a perception—and ultimately the reality—that it's prestigious to work at UPS. And we don't do that by hiring anybody that applies every week."

"Then how do we do it?" a manager asked.

"By hiring once every six weeks."

"You're out of your mind," said an area hub manager. "There's no way we can make it once every six weeks. I won't have any people left."

"You'll have to value your people more," I responded.

"How are we going to keep people waiting for six weeks?" asked a human resource director.

"The people that are really interested in UPS will wait," I said. "You have to trust me on this."

The debate over the dramatic change in hiring practice continued for thirty minutes. Al didn't say a word and the idea passed. After the meeting, Al approached me privately.

"Keep trusting your instincts," he said. "We're almost there."

Managers at UPS are evaluated solely on performance. If production is down, they don't get bonuses. If service doesn't keep increasing, they can forget about a raise. If there were too many missorts, they could lose their job. The basic fact was that if employees didn't do well, then managers didn't either.

When I informed the managers that forty-one of their new employees were coming from welfare, they were livid.

"Why don't we bring in blind and crippled people, too," cried Scott Conaway, an outbound manager.

Dan Havaford, who ran the smalls sort, was especially upset because his area was close to reaching his goals. "You're trying to sabotage my area," Dan yelled.

"The decision has already been made," I said. "You guys are going to have to trust me. This will work."

Normally, each trainee is assigned to a different area of the operation for "on-the-job training." I asked the managers who needed workers.

Silence.

I turned to Mondel, the primary direct manager. "You don't want anybody, Mondel? You have the highest turnover in the group."

"Nope," answered Mondel. "We're alright, we're good."

"Wes," I continued. "You're turning over people like flapjacks. You don't need anybody?"

"I'm cool," answered Wes.

I asked every manager and everyone said, "Nope." I shook my head. I was frustrated. Ninety-nine times out of one hundred, I wouldn't have said anything, but this time was different. This was too important.

I slammed my notebook on the table.

"Let me make sure I understand this," I said. "Nobody needs any workers? And you realize we're not getting anyone in for six weeks?"

"Nope," they said. "We don't want anybody."

"If I didn't know any better," I said, "I would think that this has something to do with the group of people that we are hiring. People coming from welfare."

Again, silence.

"But I know better than that," I continued. "Because for three months now, we've been talking about how to value our employees and what it means to give someone a chance. I know you were listening to me, so it can't be that you don't want to hire welfare recipients. Can it, Dan?"

Dan was rattled and I didn't let him wriggle out.

"Dan, that can't be what you guys are thinking. Could it?"

"Well, no," Dan replied. "I just happen to be in good shape. I'll take one if you want me to have one."

"One what?" I said glaring down at him.

"One person," he said.

"No," I snapped back. "If you say you don't want anyone, then you're not getting anyone. I just want to tell you guys, I'm very disappointed. I have a mind to tell each of you to take five people from this new class, but I'm not going to do that. It's not fair to the people who are really trying to make it. They're not here as guinea pigs. They're here to turn their lives around."

I stormed out of the room. I paced up and down the hallway.

A few of the managers thought the meeting was over and tried to leave the room.

"This meeting is not over," I said. "Just stay in there and wait until I get back."

I went down to my office to calm down. I leaned back on my chair and stared out of the window toward the operation. It was a down time. The two belts right in front of my office in Secondary Five were vacant. I racked my brain trying to think of a solution. I had forty-one welfare recipients starting in two weeks and I had managers that didn't want them. If I forced the managers to participate, the program wouldn't work.

I swung back and forth on my swivel chair, just thinking and staring. Then it came to me. I went back upstairs and walked calmly into the conference room. When the managers saw me, they stopped talking and took their seats.

"We're making Secondary Five a training area," I proclaimed. It was perfect. Not only was Secondary Five right outside my office, it was also a highly visible area. The first thing anyone coming down from the parking lot or in from the buses saw was Secondary Five. It was the ideal location for a program that I wanted everyone to recognize.

"Scott, we're going to take you off the Secondary Five red and blue belts. They're no longer going to be part of your area," I instructed. "I'm going to have them report to Nan Miland."

"What?" he said. "Are you promoting Nan?"

"No, she is just going to run this area. This is now going to be a training area."

As it turned out, this was much better than spreading the trainees throughout the operation. Nan was the ideal supervisor. She was caring and compassionate, but tough enough to get the job done.

I called Nan at home. Before I finished describing the program, she said, "I'll be honored."

I lay in bed that night feeling good. We had workers. They had a way to get to work and they had a supportive place to work.

Now for the training, I thought.

The training program was the easy part. Through all the different stops on my road to division manager, I had developed strong opinions and strategies for the best way to train workers. It had started on my second day of work, eighteen years earlier, when I learned the most important thing for any new employee: Dominic Palvino.

Every new worker deserved their own Dominic. As abrasive as he was, I remembered how comfortable I felt at work with him by my side. He wasn't my supervisor. He was just someone who gave me the inside scoop about working at UPS.

I knew that our training program needed to include this mentoring aspect. We had forty-one welfare recipients. We needed forty-one mentors.

The selection process for the mentors was rigorous. To encourage the workers to apply, I suggested that the mentor position was a stepping-stone to supervisor. "So if you want to be a supervisory candidate, I suggest you apply to be a mentor," the flyer read.

There was a great demand to be a mentor and we had more than one hundred excellent candidates apply. I outlined my vision for the mentors: "They are there to be a friend. To help the new hire get over any bumps in the road; to give practical workplace advice; or just be a sounding board or a cheerleader."

I then personally interviewed all the candidates. I wasn't looking for the hardest workers. I looked for workers with good communication skills, patience, and compassion. After a solid week of interviews and second interviews, I handpicked forty-one workers to be our first class of mentors.

"It takes courage to try to change your life," I told the training coordinators—they preferred to be called training coordinators over mentors. "Many times, it's safer to stay on welfare."

I placed incredible pressure on the training coordinators. They spent five weeks helping me create the training program. They spent two weeks mastering the flow of the blue and red belts in Secondary Five. I held them professionally responsible for the progress of the trainees.

"Don't you give them an excuse to quit," I warned. "They're waiting for you to say that they can't do it, or give them some negative vibe. That's what they've gotten their entire lives. We're going to beat them to the punch and tell them why they *can't* quit."

We made sure to keep the same basic standard for the welfare recipients as we had for other employees—no tardiness, no absenteeism.

The class would be divided into two teams—a red team and a blue team—coinciding with their belts. For each week the entire group remained on the job, they would earn a pizza party—including toppings—if no one was tardy. The extra topping incentive may seem odd, but when you're poor, mushrooms and pepperoni on your pizza is not an option. You get cheese.

If the group went a week with perfect service—no missorts— they would earn a T-shirt. Two weeks in a row earned a hat. Three weeks a UPS jacket.

Aside from learning the intricacies of the job, the training program was designed to build self-esteem. Many companies say they don't want to be social workers, and I don't think they should be. But the fact is that if you take the time to address the concerns of your employees—whether they are on welfare or not—they will feel valued, they will work harder, and they will stay on the job.

The training coordinators did role-plays concerning challenges for the jobs: the packages are too heavy. The flow is moving too quickly. And role-plays concerning non-job-related issues: I have personal problems at home. I didn't get any sleep last night because my child kept me up.

We incorporated a lesson I learned from Willow Grove. "We want the trainees to know more about UPS than most of the people in this hub," I said. "The more they know, the better they'll be able to do their jobs."

So we scheduled representatives from all facets of the organization to speak to the trainees each week. First, accounting would talk about stock programs, the 401(k) and retirement plans. Two weeks later, human resources would discuss benefits, including the difference between welfare benefits and UPS benefits.

When I was growing up, we didn't visit a doctor's office with comfortable chairs, music, and *Sports Illustrated* to browse through. Our only option was the emergency room, where we waited and waited and waited. At UPS, employees could make an appointment with a doctor of their choice. There was 100 percent prescription drug coverage.

The next week, representatives from our airline would speak about opportunities in the planes. Many people probably don't realize that UPS is the largest cargo airline in the world.

We scheduled people to talk about computers and marketing and tractor trailers. The program was choreographed so that while one group was doing on-the-job training, the other was in the classroom.

In the end, the program was created exactly as I had visualized it. It was challenging enough so the trainees would be valuable when they graduated, but forgiving enough so they wouldn't get discouraged during the process.

On July 17, 1996, a class of forty-one welfare recipients began the first six-week training program at UPS.

15. V Formation

I stood at the podium and scanned the room. I saw Billy to the right, wearing the same work boots with no laces. The woman sitting three seats down caught my eye because of the disinterested look on her face. Her name tag read Consuelo Ortiz. She had short hair with a black bandanna on her head. She had cigarettes rolled up in her sleeve and several tattoos on each arm. She looked tough.

Sitting next to Consuelo was Marva Thompson, who looked like she had come from a beauty parlor, not welfare. Her blouse was cleaned and pressed. Her makeup was perfect and her nails were filed and painted. A few seats down, sitting with perfect posture was Rashonda Lewis. Everything about Rashonda was neat—her hair, her pants. Her boots were shined. She looked like she was heading into the army.

I waited for the clock to strike 10:00 P.M.—the standard time for work to begin—then I turned around to the chalkboard and wrote the number forty-five thousand with a big dollar sign in front.

"If I were you I'd be thinking forty-five thousand dollars," I said. The class looked up.

Sam, a big, burly lumberjack-looking guy with a reddish blond beard bellowed, "I'm thinking forty-five thousand dollars."

"Good," I said. I pointed to the human resource director. "Is that what Steve said you were going to make?"

Cries of "No," "No way," "Not even close," came from the group.

"What did he say?" I asked.

"They told us we were starting at $8.50 an hour," said Rashonda.

"They didn't tell you forty-five thousand dollars?" I said. "Well if I were you, I would be thinking forty-five thousand dollars."

"Okay, we're thinking forty-five thousand dollars," said Sam. "We're all thinking forty-five thousand dollars. Why are we thinking that?"

"Because the average driver at UPS makes about forty-five thousand dollars a year," I said, my tone turning serious. "In a little over three years, you will have enough seniority to become a UPS driver and you will have the opportunity to make forty-five thousand dollars a year."

I had the group's attention now.

"Let me ask you, what can forty-five thousand dollars a year do to your life?"

"I can buy some new furniture," Salena said.

"Yes you can," I said.

"I can get a car."

"I can get my kids new clothes."

"I can move into a better neighborhood."

"Let me tell you what you can do," I said. "You can change your life."

The room was quiet. There were curious looks on many faces. People on welfare aren't used to such a clear opportunity. I sensed they were a little reluctant to trust me. I continued.

"But in the meantime," I said, "some of you may be thinking of this as simply a part-time job. Well this is no ordinary part-time job."

I told them that within a year, they would have the opportunity to work what we call combination part-time jobs at UPS, or two jobs that totaled thirty-five hours a week. "The average salary for a part-timer is between eleven and twelve dollars an hour," I said.

"Wow," said Sam. "Now you're talking turkey."

"I want everyone here to be thinking long-term," I said. "Don't think only about right now."

I named people at UPS who had advanced in the company, including Cal Darden, the senior vice president of operations. "He started as a part-timer," I said. "Jim Kelly went from driver to CEO." Then I told them about myself.

"And we have a lot in common," I said. "In 1978, I sat in a room just like this in South Philadelphia. I started part-time making five dollars an hour."

"You started where we started?" asked Billy.

"Absolutely."

"Now you're like the big boss," said Sam.

"I have a lot of responsibility," I said. "But believe me, I have enough people that boss me around."

In the past, I was uncomfortable admitting that I was once on welfare. It was my own business. I didn't see a need for others to know. But this meeting was different.

"We have something else in common," I said. "I know what it's like to go into a neighborhood store with food stamps."

"How do you know that?" Luis was suspicious.

"Because when I was a boy, my sister and I fought to see who would have to go to the store to buy food. Not that we didn't want food. But we didn't want our friends to see us pay for the food with food stamps."

"Well, how'd you get food stamps?" asked Billy.

"When I was growing up, my family was on public assistance. We were on welfare."

I was wearing a new three-piece suit. My shoes were polished. I probably looked like I didn't know a thing about poverty. "Get out of here," yelled Jeffrey, who turned out to be the joker of the bunch.

"I'm telling you," I said. "I know what it's like to have people tell you that you'll never be anything. I know what it's like to eventually stop believing in yourself." Nobody said a word.

"I have a pretty good idea of how you feel right now. I'm sure some of you have people at home thinking you're not going to make it. Your neighbors may have said, 'You'll go there a couple of nights, then you'll be back here where you started.'

"And I know that you may think that the management people here are not going to give you a fair shot. That they may look down on you. That they aren't going to understand you.

"I'll bet you're thinking that even if you do make it for a couple of days or a week, and even if the management treats you halfway decent, sooner or later you're going to have some problem. Maybe one of your children will get sick or something else may happen to cause you to miss work. You're probably thinking, 'Well, I'll go as long as I can, but as soon as I miss a day, they're going to fire me.'"

Some of the trainees had tears in their eyes. Others were shaking their heads in affirmation.

"I understand where you're coming from. You're coming from a life of being dependent on someone else. And that's a little bit farther than Camden, New Jersey.

"This is Monday," I said. "Look around. The question you need to ask yourself is, Will you be here through Friday? Don't think about six weeks, can you make it one week? Because the truth is that if you're not here at the end of the training, the reason will most likely be that you quit."

Then I paused for a minute so they could digest all the information. There was a long silence. Then Billy spoke.

"I'm not going to quit," he said.

A second later, Luis spoke out. Then another and another and another.

"Well, I ain't quitting."

"You'll never get me to quit."

"I'm not going to quit no matter what."

"I don't care how heavy the boxes are. I'm not going to quit."

"I don't care if the supervisor does look down on me. I'm not going to quit."

"I don't care if I get sleepy at night. I'll just have to drink some coffee before I come in because I'm not going to quit."

"Well," I said. "If nobody's going to quit, then let me tell you that you're in for the ride of your life and a great career. We have a big surprise at the end of this training period. But for now take some time to get to know your training coordinators down by the belts, and good luck."

Along each belt was a wire to post the description for each trailer—Upstate New York, Harrisburg, Pittsburgh. When we got to the belts, large welcome signs were in place.

WELCOME MARVA, NEW PITTSBURGH TRAILER LOADER, SIGNED, YOUR FRIEND, RONNIE.

For the next hour, the training coordinators and the trainees got acquainted. For the most part, the trainees were open and friendly.

They all exchanged emergency phone numbers—all except Connie. I was right about her. She was a loner. "I'm here to work," she told her training coordinator. "I'm going to do my job and go home. I'm not trying to be anybody's friend."

The next hour was dedicated to the belts. Packages slowly rolled down the chute. The new hires watched as the training coordinators described how to read labels and pack trailers.

"You need to tilt the label toward the light like this," said Lynn Blair.

"Make sure to use your legs like this," explained Tommy Coleman.

"Place it, don't throw it," said Velma Thompson. "It may be something breakable." Of all the training coordinators, Velma was the best. Velma was only working at UPS for the benefits. She'd had many offers to be a supervisor during her six years at the hub, but she never wanted the responsibility. As a training coordinator, she blossomed into the leader we all knew she could be.

The first night went perfectly. The training coordinators were patient and the trainees seemed interested.

I came out at the end of the shift to say good-bye.

"So, Mr. Carroll," said Luis. "What's the big surprise? Is it a bonus check?" Every time I saw Luis, he asked me about the surprise.

"Is it a pizza party?"

"Is it a new jacket?"

"Is it a day off?"

"If I told you, it wouldn't be a surprise," I said.

The night went fast. Although a few people seemed tired, many said they couldn't wait to come back the next day.

The training coordinators and I met briefly to address any potential problems. There were none. Each training coordinator believed that their trainee would remain for the entire six weeks. I knew it was unrealistic. Our normal retention rate was less than 50 percent. If two-thirds graduated, it would be a huge success. But I didn't say anything.

The second day came, but not all the welfare recipients did. Five people didn't show. Only three of the five had phones—they had missed the bus. Their training coordinators wanted to drive to Camden to pick them up.

"That's okay," I said. "This is a challenge we're going to have to deal with."

For the other thirty-six people, the training went as planned.

On the third day, all five absentees from the previous day showed—we learned that the two without phones had missed the bus as well. They were all apologetic and ready to go.

But two new people didn't show. We called. They had overslept. They were tired from the first two days and took naps before work. One didn't have an alarm clock. The other's alarm clock didn't go off because there was a power outage in their apartment—not an uncommon event when you live in low-income housing.

Although the third day also ran smoothly, the training coordinators were discouraged about the absenteeism. They expected pepperoni pizza the first week and in the first three days, there were already seven absentees.

"The people want to come," said Nan. "But you have to understand, for people on welfare, it's such a fine line. If one thing goes wrong, they can't make it."

"We have to think of something," said Velma. And they did.

First, the training coordinators purchased forty-one wind-up alarm clocks with their own money. They were those old-fashioned clocks with big silver bells on the top.

We loaned everyone an alarm clock. After the first payday, the trainees could buy the alarm clocks for a dollar.

The training coordinators then took the money to create a taxi jar—much like the Sunshine fund. A taxi ride from Camden to the air hub cost forty-eight dollars, including tip. In addition to the alarm-clock money, the training coordinators each put in two dollars to start. They created other ways of raising revenue. The use of profanity meant a quarter to the jar. Incorrect UPS terminology—a quarter in the jar.

In no time, the jar contained over one hundred dollars. If anyone missed the bus for the first time, they could use the taxi jar to pay for a ride to work. The jar was used only once.

The process allowed the training coordinators to better understand why welfare recipients may not come to work. It was not because they didn't want to work. It's the reasons that we all take for granted because we have support systems to help with things like child care and transportation. Welfare recipients have no support systems.

When Friday came, all forty-one trainees were still employed. We celebrated with eight pizzas. Just cheese.

In no time, most of the training coordinators and their trainees developed strong bonds and friendships. They saw each other after work. They went bowling. They went to church. Many of the training coordinators loaned their trainees money. They picked them up for work, or drove them home. They helped with child care. Connie was still ambivalent to her training coordinator, but she was proving herself to be a hard worker and a leader in the group.

None of the bonds were stronger than that between Marva and Ronnie. We called them the Bobbsey Twins. They both rolled their pants up above their work boots to expose their socks. They both wore a ponytail through the hole in the back of the hat. They both wore gloves to protect their hands. After the shift, they both put lotion on their hands.

Ronnie taught Marva to load heavy packages by bracing them against the side of the trailer and then using her legs to push them in.

"You go, girl," Ronnie yelled. "You got it. Use your legs, use your legs. See, sixty-five pounds. Don't tell me you can't do that."

Ronnie pushed Marva to excel. "I'm not accepting anything but one hundred on the tests," she said. "If you get ninety-nine you take it over again."

When Marva was having trouble with day care for her two-year-old daughter, Ronnie's mother agreed to take care of Marva's daughter. Their bond went beyond trainee and coordinator. They became close friends.

The program cruised into its second week. The training coordinators still did most of the work on the belt, but the trainees were slowly integrating themselves when it came to the job. Rashonda established herself as the perfectionist of the group. The trainees learned to build walls with the boxes in the trailers, and Rashonda's wall was always tight and flush and balanced. On the other end of the spectrum was Salena. Her wall fell on her. She watched the rest of the day with an ice pack on her head.

I came out to check on Salena just in time to hear a ruckus in the cafeteria. A coworker teased Connie about her clothes, which were old and tattered. Connie wanted to fight.

"If you fight, you're fired," I told Connie. "I want you to understand, there's to be no fighting. There's no self-defense. There's nothing. If you throw a punch, you're done."

"But—" she said. I cut her off.

"No buts," I said. "If someone throws a punch at you, you duck it and run. We'll fire them."

I knew that I was asking Connie to act against her nature. Connie had grown up in an area where there was no "duck and run." They had a code: You fought for yourself and you didn't tattle. We were asking her to break the code.

"Don't lose your job over this," Nan said.

It wasn't the only time the group was singled out for being on welfare. Later that week, an open package containing "How to" videotapes came down the red belt. Nan followed standard procedure, set it aside, and called quality control. After examining the box, quality control discovered that several of the tapes were missing and alerted loss prevention.

In no time, Keith Murdah, the loss prevention manager, and three of his coworkers ran into the area like the Keystone Kops. They barged into my office.

"We want to take your people off the belt and question them," he said. He already assumed that one of the welfare recipients had stolen the tapes.

"What makes you think it was them?" I asked.

"They certainly have the motive," said Keith.

"What do you mean, 'motive'?" I asked in disgust. "Let's take a look at this for a second. How many welfare recipients do you think have VCRs?"

"Well, they can sell the tapes," said one of Keith's assistants, peeking his head around from behind Keith's back.

"What tapes were missing?" I asked.

Keith checked the invoice. They were "How to Garden" instructional tapes.

"I'm sure that gardening tapes are going to be a hot commodity in Camden, New Jersey," I said.

We investigated a little more and found that the box had originated from another area in the hub that was already under investigation. It was placed on the red belt to shift suspicion.

"You're not questioning anyone in this area," I said, and Keith agreed.

We had averted a close call. If Keith questioned anyone in the group, like he wanted, I was convinced one or more would have been offended and quit. Or defended themselves and been fired. Fortunately, it had never come to that.

=

Billy was right, he wasn't the smartest guy in the world. He started the training in the Upstate New York trailer—one of the more difficult areas because of the fine splits. But by the third week, his training coordinator moved him to Harrisburg, where the volume of packages was higher, but 90 percent went to the same zip code. He flourished there.

The other trainees were getting more and more entrenched in the operation. At first, production and service numbers were high because the training coordinators did most of the work. But by the third week, the trainees shared the load without effecting the level of production or service.

At the start, I had predicted that we would retain thirty of the forty-one people. Through three weeks, we had all forty-one. We couldn't help but notice that something special was developing. The retention rates were unheard of and we quickly realized that this program should be replicated throughout UPS regardless of whether the person is on welfare or not. The fact was that our trainees were quickly developing into the better employees in the operation.

They earned hats and T-shirts and wore them like badges of honor. In no time the trainees stood out like a company softball team. Even the managers couldn't help but notice.

"When Rashonda finishes her training," said Mondel, "I'd like to have her in my area."

"That's great. But the problem with Rashonda is she has about seven or eight kids," I said sarcastically.

"No," said Mondel. "She only has one child. That's a rumor."

Slowly the managers began to become more educated about who

welfare recipients were and were not. The same managers that didn't want to risk their bonuses on a group of welfare recipients were now competing for their services.

The human resource people were also ecstatic. While our original class was excelling, other people were waiting for the next one to begin. "Okay, we'll put you on a waiting list," said human resources representatives when calls came in for employment.

"Waiting list? Give me a break. My friend worked there and got a job right away."

"Well, not anymore."

Every couple of days, I received a call.

"Mr. Carroll. They're telling us that you're not hiring anyone until after Labor Day. I know that's not true."

"It's true," I said proudly. "Even then, it's not guaranteed. We're probably only hiring fifty people and right now we have about two hundred fifty on the waiting list."

A few candidates dropped off the list, but most waited.

We knew that our training program would lead to higher retention rates, and it did. But the interesting part of the program was that working with former welfare recipients, and hearing how much it meant to have a job and be independent again, offered a unique perspective to our existing employees. We found that morale was up at UPS. People pulled together and worked as a team. There was a refreshing new spirit among all the employees involved with the program and it was due to this welfare-to-work experience.

If there was one area of the training that we didn't account for, it was the daily grind of a six-week training program. Each day there was something new to learn. Something new to understand. It was draining for even the most disciplined workers.

At the Wednesday meeting, the group looked tired. They slouched in their seats. There was no chitchat. I decided to reveal the surprise.

"Luis," I said to start the meeting, "I know you've been trying to guess the nature of the surprise for three weeks now. Unfortunately, that brand-new car in the parking lot is not going to be it. The surprise is that those of you who can make it another two and a half weeks are going to have a graduation."

Many of the trainees were like Billy. They hadn't graduated from high school and never received the satisfaction of going through a formal graduation.

"On your first day of the program, I told you to look around. If you look around now, you'll see that we're all still here. That is an incredible accomplishment. But now we have to make it to the graduation. We're calling it graduation because it's a big deal. You've graduated. You'll become full union employees."

"Are we going to have pizza?" yelled Sam.

"No. It'll be catered. We're going to have roast beef and mashed potatoes, dessert, and punch. It will be in the main conference room. You'll receive certificates and plaques, because we view this as an accomplishment. We're going to have invitations."

"My kids have never seen me accomplish anything," said Luis. "They've never seen me finish anything good."

"I'm inviting my girlfriend," said Jimmy Tyler. "She's going to be really proud of me."

"How many people can we invite?" Rashonda asked.

The graduation was going to be held right before the sort from 9:00 to 10:30 at night. I didn't figure many people would come at that time. I told them they could invite as many as they liked.

"There are only two things we need from you," I concluded. "We need a group name for your class and we need a few people to speak at the graduation."

Within five minutes, ten people offered to speak. The energy was back.

The next day Nan was waiting in my office when I walked into work.

"Ronnie's in the conference room crying," she said.

I entered the room to find Ronnie alone, staring straight ahead. She had stopped crying but I could see the dried tears on her face.

"What's the matter?" I said. I thought someone had died.

"Marva quit."

"What?" I said. I was shocked. Ronnie was devastated.

"She's never going to get off welfare now," Ronnie said. "She has blown it."

"What happened?" I asked.

Ronnie told me that Marva was getting pressure from her boyfriend for working at UPS. Apparently, Marva's boyfriend wasn't comfortable with the child-care arrangement and believed that a mother should be home to take care of her children. "It's been going on for a while now," Ronnie told me. "But I thought we had passed it."

Ronnie said she thought she had convinced Marva to leave her boyfriend. "I told her he was not supporting her. I told her that she was trying to make something out of her life. I begged her not to quit." Ronnie started to cry again. "And she was going to leave him. But then she came in and quit. He threatened to take her daughter away if she kept working."

Ronnie confessed she had confronted the boyfriend but to no avail.

"He told me to 'stay the fuck out of his business,' " she said. "I'm telling you, this man is no good. He's a dog."

I didn't know what to say, so I didn't say anything.

The loss of Marva notwithstanding, the notion of graduation served its purpose. There was a refreshing new spirit among the group and they needed it because week five was a critical time in the program. It was when the trainees entered the full-fledged flow. Hands-off training coordinators, hands-on trainees.

"How do you guys think it'll go?" I asked Nan before our Monday meeting.

"We'll soon find out," she said.

I did paperwork in my office as the shift began. They've been trained, I thought to myself. They know what they're . . . Before I finished my thought I heard a loud *buzzzz, buzzzz, buzzzz,* echoing from the sort.

It was no more than thirty minutes into the sort and the horn was sounding already. The horn meant that the belts had backed up with too many packages and needed to be cut off. I grew to hate the sound of that horn.

Forty minutes later, *buzzzz, buzzzz, buzzzz,* the belts were shut down again.

The training coordinators simply stood there and watched.

"Why don't you help me here?" yelled Salena to her training coordinator.

"You're on your own tonight," she answered.

The trainees scrambled to finish the sort that night. The horn sounded 180 times. If it wasn't a record, it was close to it. When the night ended, the belt looked like a tornado had passed through it. There were scraps on the floor, Styrofoam on the belt, and pickle juice on the floor. Many of the packages were late, which caused the plane to leave late. There was utter frustration on every face.

At the end of the night, the training coordinators and the trainees had a post-sort meeting.

"Look," said Nan to the trainees. "We can't keep carrying you. In less than two weeks you're going to be out in separate areas throughout this operation. Nobody's going to help you out there. If your packages are heavy, it's up to you to get them out by yourself. If the flow is heavy, you need to deal with it. You need to be ready."

I heard this next part of the story from Billy—now an air driver— a few years ago, but I don't doubt that it is true. According to Billy, when Nan and the other training coordinators left the room, Connie told the trainees to stick around for a second. She closed the door.

"We're better than that," she said. "And tomorrow night, we're going to prove it. We've come a long way in five weeks. Don't let it end here." With that, she opened the door.

Sure enough, all forty trainees showed up early the next night.

The reality was that if the group couldn't sort the flow on their own, the whole training program was a waste. We couldn't afford another night like the one before. I'd deflected the backlash from the late planes, but I couldn't do it again.

I was back in my office when the clock struck 10:00. I waited and waited for the dreaded horn to signal that something was wrong. But as each hour passed, I heard nothing. I forced myself not to visit the belt. I didn't want to interfere. Finally, at 1:00 A.M. I couldn't help myself. I got up from my desk and looked out of my window.

I couldn't believe my eyes. The group was working in perfect harmony. Like an alert baseball team, there was lively chatter.

"Hey come on Louie."

"Need a plastic bag."

"Plastic bag coming down."

"Only got a half hour to go. The input's almost done."

"Waiting for the Chicago plane."

"Yea, the Chicago plane is going to hit heavy in Pittsburgh."

Then I noticed something I'd never seen before. The hardest job on the sort is the splitter. The splitter makes sure the packages go down the correct belts. It's a grueling job that takes organization, concentration, and stamina.

Sam was the splitter when I first started watching. A few minutes later, he left his position. In no time, Connie took his spot. Connie came from inside the trailer—a less demanding job. She was fresh. She was sharp. The sort that never missed a beat.

Every thirty minutes the splitter rotated to an easier position while the next person rotated to the splitter's position. It was a brilliant idea.

On Friday, the pizzas came with pepperoni.

As the group filed into the bus to head home, Connie told me that she was leaving. Her brother was arrested in Florida and her family was driving down to help.

"I have to go with them," she said. I respected her decision.

It was a disappointing way to end an emotional week. We had all grown to like Connie. She was an excellent example of how a job can bring out the best in a person. Unfortunately, she was also an excellent example of how difficult it is to stay off welfare. Before I could get too down over the loss of Connie, Sam approached me with the class's name.

"V Formation," he said proudly.

"Why V Formation?" I asked.

"Have you ever seen a flock of birds?" he said. "They fly in a V formation. The lead bird flies as long as it can, then rolls to the back while another bird takes the lead in the V. That's how we view our team."

"Good enough," I said.

The next morning individually printed invitations on official UPS stationery went out, reading:

> You are cordially invited to attend the graduation of the first class
> of our new training program at United Parcel Service.
> This graduation class, entitled the V Formation,
> will hold its closing exercises at 9 P.M. on September 4.
> Please come and recognize the class for their tremendous
> accomplishment.
> We're very proud of them and we're sure you are, too.
> *Dinner and refreshments will be served.*

The security guard at the west gate must have called half a dozen times on September 4, 1996.

"I have a women here. She's got a one-year-old kid. Are we letting kids in the building?"

"Two elderly people say they are here to see their granddaughter. Could that be right?"

Our Friday-night graduation was a completely foreign concept at UPS. Visitors—particularly babies and senior citizens—were unheard of.

"Let 'em in," I said. "Let 'em all in."

Finally I sent Nan to the gate with a guest list to expedite the situation. When everyone had passed security and settled in, it was standing room only.

I stood in the back and watched the hugs and kisses and handshakes. I thought of the specific events that punctuate our lives. For most people, it's births, weddings, promotions. In a welfare recipient's life, the events are primarily negative. Deaths, evictions, divorces, terminations. This graduation represented a success. The class had accomplished something special and this was their moment to be honored.

There was an instant interaction between families in the room. Luis introduced his mom to Salena. Sam's parents congratulated Rashonda's kids.

"I never thought she would do it," Margaret's boyfriend told Ronnie. "But she proved me wrong."

"That's my dad," Luis's son, Luis, Jr., told Consuelo's daughter.

Billy was devastated when his mom couldn't attend—the commute was too much for her. But his sister was there.

"Mom would be proud of Billy today," she told me. "He's come a long way."

We've all come a long way, I thought. I stood tall, almost gloating, as if to say, "See, I told you this would work." I was full of pride because I knew that we had made a difference in the lives of thirty-nine people.

Scott Conaway was the master of ceremony. After he had welcomed everyone and their guests, Scott introduced Ronnie, one of the training coordinators. Even though Ronnie had lost Marva, she was the heart and soul of the program and she started the evening on a perfect note.

"There is a passage in the Bible which says that to everything there is a season, and a time for every purpose under heaven. It goes on giving examples of some of the seasons that may come our way; a time to love, a time to hate, a time to war, a time for peace, a time to weep, a time to laugh.

"So, a few months ago, here at this Philadelphia air hub, there came a season to train our new workers differently than before. This celebration tonight is a culmination of great efforts made by all the training coordinators, the management, and the recruits. We learned along the way that there was a time to work and then came a time to work harder, and ultimately the time came to work together for real success.

"And look how successful we have been. We did it all together. As the new employees enter the main work force here at UPS, we wish you much success. And now, as the saying goes, there's a time to speak and a time to be silent. So my time has come to shut up. Enjoy our celebration."

Al Palmer and Randy Maier were next. It was gratifying to hear that the management at UPS viewed the value of the program and its graduates as highly as I did.

"I have been here seventeen years and I have never seen anything like this group," Randy said. "I knew you guys were good, but I didn't know you were this good. You're tremendous."

"I thought about it as I was driving up here tonight," said Al. "I thought about how I could put into words what this means to the entire group and to UPS. And about the best way to do it is to compare it to my daughters—I have three daughters who go to college. I can't believe what this group really accomplished and the incredible support that you have from your management team. I hope that when my daughters find jobs, they are treated as this group is and that they get that special feeling of being part of a team, the way you all feel tonight."

With that, everyone was called up individually to receive their diplomas. Scott prefaced the proceedings by asking that all applause be held to the end. Right.

After every name was called, there were cheers and clapping.

"Yeah, Tony. You did it."

"Louie, Louie."

"Go Carla."

Kids watched with pride.

"That's my daddy."

"That's my mommy."

Parents and grandparents had tears in their eyes. Perhaps the biggest ovation was for Billy, who walked onstage with the clip-clop, clip-clop of his boots that still had no laces. We gave Billy a special award called the energizer bunny award. He had worked harder than anyone I'd ever known at UPS.

Billy held the plaque above his head and yelled, "I made it. I made it. I made it."

After the diplomas and awards were distributed, it was my turn to speak.

I thanked everyone for coming. Then I scanned the crowd much like I did on the first day of class. It had only been six weeks, but to many of us we had lived a lifetime.

"Let's take it back six weeks," I said. "There were a lot of nervous people here. I was nervous. I'm sure some of you were nervous. UPS was nervous. Why were we nervous? Because we were not sure what was going to happen. Is this going to work? Are people going to be successful?

"Remember I wrote forty-five thousand dollars on the board," I recalled.

"Yeah, yeah, we remember that," replied Sam. "We're on our way to making forty-five thousand dollars."

"You're right. You're on your way." Then I took a deep breath and paused. Much like the first day, I didn't plan on making my address personal—but how could I not?

"We all make choices every day," I said. "What kind of food to eat. What books to read. But there are choices that many of us don't get to make. Where to live. What to buy. What kind of car to drive.

"When you're dependent on someone else to survive—like we all have been—your choices get made for you.

"But today, I want to talk about the kind of choices that we all are empowered to make. My grandmother cleaned toilets and bathrooms for a living. She made eighteen dollars a day, plus bus fare. But my grandmother is one of the most honorable, dignified people that I ever had the privilege to know.

"She couldn't choose to buy this or that car. Or live in this place or that place. She chose to go out and work, even though she was at retiring age. She chose to take care of her grandchildren, even though she had already raised her own. And because she made those choices"—I started to get misty—"that allowed me to make some choices.

"One of the choices that I made, with the help of Al Palmer and Randy Meyer, was that we would have a program that would help you make choices.

"Now the ball is in your court. You are in a position to make the choices that will effect the rest of your lives and, even more important, the lives of your children. Are you going to continue to work and learn and advance until one day you're making that forty-five thousand dollars or more? Or are you going to slide back into a life where you're dependent on someone else to survive?

"Nobody here is going to follow you around and make sure you do your job. You are all qualified and capable to climb as high as you desire. But the choice is yours."

As I walked off the stage, Luis stood up.

"Mr. Carroll," he said, pointing to his six-year-old son. "This is my Luis. I want to tell you in front of everyone that I'm making the choice that my Luis will always be proud of me from now on."

I didn't give much thought to my career at UPS during the six-week program. I received a lot of positive attention for the success of our program as well. There were articles in the *Philadelphia Inquirer*, other UPS managers flew in from around the country to observe, even Pennsylvania governor Tom Ridge came to UPS for a Q&A with the graduating class. My confidence was at an all-time high.

About four months after graduation, I was asked to attend a meeting with Bill Riggans, Al Palmer, and the regional HR manager, Dave Rickerts. The regional HR manager is only called in when there's going to be a relocation, and there's only going to be a relocation for a promotion.

"You did a great job with the hub," Bill said to start the meeting.

"Thank you," I said.

"How do you think the hub will do during peak season without you here?" asked Riggans.

"I think they'll be great," I said, and I meant it.

"Well," said Rickerts. "We have a great assignment for you. We think it is something you are really going to enjoy. It's going to take place in Washington, D.C. We want to put you on special assignment with the Welfare to Work Partnership."

The Welfare to What? I thought to myself. I'd never heard of it. Just as I was about to ask what it was, Rickerts continued, "It was started earlier this year by a guy named Eli Segal. We did a company-wide search and you were selected."

"To do what?" I asked.

"This special assignment," Rickerts said.

"What's the job?" I asked.

"I don't actually know," admitted Rickerts. "I guess they'll tell you when you get there. You'll be there for at least a year. But we promised President Clinton that we would provide an executive."

Rickerts explained that I would get all the details from Kate Carr, the COO for the Partnership, at a meeting in Washington in the middle of December.

"You start January third," he said. "Good luck."

When the meeting ended, I sat alone in my office. I was disappointed. Instead of a promotion, this seemed like a lateral move to keep me busy for a year. I was concerned that being out of the UPS mainstream would hurt my momentum with the company.

Nonetheless, on December 16, I met Kate at a foundation lunch at the Women of the Arts on Twelfth and New York Avenue in Washington, D.C. After we were introduced, we walked to our table. The salads were served and Kate talked about the history of welfare and the Partnership while she ate.

She described welfare as a system in which parents lost hope in the present and children lost a chance at a future. She said that we needed a change, and in 1996 we got one when President Clinton called for an "end to welfare as we know it."

"The situation must have been dire if there was an agreement between a Republican Congress and a Democratic administration in an election year," she joked. She continued by telling me that in 1996, Congress passed the bill and on August 22 of the same year, President Clinton signed the Personal Responsibility and Work Opportunity Reconciliation Act.

The new law targeted the more than four million households who received cash assistance from the government. With dependent children, these households represented twelve million people, or almost 5 percent of our population.

The law ended cash assistance as a matter of right. It put time limits and a work requirement on all welfare recipients. It gave welfare money to the states in regulated block grants, not an open-ended, never-ending spigot of money.

According to the new law, welfare recipients could receive benefits for up to five years—and for only two consecutive years. But while they received benefits, they had to either look for work or access training. There had to be an aggressive attempt to seek gainful employment. The work requirements are strict, but at the same time, eligibility for food stamps and Medicaid remain—so there is still a basic safety net that remains in place. The key to the whole system is getting welfare recipients into the workforce—moving from a life of dependence to a life of independence.

"The new law is based in the belief that people on welfare are capable of earning a paycheck," Kate said as the waiter served the London broil. "They are capable of contributing to our economy. They can be taxpayers instead of tax users. All they need is a chance."

She then explained that when President Clinton signed the legislation, he recognized that a change in government policy would not be enough to unwind sixty years of failure. He recognized that a series of severe sanctions had to be joined with opportunities. In short, the president was saying that the answer to welfare was work. If welfare recipients were going to come off welfare, then there needed to be jobs for them to move into.

And that is why the Welfare to Work Partnership was formed. The Partnership was launched with the full blessing of the administration and Congress on May 20, 1997. The timing could not have been better. With the economy growing and the unemployment rate falling, businesses in all industries across the country were looking for a new source of entry-level employees. And with the new welfare laws, millions of former welfare recipients were looking for jobs.

Kate had the speech down pat. She finished her explanation at the same time she finished her steak. I hadn't eaten a bite. I was trying to take it all in, but my head was spinning with all the information.

I was not a political guy when I first moved to Washington. I never watched C-SPAN and although I voted, I rarely followed the specific issues. I didn't even know that there was a new welfare act passed in 1996.

"Are you finished with that?" the waiter asked.

"Oh, yeah, I guess," I said, realizing Kate had given me enough to digest.

"Don't worry about it," Kate said. "I'll send over some information about the Partnership. Read it and when you come back into town, we'll talk about it."

A week later, I moved into an exquisite three-level town house on Third and A street in Washington, four blocks from the Capitol. It was owned by UPS, so I was able to live there rent free. I was still very anxious because I didn't know exactly what I'd be doing.

Fortunately, Keith Jones, who held the job at the Partnership before me, agreed to spend a few days with me before I started to fill me in on all the details. Keith was a well-respected HR manager at UPS. He worked at the Partnership for eight months and then was promoted to a position in San Francisco.

"There is never a dull moment at the Partnership," Keith said. "Things are happening quick. It's going to be a great experience for you. You will have a great resource in Eli Segal. Listen to him and you will learn a lot."

"But what will I be doing?" I asked.

"Your job is to go talk about welfare to work," Keith said. "Encourage other businesses to get involved. Talk about what you did at the air hub and what UPS does."

"Okay," I said. "I can do that."

I didn't get my first chance until a month into the job. The U.S. Conference of Mayors was having a meeting in Washington, D.C. Eli asked me to speak about the Partnership. This would be a great opportunity to encourage the mayors to create and implement programs to help businesses hire people off welfare.

When I got to the meeting, I noticed the other speakers on the panel. One had a slide presentation, another had handouts, one had a PowerPoint presentation.

When it was my turn to speak, I walked up to the podium.

"I don't have any materials or slides," I said. "But I do have something I want to tell you."

I paused for a second and then told them about Billy. When I finished, the audience was dead silent. Then all of a sudden there was a smattering of applause. Following the meeting, there was a line of people waiting for me to say how much they enjoyed my story.

It was then that I knew this opportunity at the Welfare to Work Partnership was going to be something significant in my life. I didn't know where it was going to lead, but I knew it was where I was supposed to be.

16. Large Order of Wings

It was a year and a half later and I could still hear Scott Conaway announce, "I present to you the first class of our new training program at United Parcel Service: the V Formation graduation class."

I still shook my head in disbelief when I thought about everything I went through to get there.

There must be a reason for all this, I thought.

I walked into the warehouse after my excursion to Cabrini-Green, and was handed a letter made out to the Welfare to Work Partnership. It was from Kelly Shaheed, a former welfare recipient who had come to Chicago from Los Angeles to participate in a part of the conference called Faces of Welfare Reform. Kelly is a mother of three. She was on welfare for thirteen years before the new law forced her to look for work. Kelly's mother was on welfare before her and together they found a way to get through life on $140 a month.

It's easy for society to look at Kelly and see only her thirteen years on welfare. People on welfare face the stigma all the time. After a while, many start to believe it. But Kelly never did. Kelly loves to write poetry. She has her own collection of poems that reflect her life on welfare, from her marriage to an addict, to her first day on the job. After going to a job club in Los Angeles, Kelly was hired for an entry-level job at Sears as a sales representative. In less than a year, Kelly was promoted to a commissioned sales associate in the hardware department. Kelly woke up at 5:00 A.M. to get her three children ready for school—they now attend a school an hour outside the city—before taking public transportation to work. She takes a bus to catch a train before walking a mile and a half to Sears.

I took her letter to the corner of the warehouse and sat in one of the empty chairs. I opened the envelope and unfolded a note in beautiful cursive handwriting. It read:

> *Wondering what I did to deserve all of this; I have been deeply reflecting. Looking back at the struggles, and being able to see the rewards has always been a pleasure, but this time I am clearly seeing the rewards multiplied. What an excellent opportunity! Many would not participate in such an activity because they would not want the world to know they were on welfare. I wasn't proud to be on welfare but I wasn't ashamed either. Although I didn't work a 9–5, I was still a hard worker. I wasn't working but I wasn't stagnating either. I discovered myself, something worthy and priceless.*
>
> *Working at Sears and participating in this conference gives me an opportunity to give back to the system that gave so much to me. Everything I have said and done and can say or do will make me a better person. Working makes me a better person because it's positive, rewarding, different from being home, it's an added responsibility, an opportunity to grow and give a little more.*
>
> *I don't know exactly why I was chosen; but I do feel the efforts I have made to be a good Sears employee are being rewarded and I feel truly appreciated. The chance to see the president and other bigwigs are really the small joys. The big rewards are the people I meet. Those who directly touch my life, who openly and genuinely share of themselves. The fun I'll have can be paid for, but the feeling all of this has given me is priceless.*
>
> *—Written from a House of Blues Hotel room in Chicago during the One America Welfare to Work Partnership conference. August 1999.*

I reread the letter a few times. It reminded me of why we were here. Why the president was here. Because when it comes down to it, Welfare to Work is about people like Kelly. People who understand that a job can lead to bigger and better things.

Reading Kelly's letter and remembering Lucky, Billy, and Robert Speaks made me rethink my decision to skip the town hall meeting. Maybe Sharon from the White House knew best. Why don't I just do it the way she wanted? I could ad lib a little bit. I could stand in the right place and work with the president. And at least I would be there to help the other participants feel comfortable.

Normally, I'd talk this through with my boss and mentor Eli Segal, but he wasn't arriving until late in the evening because one of his best friends had died unexpectedly. Eli, President Clinton, Vice President Gore, and other friends and family were in Colorado for the funeral on Monday afternoon. I didn't want to bother him when he returned.

Eli was the first person, other than my grandmother, who has made me feel like I could accomplish my dreams. After a speech I gave at the Alliance to End Homelessness, Eli told me I was one of the greatest speakers he had ever heard.

"There's Clinton and then there's you," he said. "I don't know what happens to you, but when you get up there, you really connect with the audience. We need to get you and the president on the same stage someday."

It's difficult to quantify what Eli's rare combination of brilliance and compassion have meant to the country. He has dedicated his life to effecting social change. After his inauguration, President Clinton had asked Eli to start the Corporation for National Service, called AmeriCorps. In only four years, there were one hundred thousand young people serving in our communities while earning money to go to college.

When President Clinton was searching for the person to head the Welfare to Work Partnership, he had insisted on Eli, who he referred to as, "The best start-up guy on the planet." For the last three years, Eli has devoted himself to the Welfare to Work Partnership without taking a nickel of salary in return.

Eli had dedicated his professional life to helping other people. From the time he graduated from law school in 1967 he dedicated himself to getting a Democrat elected as president.

"Maybe you've heard of my candidates," Eli always joked. "They are President McCarthy, President McGovern, President Ted Kennedy, President Dukakis, President Hart, President Hart, and President Hart."

Despite the lack of success till then, Eli kept trying and in 1992, Arkansas Governor Bill Clinton asked Eli to be his chief of staff in his campaign for president. "Nobody really knows him," Eli remembers telling his wife, Phyllis. "But we'll give it a run."

When I moved to Washington, I knew very little about the political scene. After two months at the Partnership, Eli called me into his office and told me that he thought I could be a great secretary of transportation. At that point, I had no idea what the secretary of transportation did or whether or not it was something I wanted to be. But here was an expert in politics telling me what I could do, instead of what I couldn't.

It's his willingness to believe in others and help others believe in themselves that makes Eli so special. He focuses on how something can get done, not why it can't. It's that belief that people on welfare are not used to.

I decided that regardless of the circumstances, when Eli got into town, I would take a stand. I'd take Eli aside and explain that I couldn't do the town hall the way the White House wanted and if I tried, I wouldn't be true to him, the president, or myself. Then I'd tell him that either I do the town hall my way or not at all—"Give me liberty or give me death,"—to a slightly lesser degree, of course.

"I'm glad you're being honest with me," I imagined Eli telling me in response to my ultimatum. "We'll get someone else to do it."

I heard my stomach growl. It could have been the nervous feeling about the possibility that I was making the biggest mistake of my life, but for my sanity's sake, I assumed it was hunger. Unfortunately, I didn't have time to enjoy a quick bite at the rooftop banquet because I was scheduled to meet the rest of the participants in the town hall. We all left the earlier rehearsal with an uneasy feeling, so tonight's gathering was to answer any last-minute questions and hopefully make everyone feel more at ease. Sharon wasn't going to be there, so the atmosphere would be more relaxed.

I was a few minutes early and as the rest of the group filtered in, I saw Maria Mercado sitting alone in the bleachers behind the stage. She was in the exact spot she was supposed to be in for the town hall. I wondered if she had ever left, because I could see the fear still on her face. As I came closer, I would've bet even money she thought I was either going to tell her that she was out of the town hall thing or I was going to hammer her about what a poor job she was doing.

"Is this seat taken?" I asked, and sat down when she nodded. "Listen. Relax. You're going to do wonderfully tomorrow."

A small smile appeared on her face.

"You have an incredible story to tell. I know you're nervous because we are all nervous. Just tell your story. Tell them how you feel. Can you do that?"

"But the other lady . . ." Maria said.

I cut her off. "Don't worry about the White House lady," I said. "She's just doing her job. But she won't be with you tomorrow. It will just be me, you, and the president."

"What if I get nervous?" she asked.

"Just take your time and talk nice and slow." I tried to show her. " 'My—name—is—Maria—Mercado.' And take a breath. 'I'm—very—happy—to—be—here.' "

"Isn't—that—going—to—sound—funny?" she said, mocking the pauses. We both laughed.

"Your nervousness will make it go faster than it seems," I said. "Trust me, in your mind it will be slow, but for us it will be perfect. Take a deep breath. Collect your thoughts and just tell your story. Everyone is with you."

Maria and I were interrupted when Bobby Peedie, a sound technician, called everyone over to the stage to review a few last-second details.

"Make sure to speak into the microphone," said Bobby. "Place the microphone close to your mouth. Don't put your hand over the wire. Don't look into the television camera."

I saw a confused look on Maria's face. The same look spread to the other participants. I jumped in.

"Listen," I said. "Don't worry about the microphones. Don't worry about the television cameras, and don't worry about the president. Just be yourselves. You're here because we want *you* here, not an actor or a robot. Tomorrow, I'm going to be right here with you. I'm going to ask you, 'How are you doing?' If you're nervous say, 'Hey, I'm a little nervous.' It's okay. The most important part of tomorrow is that the world hears your story. That's what it's all about. That's what the president is here for. That's what the television cameras are here for, and that's why we're here."

I told everyone to take a deep breath, and Bobby gave a few more logistical details before the meeting ended. As the group filed out, I decided to take matters into my own hands. I chased down a few more people to offer some personal advice.

I told Bill Simmons not to worry about the thirty-second time limit. His story was so compelling that I wanted him to take his time and not leave out a single detail.

"No problem, Rodney," he said. "I'll follow your lead."

I told Rita Burns to include the story about her welfare-to-work hire. "I'll take care of the time, you just tell the story."

"Okay," she said.

Finally, I caught up to LaTonya Stephens. Bank of America pays her mother to take care of her children. It's one of the many innovative solutions Bank of America has implemented to help their welfare-to-work program succeed. "Talk about your mother and kids," I told her.

"No problem," she said.

I turned around and almost ran over Wendy Waxler.

"Wendy," I said. "Sorry about that. Is everything okay?"

"Fine, Mr. Carroll," she said. "I wanted to ask you what you thought about my speech."

Wendy was one of the people I didn't have to worry about and I told her that. It was obvious from the morning rehearsal that she was an intelligent, confident woman who was somehow balancing a job and taking care of her child. As she walked away, one thought occurred to me and I called her back. In the morning rehearsal, she had told us that she was a workaholic. Sharon insisted that she stay on message, but that word stuck with me.

"I'm a workaholic."

I thought it was a critical message. There's a perception out there that people on welfare don't want to work. That they're lazy. Here's a woman whose first statement out of her mouth is: "I need to work." It wasn't in the script. But I told her to include it when she spoke. She said she would.

As the room emptied I felt much better about the town hall. I knew that the governors and mayors would be fine and I was confident about the corporate executives. Now I knew Bill Simmons would be great. LaTonya Stephens would be fantastic. I already had a good feeling about Wendy Waxler. Rita Burns would do well. I was still a little nervous about Maria Mercado.

I remember watching the NBA playoffs a few years back when I saw an interview with Karl Malone, the power forward for the Utah Jazz. In the interview, Malone was asked a question about pressure.

He said most people didn't understand what real pressure was. Real pressure meant that everyone was depending on you to come through in the clutch. Day in and day out.

I realized that Malone was only half right. It's true that many people didn't understand what real pressure was. But it wasn't making a game-winning shot at the buzzer. What many people don't understand is that there is little pressure greater than trying to lift a family out of welfare. A family that depends on you every single day. Real pressure was what welfare recipients on this stage and throughout the country were trying to overcome every day. The quiet work of transforming their lives. The hard work, day in and day out, of making a better life for their families.

I was honored to be with this group of people in the town hall. Then I remembered that chances were that I wasn't going to be in the town hall at all. I laid down on the bleachers, put my hands over my face, and took a deep breath. The truth was I had no idea what was going to happen. The only thing I could do was wait to speak with Eli.

Luckily someone brought cheeseburgers and french fries to my final meeting of the day and the rest of the staff and I ate while we waited for Eli. It was about 10:00 P.M. and I had inhaled one burger and was working on the second when Eli walked in. He appeared emotionally and physically tired, but Eli is never one to dump his problems on others and as soon as he saw us, he was all smiles.

After the staff greeted Eli and conveyed their condolences, we had a chance to be alone while people finished eating. I walked him to the front of the warehouse to see the ten-by-ten-foot display of our business partners and success stories. The display was his idea and I knew he'd be excited to see it.

"Looks great," Eli responded. "Now, what's making you anxious?"

With the staff waiting, it was not the right time to delve into my problem. "There is something I want to talk to you about," I answered. "But I don't want to talk about it here."

"I'll tell you what we'll do," Eli said as we walked back to the group. "After our meeting, why don't we go back to the hotel room and talk there? Maybe we'll get something more to eat."

"That's perfect," I said. I was still hungry.

The meeting went quickly, and by 11:00 P.M. we were in Eli's suite in the House of Blues Hotel in downtown Chicago. Jonathan Tisch, the president and CEO of Loews Hotels, is on the Partnership's board of directors, and he and Eli are good friends, so he hooked Eli up with a fabulous suite.

We sat in the living room. There was an office with a computer and fax machine off the living room where Eli's assistant was working. Eli sat down on the leather couch and I pulled an ottoman to the other side of a coffee table.

"I'm just going to have a salad," Eli said, handing me the room-service menu. "What do you want?" Eli is always on some sort of a diet, but he loves junk food. Usually, all he needs is a little nudge to get him off track and I'm just the guy to do it.

"I think I'll have the chicken wings," I said.

"Ooh, chicken wings," Eli said as his eyes lit up. "Why don't we order a large?"

Eli picked up the phone and started to order. "We'll have a salad, and give us a large order of chicken wings. And, on second thought, no salad. Just throw in some fried shrimp and, uh, some chicken fingers."

While we waited for the food I figured Eli was going to be anxious to talk, but we didn't have a chance. As soon as Eli hung up, his assistant brought in a copy of the president's speech for the next morning. We sat on the couch and Eli started reading the speech aloud.

I thought this was pretty cool because we were reading tonight what the president was going to say tomorrow. It wasn't a big deal to Eli; he made some changes and gave it back to his assistant to fax back to the White House.

There was a knock on the door. The food had arrived. It was almost 12:30 and I was getting nervous because we still hadn't talked. The town hall was nine and a half hours away, the president's speech was complete, and I had no idea what I was going to do tomorrow.

"So what is it you want to talk about?" Eli asked as he dipped a chicken finger into a bowl of honey mustard sauce.

I didn't know where to begin, so I blurted out, "The rehearsal for the town hall was a disaster." Eli looked up. "We had people crying, the real stories weren't coming out, and there was all kinds of confusion."

I thought Eli would be taken aback to hear all this so late, but he was calm. "Hold on. Let's start at the beginning. What are you talking about?"

I calmed down a little and leaned back in my seat. I figured I'd start slowly.

"Number one," I said. "They want me to read what I'm going to say."

"Absolutely not," Eli interrupted. "That's not going to happen. You are much better when you speak from the heart. What's next?"

That went well, I thought to myself.

"Okay," I went on. "Number two. I'm supposed to cut the president off if he's talking too long."

"That's ridiculous. You're going to tell the president of the United States that he's talking too long?"

"That's what they want me to do," I said, lifting my shoulders.

"You can't do that," Eli said. "The president is sharp enough. He'll know when he's talking too long. If he's got something to say, then the American people want to hear it. Don't even give that a second thought. What's next?"

At this point I felt pretty good. I cut to the chase.

"I'm supposed to get up on the stage and not say anything about my own experience. I'm supposed to start off by saying, 'Here we have Wendy Waxler from Xerox.' "

"Oh no. No. No. Absolutely not," Eli said, raising his voice. "You gotta go up there and give them Rodney Carroll."

"I agree," I said. "But the White House staff does this all the time and they said I should follow the script."

"The White House staff?" Eli responded. "They don't know Rodney Carroll. I know Rodney Carroll."

"I'm telling you," I tried to explain. "They said this isn't about me. It is the president's show."

"Look," Eli said. "You have to trust me. I don't know exactly what happens to you when you get up in front of an audience. But you're brilliant. You gotta get up there and be yourself."

"I should just ignore their instructions?" I said innocently, like I hadn't been thinking of doing it the whole time. Then I said, "The problem is nobody will be prepared for me to speak. We didn't go over it at rehearsal. The president won't expect it."

"You have to trust me on this," Eli said. "I'll talk to the president tomorrow morning."

A small part of me was hoping Eli wouldn't be so accommodating. Now that I had made my demands, all the crutches were gone. If I messed up, I'd have no excuses. For the first time, I was a little nervous.

I stammered for another excuse.

"But-but, do you know that I won't be able to use the podium?" I said and explained the reasoning.

"Then don't use the podium," Eli said, dismissing the excuse.

"Well, well, it's a circular stage," I explained. "We have people in a 270-degree circumference and I'm never supposed to be behind the president or in front of the president. It's impossible." At this point it was obvious that I was simply making excuses.

"Look," Eli said matter-of-factly. "It's not that hard. Just use common sense. Don't stand directly in front of him. There're three or four different cameras, they'll pick up the right angle. You're working with professionals. You'll be fine. You're worrying for nothing."

There was nothing else to say. Eli had taken care of every concern.

We both sat back. I leaned my head back and stared at the ceiling fan. Eli was polishing off the last chicken wing. After a few minutes of silence, he looked at me and said, "Are you alright with this?" I didn't say anything.

It was 1:30 A.M. Eli had just returned from one of his best friends' funerals. He hadn't slept in almost twenty-four hours and his organization was in the middle of the biggest conference in the history of welfare to work. But instead of focusing on his own problems, Eli was worrying about mine. He leaned forward and placed his glass on the coffee table.

"This is the opportunity of a lifetime," he said, looking me right in the eye. "It could last for ninety minutes, for three days, or the rest of your life. But you have to be prepared to go after it. A lot of people never get a chance to show what they are capable of. They think about it. They talk about it. But they find some way to avoid it. The truth is, unless you are prepared to fully expose yourself, you'll never know how good you can be.

"Tomorrow, you and the president of the United States are going to be working hand in hand on a topic that nobody in the country knows better than you. There are people in the audience that will be amazed. They'll be amazed at where you started and they'll be amazed at how you got here. But you can never let an opportunity pass. Because there's no guarantee it's going to ever come back.

"There are millions of people that are going to be encouraged and inspired by the stories they hear tomorrow, but only if you are there to bring them out. I have tremendous faith in you. You're made for this. This is your time. This is your shining moment."

By the time I got back to my room, it was 1:45 A.M. I had a radio interview at 6:00 so I got a wake-up call for 5:45. My mind was racing. What was I going to say? How was I going to remember everyone's name? What if Eli couldn't talk to the president? What if I let him down? I was in no shape to write my speech so I decided to grab a quick shower and get some sleep.

I hit the pillow by about 2:00 A.M. and at 2:30 I noticed that I wasn't asleep yet. I had a full day ahead of me—after the radio interview, I had a board meeting at 7:00 A.M., a breakfast at 8:00 A.M., the town hall at 10:20, Faces of Welfare Reform at 3:00 P.M., and a dinner honoring Gerald Greenwald, the Chairman of the Board of Directors for the Partnership at 6:00 P.M.

I figured that if I wasn't going to sleep, I better do some work, so I got out of bed, sat at the desk, turned on the light, and grabbed a pencil.

"Okay," I said out loud. "The first person I'm going to talk to is Wendy Wilson. Wendy Wilson." I can't think. "Who's Wendy Wilson?" I threw the pencil over my shoulder. "I can't believe it," I said. "I'm gonna say, 'Wendy Wilson' and her first words are going to be, 'No, my name is Wendy Waxler.' "

I decided not to take any chances so I grabbed the White House notes and started writing down everyone's name on a sheet of paper. I figured that at the very least I'll get the names right. The writing made me tired and at 2:50 I put my head down on the pillow. Next thing I knew, the phone rang for my wake-up call.

It seemed like two minutes, but I got right out of bed. This is it.

I got a glass of water to clear my voice and called the radio station in New York a few minutes early. The interview went well. I turned on the shower. As the bathroom steamed up, I cleared a circle in the mirror to brush my teeth. I looked closely in the mirror and was reminded that my bottom teeth were crooked. It was a healthy reminder of where I had come from. When you grow up on welfare you don't see a dentist unless it's an absolute emergency. I didn't go to a dentist until I was seventeen years old. If I had a toothache my grandmother made a concoction of warm salt water and honey to take the pain away.

I took a shower and put on a double-breasted, pin-striped suit and a gold tie with red polka dots. The tie was flashier than I normally wore, but I knew the president always sported nice ties and I wanted to fit in. I placed the sheet of names in my inside coat pocket and was about to leave the room when I stopped.

I learned my faith from my grandmother. My whole life I saw a woman who lived in heartbreaking poverty and stress, yet she was always happy and at peace. Her spirit was always alive. One time I asked her, "Don't you ever get sad?" And she told me about the true meaning behind faith.

"It's the peace and strength that comes from within," she said.

I began to seek that out. I started to believe that if I tried to do the right thing then God would direct my path. It's hard, because sometimes I couldn't see it right away, but today I saw things clearly. Before I left the room, I said a prayer.

God, ever since I can remember, I've been interested in people with great character and how they became influential in our society. I believe that from the time I was little, God, You've been preparing me for this moment. Because as I look back at it, that's the only way I can make sense out of my life. It's too much to be a coincidence. So I'm going to trust in You. In Jesus' name, I pray. Amen.

The staff met in the lobby at 6:50 A.M. and when Eli walked in, I ran at him asking if he had talked to the president yet.

"Are you joking?" Eli said. "It's seven o'clock in the morning."

"Oh, yeah," I said, sheepishly.

Following the board meeting, I met Secretary of Transportation Rodney Slater, Wisconsin governor Tommy Thompson, and Chicago mayor Richard Daley in the holding room before the breakfast. After some brief pleasantries, they all rehearsed their speeches, so I pulled the paper from my pocket to review the names in my head.

Athletes often talk about being in the zone. Basketball players say it's when the basket looks like it's five feet wide and everything they shoot goes in. Football players say it's when the defense looks like they're running in slow motion, and baseball players say it's when the ball looks like it's the size of a grapefruit.

I had only been in the zone once before, but for some reason, I was now in the "town hall" zone. The names rolled off my tongue with the rhythm of a metronome: "Wendy Waxler, Rita Burns, Tiffany Smith, Antoinette Patrick, Bill Simmons, Tyler Left Hand, Governor Tom Carper, Mayor Wellington Webb, Joanne Hilferty, Ted English, Maria Mercado, LaTonya Stephens, Cathy Bessant, Jonathan Tisch, Consuelo McGlound."

There was no hesitation in my voice. It was like the participants were lined up in my mind's eye with giant name tags. I tried it again, with the same results.

I'm all over this, I thought. Unbelievable.

I listed them by topic: "Wendy Waxler and disabled child at big company; Rita Burns and small company; Tiffany Smith and transportation issue; Antoinette Patrick and training program; Bill Simmons and alcohol and substance abuse; Tyler Left Hand, a Native American and a single father; Governor Tom Carper and his father's program; Wellington Webb and cities; Maria Mercado and an industry-based training partnership with Goodwill; LaTonya Stephens and subsidized child care and home ownership at Bank of America; Jonathan Tisch and hotel association banding together to hire welfare recipients in Miami-Dade County with America Works."

I reviewed different scenarios: If Wendy Waxler doesn't remember to say disabled child, I'll say, "I bet your daughter is very proud of you. And I know all children are special, but your child is even more special."

If Maria Mercado starts crying, I'll say, "Maria, there are many times where I had my own tears trying to make sense of this or hoping I got an opportunity, and I know your tears are tears of joy."

I felt confident. Now all I had to worry about was Eli talking with the president.

The morning cruised by. It was less than thirty minutes till the town hall. After breakfast, the CEOs, cabinet secretaries, and other elected and appointed government officials were rushed up the steps and into yet another holding room to wait for the president. Then all of a sudden, President Clinton and Eli entered the room. We took a quick picture before Eli started introducing President Clinton to everyone—starting on the opposite side from where I was.

Just before they got to me, I pulled Eli aside like a little kid.

"You have to talk to the president," I begged him.

Eli grabbed my arm. "Mr. President, this is Rodney Carroll."

"Oh, yes," said President Clinton. "It's going to be an honor to do the town hall with you." That was the first time I truly believed that this was really going to happen.

"No, sir," I said. "The honor will be all mine."

Then Eli made good on his promise. "Mr. President," Eli said, "Rodney is one of the greatest speakers that I've ever heard. I think we should let him say a few words in the beginning. You won't be disappointed. You have my word on it."

I was frozen while the president thought for a couple of seconds. Then he turned to me and said, "Okay, I'll tell you what we'll do. You go ahead and take charge out there. If you get stuck, I'll jump in. But other than that, it's your show."

17. It's God's Fault

I was extremely nervous. My seat was in the front row on the right of the stage, about fifteen feet from the president's podium. Eli, Mayor Daley, and the president were scheduled to open the event with brief comments. After the president spoke, the podium would be removed and we would use hand microphones. The microphones were next to three bottles of water on a small coffee table between two chairs on stage.

Wait a minute, I thought as I found my seat. I need the microphone to deliver my speech.

"I don't have a mike," I mouth to Bobbie Peedie, the sound technician. All of a sudden, a voice comes over the loudspeaker.

"Ladies and gentlemen, the founding partners of the Welfare to Work Partnership, Gerald Greenwald of United Airlines, Paul Clayton of Burger King, Bill Esrey of Sprint corporation, Jim Kelly of United Parcel Service of America, and Bob Shapiro of the Monsanto Company."

The crowd applauded.

"Ladies and gentlemen, Mayor Paul Helmkie, Mayor Wellington Webb, Mayor Marc Morial, Mayor Beverly O'Neill, Governor Tom Carper, Governor Tommy Thompson, and Governor George Ryan."

Applause.

"Ladies and gentlemen, Secretary of Commerce William Daley, Secretary of Labor Alexis Herman, Secretary of Transportation Rodney Slater, and Administrator Aida Alvarez of the Small Business Administration."

Applause.

"Ladies and gentlemen, the President of the United States, accompanied by Mayor Richard M. Daley and Eli Segal."

As the president walked out from behind the large blue curtain in the back of the stage, there was a standing ovation. I could feel the electricity in the room. During the ovation, Bobbie grabbed one of the two microphones.

"Good luck," he told me and handed me the mike. "You're going to need it."

Beads of sweat dripped off my forehead. My hands were damp. The collar of my shirt felt tight. I heard my heart beating through my suit. I tried to relax but I couldn't. When the crowd settled down, Eli calmly walked to the podium to commence the event.

"Good morning, everybody. When Congress passed and President Clinton signed the new welfare law, President Clinton challenged the American business community to help end welfare as we know it. Now, three years later, more than twenty-five hundred Welfare to Work leaders, including over one thousand businesses from across the country, have come to Chicago to say that we are on our way."

The audience applauded. Eli paused suitably and continued.

"By choosing partnerships over partisanship and citizenship over cynicism, we know that Welfare to Work is working."

Again, applause.

"But today, my friends, is not about self-congratulation. Today has to be viewed as an end to the beginning and the beginning of the end of welfare as we know it.

"During this conference, we have the country's most innovative minds and creative spirits all gathered in one place. By working to-gether, my friends, we can complete this job. You know, when you get right down to it, Welfare to Work is not all that complicated. Busi-nesses need workers, and people need jobs. Let's continue to fight for a better future for all Americans. Thank you very much."

Mayor Daley was the next to speak. He was a pro. He welcomed the crowd, his fellow mayors, and the president to Chicago, discussed the bipartisan nature of Welfare to Work, and thanked the president for "providing the leadership and common-sense legislation." Again, the crowd applauded. Mayor Daley then introduced "the man whose vision has given so many of our fellow citizens an opportunity to real-ize the American dream, our president, the President of the United States, William Jefferson Clinton."

Already, I thought to myself. Eli was fast. Mayor Daley was really fast and I'm next. The last twenty-four hours seemed to last a lifetime, now in a matter of minutes, my opportunity of a lifetime would be here.

I tried to listen to the president's speech, but I couldn't. I was too nervous. I tried to focus on what I was going to say and how I was going to say it, but my mind kept wandering.

First to Rodney Slater and Bill Daley and Jim Kelly and Gerald Greenwald—all the people I respected who were going to have to sit and listen to me speak. I thought about all the welfare recipients I represented. I thought about the companies in The Partnership. I thought about all the people in the audience and the millions more watching on television. I thought about Maria Mercado and Reta Burns and Consuelo McGlond and the rest of the participants in the town hall. If I was this nervous, how must they be feeling?

Then I realized that nobody except the president and Eli expected me to give a speech. The White House, the Partnership staff, even Eli thinks there is supposed to be a dialogue between the president, the town hall guests, and me. What are people going to think when the president doesn't speak?

It's not going to work, I thought. This is crazy. This is stupid. Everyone will be wondering why the president isn't talking. How can he just sit onstage for so long and not say a word?

I tried not to perspire, but the harder I tried, the more I did. I was drenched. I took deep breaths but it didn't help. I took quick short breaths, but that didn't help either. The president was cruising though his remarks, describing his vision for the future of Welfare to Work.

"We have to strengthen our commitment to child care. For years, mothers on welfare chose not to work because, to do so, would literally have hurt their children because it would have cost them more in child care than they could make on the job. In 1996, we added four billion dollars to our child-care subsidy, but believe it or not, we have only met one-tenth of the need."

He spoke with grace and ease. What was Eli thinking? I was not in the president's league. The crowd was more enthusiastic than ever and I was more anxious than I have ever been in my life. Finally, I couldn't take it anymore. I was putting too much pressure on myself. I needed a release.

"God," I said. "I'm putting this in Your hands. You brought me this far and if I screw up, it's Your fault."

I don't know exactly why that simple statement made me feel so calm, but it did. Suddenly, the sweat dried up, my heartbeat slowed down. I was at ease. I was confident. I was in the zone. An instant later, the president finished his remarks.

"The great Russian writer, Leo Tolstoy, once said that work is the true source of human welfare. In this era of unprecedented prosperity, we still have some work of our own to do to make sure that we embrace all Americans in this prosperity and to give every American the chance to succeed at work and to succeed at home.

"I thank every one of you for what you have done, and I ask you to support the initiatives I outlined with the Congress and to stay at the job until we can literally say we have completely ended welfare as we know it and America is a better place because our families are stronger, our children are growing up in more stable homes, and every adult American who is willing to work has a chance to do so.

"Thank you very, very much."

He waited through the shower of applause.

"Now we get to the interesting part of the program," the president said. "I'd now like to introduce a man who knows about welfare reform from every conceivable perspective. He was on welfare as a child and as a young adult. As a businessman he built a first-of-its-kind welfare-to-work program that has helped countless Americans reclaim their independence and he is now leading the country to help end welfare as we know it. He's a truly remarkable man and we are grateful for his services. I would like to ask him to come forward now and take over the program."

This was my moment. There was no turning back. I approached the stage cautiously. The stage was raised about three feet off the ground. I knew my toughest hurdle may be getting on stage without tripping, so I made sure to lift my leg extra high. I headed for the president with my hand outstretched.

"Thank you, Mr. President," I said, although nobody heard me because my microphone was not turned on. The problem was immediately fixed. I switched the mike to my left hand, gave the president a strong, firm handshake, and switched the mike back to my right hand. The president sat down on one of the stools. At that point I wasn't concerned with any of the rules that Sharon had lectured me about during rehearsal. I wasn't concerned with anything. I turned to the audience to begin my remarks.

"Mr. President and members of this audience, I am not sure if you can see this or not, but in my hand, there is a glass. Now, if you can't see this glass in my hand with your eyesight, perhaps you can see it with your insight. For those of you who have either limited eyesight or insight, I will describe this glass for you.

"The glass is about so high, and in it there is water up to the halfway mark. Of those of you that can see this glass, some will see it is half empty, others will see it is half full. Same glass, same water in the same glass, yet two different perspectives."

President Clinton and Eli were the only people who knew I was going to speak. I looked around to see confused faces in the audience—they had no idea what I was talking about. My colleagues at the Partnership were bewildered—this was not part of the script. Sharon stood by the curtain that concealed the technical equipment. It was her job to signal to me if the program was running too long or too short. She looked absolutely appalled. But I remained confident. I knew what I was doing. I took my time and continued.

"I would like to open this town hall by talking to you on the subject of perspective. It seems that everyone has his or her own perspective. Remember what I said about the glass of water—half full to some, half empty to others. And let us apply that same analogy to welfare recipients. Two different companies could view a welfare recipient from two different perspectives. One company might think hiring a welfare recipient would be a liability. Yet, another company might see the same welfare recipients as an asset. Some companies may see the problems involved in training. Others see the training as an obstacle, but they know that given proper training, welfare recipients by and large can make good, productive employees. Same person, two different perspectives. Why?

"Does it have to do with age, gender, race, religion?

"I grew up in Philadelphia. In Philadelphia on the Parkway, there is a building called the Philadelphia Art Museum. About twenty years ago, I used to have a friend who always tried to talk me into going to the art museum. We would negotiate back and forth, but finally she won and we took in an exhibit.

"So we get there, and we take in the art. We look at the paintings. I remember one and her saying, 'Unbelievable.' 'Sure,' I said, 'it's unbelievable they would charge that much money for that painting.'"

The crowd laughed. It was music to my ears. I glanced back to see the president cracking up. I saw Alexis Herman, Gerald Greenwald, Eli all smiling. Rodney Slater, whom I consider to be one of the country's greatest speakers, even seemed engaged. Sharon, of course was aghast.

"What the heck is he doing?" she asked Elissa Johnson, one of my colleagues at the Partnership.

"He's doing great," Elissa responded. I didn't look Sharon's way for the remainder of the program. I focused on my story.

"I remember yet another time, there were these large pieces of art. They had a lot of colors, I guess this was a showpiece of the exhibit, and I remember her saying, 'This piece of art is speaking to me.' I said, 'What?' She said, 'It is speaking to me.' I said, 'Well, what is it saying?' She said, 'This piece of art says that I am alive and I can soar and I can do things in my life.' I said, 'That piece of art is saying that to you?' She said, 'Yeah.' I said, 'Well, you know, it's speaking to me, too.' She said, 'Well, what is it saying?' I said, 'It's telling me that if you hurry, you can still catch the second half of the game.'"

Again, laughter. This was getting better and better. I was in a groove. I could go on and on but I stopped myself. There were still seventeen success stories left to be told and I knew my job was to make sure they were heard.

"I probably neglected to tell you that while she was in college, my friend had taken three or four semesters of art history. As a matter of fact, she had studied art abroad. What I would like to suggest to you this morning is that perhaps one reason why different people see things from different perspectives has to do with education or their comprehension of the subject. In other words, companies that understand who welfare recipients are, and more important, who they are not, generally have a different approach to hiring."

Applause.

"Now take this person standing here next to me. I am not sure how you see this person, but let me tell you what you should see. You need to see a person who is living in poverty, a person whose life is filled with despair. Even in a time of unparalleled prosperity, this person is still not able to participate. This is a person just looking for an opportunity, looking for a chance, in some cases a second chance. All that this person wants is what all of us want. The dignity and pride that a good job brings."

Applause.

"You might be wondering how it is that I see the glass. You probably guessed that I see the glass as it relates to this as half full. But you see, that would not quite be correct because, when it comes to transitioning people's lives from dependence to independence, from reaching down and giving someone a hand up, or in this effort as far as Welfare to Work, not only do I see the glass as half full, but I can clearly see the waiter on his way to my table to fill the glass.

"Thank you."

I listened to the applause and I was satisfied with the speech. It hadn't been long, and I was in good shape to present the success stories. I thought to myself, "God, so far so good."

I was glad that Wendy Waxler was the first. She was poised during the rehearsal and she was even better now.

I addressed the audience. "Now I'd like you to hear from some of the extraordinary people who are the true heroes behind welfare reform. Our first speaker is Wendy Waxler.

"Wendy, how about telling us of your own experience, and how you like your job." Wendy stood up, took hold of the microphone with both hands, and said, "I consider myself a workaholic." She talked about her daughter's disability, what it meant to be self-sufficient, and how Xerox continued to support her in every way. "This company not only took me in as an employee, it took me in as a member of the family. It treated me like a daughter."

With that, Wendy had set the perfect tone for the day. That word "workaholic," did it. Who would ever associate such a word with a welfare recipient?

I didn't have to worry about the next speaker. Bill McDermott was a senior vice president at Xerox. He was articulate, charming, and smart. In today's competitive business environment where executives tend to focus more attention on balance sheets than on balanced lives, it spoke volumes for a company when one of its employees feels like she was being treated like a "member of the family," as Wendy had put it. Bill McDermott spoke eloquently about the specifics of a Xerox program that had hired some four hundred people from welfare ranks with an impressive 76 percent retention rate.

"On day one, when a welfare recipient comes to work at Xerox, that person has a mentor. They help them through the training. This is the digital economy.

"The second thing we do is focus on the aspirations of the person. Hopes and dreams belong to everybody in America. We have now opened up a line of credit for all the former welfare recipients who have moved to meaningful work at Xerox. We have given them a free Visa credit card, and we provide personal financial planning to them so they, in fact, can get their piece of the American dream."

The program sailed on smoothly.

Reta Burns represented both small business owners and welfare recipients admirably when she told the story of an employee who had been hired as general office help.

"One day she came to me and asked me why we wouldn't go after a certain contract. 'We're a small business,' I explained. 'It's lack of resources.' She offered to take the project on, on her own time, working with some of our technical folks. And she won that contract. She has won several since. The interesting thing is she is a single mother of five kids without a high school diploma."

Before Tiffany Smith spoke of her plan for a long career at UPS, I took the opportunity to address Jim Kelly.

"Now, there is one company I know a little bit about because I have been fortunate to work there for over twenty-one years, and that is United Parcel Service. Here today with the United Parcel Service is the chairman and CEO, Jim Kelly. I would like to take this moment to publicly thank Jim Kelly and the UPS team for allowing me to have this great experience. Thank you, Jim."

Jim Kelly acknowledged the applause. I went back to Tiffany.

"Tiffany, I understand you have some ambitions of your own. This is a good time to talk about them, so the chairman can hear it."

Tiffany turned to Mr. Kelly. "I'm starting night school for my GED in September and I have filed a letter of intent to become a supervisor at the United Parcel Service for day hub. And from there on, I hope to go further."

I could see President Clinton giving his undivided attention to every speaker. He turned in his seat to hear Rosemary Mede, senior vice president from CVS Pharmacy, describe her company's apprenticeship program, which puts welfare recipients into promotional-track jobs.

"It is a two-year program that combines work under the guidance of registered pharmacists and learning. There are over six hundred classroom hours that our apprentices put in. It is a three-track program. So we have three levels of achievement ending in lead technician, and then if our apprentices choose to go on to a career in pharmacy, they can take advantage of our educational benefits and loans, or if they choose store management, they can move into assistant store manager. By the way, we hired over four thousand people in the last three years. Our retention rate is about seventy percent, which is way off the charts for us, double the average."

Rosemary then introduced Antoinette, a graduate of the program.

"I put myself in their shoes," Antoinette said, speaking of the customers. "Because I know they are in pain and I try to fill their prescriptions accurately and quickly."

"That is wonderful," I said. "Thank you very much."

Bill Simmons from Master Lube was entrancing. Tyler Left Hand, who grew up on the Crow reservation, captivated the audience when he described his journey off the reservation.

"I had to struggle through a lot of hardships. And I don't want my daughter to go through all that. So I had to take her off the reservation with me. It is an honor to be here to represent Master Lube and the Crow tribe."

"That's outstanding," I said. "Give him a round of applause."

By the time we got to Delaware Governor Tom Carper, the town hall was on cruise control. The other participants and I had developed a rhythm. The crowd was responsive all the way. I could feel it. President Clinton was having a ball. He laughed. He was engaged. I made sure to keep a close eye on the president's microphone that lay on the table next to him. So far, it hadn't moved.

Governor Carper's commitment to welfare reform is well documented. Thanks to his "A Better Chance" program, the welfare rolls in Delaware have decreased by 46 percent. He focuses most of his attention on reaching noncustodial fathers. He has created a bridge

program to provide intensive case management to eliminate substance abuse as an obstacle to successful employment. And he is
helping those who have found work stay on the job with mentoring
and transportation programs. Along with all that, he is one of the
most genuine, caring people that I have ever met.

I knew that Governor Carper was anxious to discuss his father's
program in Delaware, but he caught me off guard with the way he
began his remarks.

"Rodney Carroll, I don't know how you are doing it," he said.
"This guy is doing all of his introductions and everything without a
script. How do you do this?"

The crowd applauded.

"I am looking at the president to see if his lips are moving when
you speak. You are amazing. You are amazing. Do you want to move
to Delaware?"

Again the crowd applauded. I was embarrassed. It was nice, but I
knew if I got cocky, I might get too relaxed and make a mistake.
There were still six people to go.

Governor Carper dedicated the rest of his remarks to a heartfelt
testament to the importance of fathers.

"The president mentioned child-support enforcement. It is important that the dads who owe money to their children meet their financial responsibilities, but it is also important to note that those
of us who become dads—I became a first-time father at the age of
forty-one—don't just have an obligation to put food on the table.
We have an obligation to love that child. I love being governor of
Delaware. I love being chairman of the National Governors Association, which our president used to be. But the thing I love most in my
life is being a dad."

With that, I felt we were right back on track. But Denver mayor
Wellington Webb—the president of the Conference of Mayors—
started his remarks the same way as Governor Carper.

"First, let me say that UPS has a secret weapon they have been
using, Mr. President. His name is Rodney Carroll. And to Jim Kelly, I
just want to add that when Rodney Carroll came to Denver, we had a
Welfare to Work Partnership meeting with our chamber of commerce, trying to get our employers involved in providing jobs and opportunity. Rodney was the keynote speaker, and by the time he

finished, we had them lined up at the desk. Rodney, I want to thank you for coming to Denver for that."

I smiled to acknowledge the compliment—Mayor Webb is one of the most respected mayors in the country. But I didn't want the attention on me any more than it already was. Fortunately, Mayor Webb's speech focused the attention right back where it needed to be.

"As president of the U.S. Conference of Mayors, one of the goals that we have and we are very much concerned with is that we want Congress to hear the message that the president has put forth in the budget—a billion dollars to provide support for a program that works. Let's not challenge the success. Let's not punish success.

"The welfare rates are going down, but the people who are left, most are in our cities, and many of those are the hardest to place. They need more resources. We need more resources, not less resources, and we need to get that message to Congress."

After Mayor Webb, the program shifted toward partnerships between businesses and community-based organizations in helping transform people's lives.

"One such example exists between TJX and Goodwill," I said. "And we have representatives Joanne Hilferty and Ted English here today. Joanne, welcome."

Joanne talked about the importance of industry-specific or industry-based training for retail.

"We work collectively with the Boston Private Industry Council. The program starts with a three-week training program in the classroom, and in that, we address work readiness. We address all of the issues around customer service, and we help people get their lives organized for going to work, but we don't stop there.

"It then moves to a five-week internship in a TJX or Goodwill store, where the individual is paid for that internship and has a chance to work out many of those issues related to starting to go into work, if you haven't worked in a long time.

"The carrot is the guaranteed job with benefits if you can complete that internship. We have had a tremendous success rate with that."

Ted English then announced that TJX was experiencing a 90-percent retention rate among its early graduates from the First Step program.

"And twenty percent of those associates have already been promoted," he added. "Based on this success, we are currently in the process of implementing a First Step Program in Atlanta, and right here in Chicago. We are very pleased with our association with Goodwill, and with their help, we are sure going to put a lot more people back to work."

As Ted English concluded, I glanced at Maria Mercado. She was next. I prepared myself for anything. If she couldn't speak, I was going to tell her story the best I could. If she spoke too fast, I was going to say, "No rush, we have plenty of time." Just as we had practiced in rehearsal, she stood up and took the microphone as I introduced her.

"Maria Mercado is also here," I said. "She is one of the graduates of the program at TJX. How are you doing, Maria?"

"Fine," Maria said. "And you?"

There was a light chuckle from the crowd.

"I am doing just fine. Thanks for asking. Tell us a little bit about the training program at TJX and how you like working there."

Maria paused for a split second. I could tell she was organizing her thoughts. Then she took a deep breath.

"The first decision that I made was to participate in the First Step Program, to prepare myself to go back to the real work," she said slowly and clearly. "The day my internship came at one of the stores, Marshalls in Boston, I started as a cashier. After a week, I was made a full-time employee. After two months, I was promoted to sales associate in the ladies department. Now I am participating in a program that is called Come and Grow With Us. This program has given me the opportunity and the training to become a coordinator of the ladies department area."

The audience loved it. How could they not? Maria might not have been the most eloquent, but she was a good communicator. She was genuine. I know people who work in corporate America every day who couldn't give a two-minute speech in front of the president of the United States, but here was a woman who had been slighted her entire life, who the day before had been told that she may be removed from the program, who had every excuse to collapse, but hadn't. Instead she was strong and confident. The fact is that if someone can overcome poverty and hopelessness, then they can do anything, and Maria was living proof of that.

"That's wonderful," I said. But Maria wasn't done yet. When the applause died she continued to speak.

"I am very proud of myself for having accomplished so much in such a short time, and have become a dependable person, with the support of my two beautiful daughters, my family, Goodwill, and Marshalls. And thanks from the bottom of my heart to the TJX company."

Again, the crowd erupted. The president beamed. I didn't have to worry about the attention falling on me anymore. Maria had clearly stolen the show.

"Thank you very much," I told her. "Well done. Very well done. Fabulous."

Eli was sitting four rows below Maria. As I was about to introduce the next speaker I saw Eli pointing frantically at the president. I shot Eli a glance as if to say, "What is up?" He continued to point and then mouthed, "Get the president involved."

"I can't believe the president isn't saying anything," he whispered to Mayor Daley. "This is a disaster."

"Are you kidding me?" Mayor Daley whispered back. "This is the best thing I've ever seen. The president is loving it."

I looked at the president—he was grinning from ear to ear. I looked at his microphone—it was still lying in the same spot on the table. I began my next intro by trying to include him.

"Mr. President, I know one of your concerns, like all of ours, is child care. Bank of America has a great story." I paused, waiting for him to comment. But he said nothing. He winked and casually turned his chair thirty degrees clockwise to face LaTonya Stephens. I felt completely at ease.

"Mr. President, I would like to introduce to you LaTonya Stephens, who works for Bank of America. She has been a banking assistant in Dallas, Texas, for about a year. Bank of America offers an incredible array of services to train and retain former welfare recipients. They also offer tuition assistance and even home-buyer assistance."

Like everyone else in the program, LaTonya described her feelings about moving from welfare to work. She had won a trip to Beverly Hills for having the top performance in her unit and, "I was able to finally get my own car," she said.

Cathy Bessant, President of Bank of America, then summed up the value of Welfare to Work brilliantly by saying, "Companies that are successful really do a couple of things. They take great care of their customers they have today, and they work like crazy to build markets of the future so that they have got customers to service tomorrow. We think having great people who are dedicated to our company and really committed to what they do is critical to getting at both of those things.

"We know though, from experience, that it takes more than just a job. It takes more than what some people might call a slot in a company, and that is particularly true with our Welfare to Work associates.

"We know that it takes things like transportation—how am I going to get to work? It takes child care—do I feel comfortable with where my children are? It takes the knowledge that there is a roof over their heads that people feel confident and happy to go home to every night. And so our benefits programs, our stock options efforts that help us build wealth at the same time that we are building income, our work to do child-care reimbursement like LaTonya was talking about, tuition reimbursement, our home-ownership program, which provides a five thousand dollar loan that is forgivable over five years for any associate, to help people feel confident and comfortable about the house they can go home to.

"LaTonya to me is living proof of what it is all about. We have got great programs, great benefits, and great associates who make our programs work for themselves, for our communities, and really important, for our shareholders."

Cathy was every bit as impressive as the program she had described. The next two people in the program were the last two. We made it. Everyone was going to get to speak. Everyone was going to tell their story.

I could even enjoy it a little, when Jonathan Tisch, the president and CEO of Loews Hotels, began his remarks by saying, "Jim Kelly, CEO to CEO, no one is listening. We have a hotel under construction in Philadelphia. I will offer you two future draft choices for Rodney Carroll to come join us."

I smiled. President Clinton slapped me on the arm.

Jonathan then talked about his hotel in Miami's Dade County, where Jonathan worked with the mayor's office, Miami WAGES, and forty-four other hotels to commit to hiring five hundred welfare recipients over a two-year period. Jonathan Tisch is someone with passionate beliefs and the courage to make them work. He is one of our country's great businessmen. The amount of success that he has earned through his work is rare. But even more rare is the way he uses his success to help others. He is living proof that you can be socially responsible and still improve the bottom line.

I could not think of a better person to conclude the success stories than Consuela McGlond, who worked in the Miami Loews Hotel. Consuela is a single mother of three, who hadn't worked in about two years. She spent ten months at America Works learning about all the issues that are so important to making the transition from welfare to work. Loews had hired her as a night operator at the hotel in 1998, and Consuela has been with Loews ever since. She works the night shift from 10:30 P.M. to 6:30 in the morning, goes home, takes care of her children, and every two weeks takes home a paycheck.

"First of all, let me say I rarely see the sun," Consuela joked. Then she got serious. "I love working at Loews. Working for Loews has given me stability in my life. It has given me loads of confidence that I hadn't felt before, and I also feel like I can go out and conquer just about anything. There are so many things that I want to do. There are so many things that I want to learn. One of the things that I am going to be doing in just a few short weeks is getting my driver's license. I am so grateful to programs such as America Works and the Wages Coalition in Miami for helping people like me to go out and have a better chance of reaching their goals. I am just so honored to be here."

Consuela started to cry. She wasn't the only one. The president's eyes were also watery. When she sat down, it occurred to me that I had no idea how the program was supposed to end. We had never discussed it. I guess nobody had ever thought it would get this far. There was a moment of silence. Then I turned to President Clinton.

"Well, Mr. President and members of the audience, these are just some of the stories we have to tell. It has been a fascinating experience so far. We know we have a ways to go. However, we believe that by working together for the same purpose, we will be able to accomplish our goals. It has been an honor for me to be here today. I appreciate it very much. Thank you so much."

The crowd applauded. For the first time in over an hour, the president grabbed his microphone.

"I have been asked to announce that as soon as we adjourn this meeting in this very spot, Rodney will be offering memory training to everyone who would like to stay." The crowd laughed. As they did, I had a second to catch my breath. The last ninety minutes were a complete blur.

"Rodney," continued President Clinton, "I want to thank you for your devotion to this cause, and, Jim Kelly, thank you for giving us this fine man. I just want to ask you all to think about it. While Rodney was talking to all the people here, I just got to sit here in the middle so I could see everybody else. I would turn around, and I would look. Every time someone was talking, I would look at every face in this section, and what I saw was that all of us had the natural human emotion. We were exhilarated by the stories that these people told. We were gratified by the enlightened self-interest of the employers.

"I had a funny thing happen to me a couple of weeks ago. We were in an unrelated fight in Washington, and one of the people who took the opposite position from me said, 'The president is always up there telling stories. What has stories got to do with this?' Well, we found out today, didn't we? I mean, all of our lives are nothing but our stories.

"We should recognize that we can pass these programs to empower people, but it takes human beings with real commitment, like the employers we have honored today and all the others in this room, and all those like them around this country. And then it takes people with courage to stand up and say, 'I am going to change my life.'

"All over this country today, there are people just like them who still don't have the lives they deserve, and we can reach them, too. If we do it, America will be a better place. We will be closer to the one America of our dreams when we start this new century. We will have a stronger economy.

"Rodney, we will follow your lead. We will follow the lead of our founding companies, but I ask you all to leave here with a renewed sense of energy and commitment and go out and tell other people about what you have seen and what you have participated in and what we can do. If you do that, we will finish this job, and we will hear a lot more of the stories that make our hearts soar. Thank you, and God bless you all."

"Thank you," I whispered, glancing to the sky.

18. The Good and the Not So Good

When I was five years old, I got lost after church. While the rest of the congregation socialized outside, I wandered off. I was searching for something, but I didn't know what. I was oblivious of the time, and my mother and grandmother back at the church. I was in my own world. I zigzagged up and down streets, staring into the clear blue sky. I strolled through the neighborhood thoughtfully observing the residents.

An hour passed before I realized that I was completely lost. I was a five-year-old kid, alone in the city, but I wasn't scared. I coolly asked several adults for help, but the more directions I got, the more lost I got.

"Do you know where the church is?"

"There's a church right around the corner," a man said. Wrong church.

Finally, I asked a police officer for help. He put me in the front seat of his car.

"Can I put on the siren?" I asked.

"Sorry, we can't do that," he replied. "There are rules I have to follow."

As we turned down my street, the cop looked at me and smiled. "Okay, we can put the siren on now." He flipped the switch next to the steering column. I felt like a king going down my street in a police car with the siren blaring.

An immediate spanking from my mom snapped me back to reality. She and my grandmother were worried sick. I got a spanking from my mom. To me, it didn't seem like a big deal. When my mom left the house, my grandmother talked to me. She explained all the horrible things that could have happened to me. She described how scared she and my mom had been at the thought of me alone in the big city.

"Weren't you scared?" she asked.

"No," I said. "I wasn't afraid. I was just looking around."

"What were you looking for?" she asked.

"I don't know," I said. "I figured I'd know it when I saw it."

It seems I spent most of my life looking for something without knowing exactly what it was. The search led me down many paths that I didn't understand at the time. In my wildest dreams, I didn't believe the town hall could have gone so well. In the end, it answered a lifetime of questions.

When President Clinton said, "Rodney, we will follow your lead," I knew that I had finally found what I had been looking for all those years. I knew how I was going to make my impact. In that instant, I understood that everything that I had been through in my life—the good and the not so good—had prepared me for my future. It taught me about people. Instead of simply seeing the surface, I was able to understand the substance. Through it all, it had allowed me to believe in the tremendous potential within each person, and what needed to happen so that everyone could see the potential within themselves.

Lucky had been right about one thing: I was a dreamer. There was a time in my life when I forgot how important that was. There comes a time in all our lives when we understand that life can be a lot like a boxing match. Sometimes you get hit to the right, sometimes you get hit to the left, sometimes you get knocked down. But the key to winning is that we continue to get up and fight—and dream. It's not easy. It takes belief in yourself and, just as important, it takes belief from others. But we all can do it. Just because a person is struggling or unmotivated or disillusioned at some point in their life doesn't mean they can't become inspired. There are millions of people, like Maria Mercado, like Billy, like my brother—like myself—who remind me of that every day.

The day after the town hall I called my grandmother.

"I knew you'd do well," she said.

Three months later, my grandmother had a stroke. It wasn't so slight. She had told me a month earlier that she was ready to go to heaven. She was ninety-five years old. When I got to the hospital, she was in a coma. She looked at peace. I held her hand in mine.

"Can you hear me?" I said quietly. I felt her flinch. I knew my next words would be the last words I spoke to her.

"God bless you," I said. "I'll try to make you proud."

I often think about my grandmother and how her patience and perspective have helped me become the person that I am today. She had taught me to believe in myself. She had taught me to follow my dreams. And she had taught me that anyone can change their life for the better if they don't give up.

Thanks to her, I am dedicating my life to helping others get the opportunities that we all deserve. The opportunity to work and be self-sufficient—and dream. Because I am convinced that all of us are capable of achieving our dreams. All around us there are people who once struggled to survive and who are now successful. They own companies. They are actors and politicians and teachers. They all have one thing in common. They continue to try. When things are at their worst, they persevere. They keep their spirit alive. And as my grandmother always said, "That's the most important thing."

For more information on welfare reform or starting a welfare-to-work program at your company please contact the Welfare to Work Partnership at 1-888-USA-JOB1 or visit our Web site at www.welfaretowork.org.

A portion of the proceeds from *No Free Lunch* will be donated to the Welfare to Work Partnership, a 501(c)(3) organization.